Civilization is Possible

Louis,

In solidarity

Blase Bonpane

July 23, 2010

Civilization

⇶ *is* ⇴

Possible

Blase Bonpane

Radio commentaries and interviews directed
to the formation of an international peace system

Red Hen Press *Los Angeles 2008*

Book design by Mark E. Cull

ISBN 978-1-59709-123-7

Library of Congress Catalog Card Number 2008927583

The California Arts Council and
the National Endowment for the Arts
partially support Red Hen Press

First Edition

Red Hen Press
w w w . r e d h e n . o r g

To our precious grandchildren,
Ossian, Blase Jairo, Chiara, Nola and Gianna.

May they live in a civilized world.

Contents

World Focus Commentaries

KPFK 90.7 FM / Los Angeles, California

World Focus Interviews

Prologue

This volume completes a trilogy of commentary and analysis on the everlasting war in Iraq and the culture which sustains it. The books are: *Guerrillas of Peace on the Air*, Pacifica Radio Commentaries and Reports on Peace Actions in the Americas. (Red Hen Press, 2000) and *Common Sense for the Twenty-First Century*, Pacifica Radio Commentaries and interviews with: Chalmers Johnson, Jonathan Schell and Rev. James Lawson (Red Hen Press, 2004).

And now, *Civilization is Possible*; Pacifica Radio Commentaries and interviews with Robert Fisk, Greg Palast, Peter Laufer, Chalmers Johnson and Noam Chomsky.

There is no sign of civilization or intelligent life in the creators and sustainers of the rape of Iraq. On the contrary, what is demonstrated in these years of inhuman and illegal massacre is the amoral performance of the corporate mind. Structures with no democracy, and no humanity that is corporations, which manifest their power by shares, not by one person, one vote, are now governing directly in opposition to the will of the people. Corporate lobbyists purchase elected officials who sell themselves quite cheaply. It is really a bargain for the corporations. By investing a few hundred thousand dollars in members of two giant political parties, they are rewarded with billions in windfall profits. After an election these masters of greed say to whomever won, "Don't forget who put you where you are today." This is why some people are surprised when Democrats who are now a majority seem only slightly different from the Republicans who came before them. Quite simply, we have two corporate capital parties. Citizens are not powerless, however, but they must know these facts of life before they are capable of making necessary changes. The majority of our people want single payer health care. But insurance corporations, wielding real political power, will not let them have it. We the people must rebel against corporate insurance power.

The majority of our citizens want gun control, but the largest purveyor of violence in the world, the military/industrial/ arms business/ prison/ pharmaceutical/congressional complex will not let them have it.

We the people must rebel against the military industrial government which is destroying democracy.

Citizens want their public sector back. Remember when colleges were public as well as high schools and elementary schools? Remember public libraries, public parks, public hospitals, public beaches, and yes, even public sources of employment when the economy was depressed? Remember public utilities? The public sector has been Enronized by a rigid ideology of privatization. The infrastructure of the United States is in shambles. Sewer systems, water systems, dams, bridges, highways, school buildings; electrical grids are deteriorating together with the quality of the air. Think about the air. The delicate gas which makes this planet inhabitable is in a state of decline. But some banal, servile and mindless people are ready to deny the coming environmental holocaust.

China has the economy of the United States in its hands. Many nations are turning to the Euro as their currency of choice.

In the midst of this we have become the world's largest prison state. With 4 to 5 percent of the world's people, we boast of 25 percent of the world's prisoners. We are now international number one in both adult and child prisoners.

Fear of the military/industrial power has become the driving force in our political culture. "Support our troops" becomes an asinine mantra of the Bush Administration. Does anyone think that the troops decided to be where they are? Does anyone think that the troops want to be where they are? The only way to support our troops is to remove them from the chaos our "leaders" have created.

What our founders called "the last refuge of scoundrels," militaristic patriotism, is still a mechanism to frighten legislators into compliance with war mongers. Chalmers Johnson has defined the United States as "An empire of bases." We currently have 737 military bases in 130 countries. We agree with his conclusion that our country can either be an empire or a democracy. It cannot be both.

Police culture is a domestic parallel to the military national culture. Police have been militarized and have many urban communities living in fear. Unwritten laws have developed a culture of policing which includes:

- Punishing people for alleged crimes prior to the decision of a court.
- Using deadly force and following a policy of, "One shoot, everyone shoot."
- Police perjury as undoubtedly the most widely unpunished crime in our country

Worn out epithets continue; one who opposes war is called unpatriotic, one who opposes police violence is called anti-police. It does not require a genius to understand that civilized people do not approve of our state terrorism or police brutality.

Civilization is possible. But it is only possible by breaking away from nationalistic fundamentalism and the bankrupt mythology that goes with it.

The Universal Declaration of Human Rights is an international Declaration of Interdependence. It is, at the same time a formula for a functional international civil society. Now there is no need to say, "Your human rights are not my human rights."

Here we have an international consensus on what is possible. Therefore I offer The Universal Declaration of Human Rights as a preface to this book. Yes, civilization is possible. One planet, one race, one family that will survive only if we accept our unity.

Universal Declaration of Human Rights

Adopted and proclaimed by General Assembly resolution 217 A (III) of 10 December 1948

On December 10, 1948 the General Assembly of the United Nations adopted and proclaimed the Universal Declaration of Human Rights the full text of which appears in the following pages. Following this historic act the Assembly called upon all Member countries to publicize the text of the Declaration and "to cause it to be disseminated, displayed, read and expounded principally in schools and other educational institutions, without distinction based on the political status of countries or territories."

PREAMBLE

Whereas recognition of the inherent dignity and of the equal and inalienable rights of all members of the human family is the foundation of freedom, justice and peace in the world,

Whereas disregard and contempt for human rights have resulted in barbarous acts which have outraged the conscience of mankind, and the advent of a world in which human beings shall enjoy freedom of speech and belief and freedom from fear and want has been proclaimed as the highest aspiration of the common people,

Whereas it is essential, if man is not to be compelled to have recourse, as a last resort, to rebellion against tyranny and oppression, that human rights should be protected by the rule of law, Whereas it is essential to promote the development of friendly relations between nations,

Whereas the peoples of the United Nations have in the Charter reaffirmed their faith in fundamental human rights, in the dignity and worth of the human person and in the equal rights of men and women and have determined to promote social progress and better standards of life in larger freedom,

Whereas Member States have pledged themselves to achieve, in co-operation with the United Nations, the promotion of universal respect for and observance of human rights and fundamental freedoms,

Whereas a common understanding of these rights and freedoms is of the greatest importance for the full realization of this pledge, Now, Therefore THE GENERAL ASSEMBLY proclaims THIS UNIVERSAL DECLARATION OF HUMAN RIGHTS as a common standard of achievement for all peoples and all nations, to the end that every individual and every organ of society, keeping this Declaration constantly in mind, shall strive by teaching and education to promote respect for these rights and freedoms and by progressive measures, national and international, to secure their universal and effective recognition and observance, both among the peoples of Member States themselves and among the peoples of territories under their jurisdiction.

Article 1

All human beings are born free and equal in dignity and rights. They are endowed with reason and conscience and should act towards one another in a spirit of brotherhood.

Article 2

Everyone is entitled to all the rights and freedoms set forth in this Declaration, without distinction of any kind, such as race, colour, sex, language, religion, political or other opinion, national or social origin, property, birth or other status. Furthermore, no distinction shall be made on the basis of the political, jurisdictional or international status of the country or territory to which a person belongs, whether it be independent, trust, non-self-governing or under any other limitation of sovereignty.

Article 3

Everyone has the right to life, liberty and security of person.

Article 4

No one shall be held in slavery or servitude; slavery and the slave trade shall be prohibited in all their forms.

Article 5

No one shall be subjected to torture or to cruel, inhuman or degrading treatment or punishment.

Article 6

Everyone has the right to recognition everywhere as a person before the law.

Article 7

All are equal before the law and are entitled without any discrimination to equal protection of the law. All are entitled to equal protection against any discrimination in violation of this Declaration and against any incitement to such discrimination.

Article 8

Everyone has the right to an effective remedy by the competent national tribunals for acts violating the fundamental rights granted him by the constitution or by law.

Article 9

No one shall be subjected to arbitrary arrest, detention or exile.

Article 10

Everyone is entitled in full equality to a fair and public hearing by an independent and impartial tribunal, in the determination of his rights and obligations and of any criminal charge against him.

Article 11

1) Everyone charged with a penal offence has the right to be presumed innocent until proved guilty according to law in a public trial at which he has had all the guarantees necessary for his defence.

(2) No one shall be held guilty of any penal offence on account of any act or omission which did not constitute a penal offence, under national or international law, at the time when it was committed. Nor shall a heavier penalty be imposed than the one that was applicable at the time the penal offence was committed.

Article 12

No one shall be subjected to arbitrary interference with his privacy, family, home or correspondence, nor to attacks upon his honour and reputation. Everyone has the right to the protection of the law against such interference or attacks.

Article 13

(1) Everyone has the right to freedom of movement and residence within the borders of each state.

(2) Everyone has the right to leave any country, including his own, and to return to his country.

Article 14

(1) Everyone has the right to seek and to enjoy in other countries asylum from persecution.

(2) This right may not be invoked in the case of prosecutions genuinely arising from non-political crimes or from acts contrary to the purposes and principles of the United Nations.

Article 15

(1) Everyone has the right to a nationality.

(2) No one shall be arbitrarily deprived of his nationality nor denied the right to change his nationality.

Article 16

(1) Men and women of full age, without any limitation due to race, nationality or religion, have the right to marry and to found a family. They are entitled to equal rights as to marriage, during marriage and at its dissolution.

(2) Marriage shall be entered into only with the free and full consent of the intending spouses.

(3) The family is the natural and fundamental group unit of society and is entitled to protection by society and the State.

Article 17

(1) Everyone has the right to own property alone as well as in association with others.

(2) No one shall be arbitrarily deprived of his property.

Article 18

Everyone has the right to freedom of thought, conscience and religion; this right includes freedom to change his religion or belief, and freedom, either alone or in community with others and in public or private, to manifest his religion or belief in teaching, practice, worship and observance.

Article 19

Everyone has the right to freedom of opinion and expression; this right includes freedom to hold opinions without interference and to seek, receive and impart information and ideas through any media and regardless of frontiers.

Article 20

(1) Everyone has the right to freedom of peaceful assembly and association.

(2) No one may be compelled to belong to an association.

Article 21

(1) Everyone has the right to take part in the government of his country, directly or through freely chosen representatives.
(2) Everyone has the right of equal access to public service in his country.

(3) The will of the people shall be the basis of the authority of government; this will shall be expressed in periodic and genuine elections which shall be by universal and equal suffrage and shall be held by secret vote or by equivalent free voting procedures.

Article 22

Everyone, as a member of society, has the right to social security and is entitled to realization, through national effort and international co-operation and in accordance with the organization and resources of each State, of the economic, social and cultural rights indispensable for his dignity and the free development of his personality.

Article 23

(1) Everyone has the right to work, to free choice of employment, to just and favourable conditions of work and to protection against unemployment.

(2) Everyone, without any discrimination, has the right to equal pay for equal work.

(3) Everyone who works has the right to just and favourable remuneration ensuring for himself and his family an existence worthy of human dignity, and supplemented, if necessary, by other means of social protection.

(4) Everyone has the right to form and to join trade unions for the protection of his interests.

Article 24

Everyone has the right to rest and leisure, including reasonable limitation of working hours and periodic holidays with pay.

Article 25

(1) Everyone has the right to a standard of living adequate for the health and well-being of himself and of his family, including food, clothing, housing and medical care and necessary social services, and the right to security in the event of unemployment, sickness, disability, widowhood, old age or other lack of livelihood in circumstances beyond his control.

(2) Motherhood and childhood are entitled to special care and assistance. All children, whether born in or out of wedlock, shall enjoy the same social protection.

Article 26

(1) Everyone has the right to education. Education shall be free, at least in the elementary and fundamental stages. Elementary education shall be compulsory. Technical and professional education shall be made generally available and higher education shall be equally accessible to all on the basis of merit.

(2) Education shall be directed to the full development of the human personality and to the strengthening of respect for human rights and fundamental freedoms. It shall promote understanding, tolerance and friendship among all nations, racial or religious groups, and shall further the activities of the United Nations for the maintenance of peace.

(3) Parents have a prior right to choose the kind of education that shall be given to their children.

Article 27

(1) Everyone has the right freely to participate in the cultural life of the community, to enjoy the arts and to share in scientific advancement and its benefits.

(2) Everyone has the right to the protection of the moral and material interests resulting from any scientific, literary or artistic production of which he is the author.

Article 28

Everyone is entitled to a social and international order in which the rights and freedoms set forth in this Declaration can be fully realized.

Article 29

(1) Everyone has duties to the community in which alone the free and full development of his personality is possible.

(2) In the exercise of his rights and freedoms, everyone shall be subject only to such limitations as are determined by law solely for the purpose of securing due recognition and respect for the rights and freedoms of others and of meeting the just requirements of morality, public order and the general welfare in a democratic society.

(3) These rights and freedoms may in no case be exercised contrary to the purposes and principles of the United Nations.

Article 30

Nothing in this Declaration may be interpreted as implying for any State, group or person any right to engage in any activity or to perform any act aimed at the destruction of any of the rights and freedoms set forth herein.

Civilization is Possible

Pacifica

Ψ

Radio Commentaries

KPFK 90.7 FM

Los Angeles, California

April 15, 2004 to November 28, 2007

Hello, this is Blase Bonpane with a comment . . .

The Nature of Defeat

April 15, 2004

Daniel Nelson is Dean of the College of Arts and Sciences at the University of New Haven. His most recent book, *At War with Words*, is significant at this time of perpetual conflict. Both Nelson and Michael Moore are concerned about the bastardization of language.

Our media speak of contractors in Iraq. These are actually mercenaries or soldiers of fortune. They are not there to fix the roof.

Halliburton and Bechtel are not companies doing business in Iraq. They are war profiteers bilking billions from average Americans together with the blood of our troops.

Iraqis who have risen up against us are not a small group of fanatics, they are the revolution and their numbers will grow.

When we get a press release from Iraq we are actually getting a statement handed out by the U.S. occupation forces which is repeated to us as news.

When we are told we are winning the hearts and minds of the people . . . the exact opposite is true.

Here are some thoughts from Daniel Nelson as he writes about the nature of defeat:

Defeat is made possible by: ignorance and gross policy errors that enlarge threats and squander capacities. This includes not knowing other cultures, histories or environments.

Defeat comes through arrogance with the assumption that power is deserved and that deserved power embodies one with missionary zeal. The conceit of power or hubris is the formula for certain defeat. The utterance of arrogant power generates fear, alienation and ultimately countervailing force.

Distrust of friends and dread of presumed enemy plots, join to produce the self flagellation of paranoia. "Report suspicious behavior," flashes a sign above the beltway in Washington, D.C.

Greed is also a quick route to defeat. Believing in nothing but today's material interests is another way of believing in nothing. Lying about motives, deceitfully spinning information and concealing data or events are also signs of defeat.

This is George Bush's America. With each pre-emptive step toward global unilateralism, enemies multiply, friendships wane and the imbalance between threats and capacities escalates. The smell of defeat hangs in the air.

The Tet Offensive

April 22, 2004

Do you remember the Tet Offensive?

On the evening of January 31st, 1968, 70,000 North Vietnamese soldiers launched Tet. It is ranked as one of the greatest campaigns in military history.

Guerrilla fighters surged into over one hundred towns and cities including Saigon.

The purpose of the attack was threefold:

First, to demand an end to the ceaseless bombardment of North Vietnam where operation Rolling Thunder dropped more bombs than were used in the entire Second World War. Twenty-two tons of explosives were dropped for every square mile of territory, 300 pounds of bombs for every man woman and child. In totality, 7 million tons of bombs and dioxin defoliants were dropped and a total of 2.6 million Vietnamese were killed.

The second reason was to force the United States into negotiations.

The third reason for the Tet Offensive was to drive the U.S. out of Vietnam altogether and open the path to unification and liberation of Vietnam.

After a small group of commandos arrived by taxi and took over the U.S. Embassy in Saigon, President Johnson realized that military and political defeat was in the air. He finally had the sense to end his candidacy for a second term, and to authorize negotiations with the Vietnamese. In spite of this and because of the blind denial from the Secretary of Defense and the Generals, troop levels remained at some 500,000 and the war dragged on for another five years. More U.S. soldiers were killed after the Tet Offensive than before.

Text books in current use at West Point describe what happened here as an intelligence failure on a par with Pearl Harbor.

Thirty-six years after the Tet Offensive the Vietnamese continue to die of dioxin, land mines and other unexploded ordnance. And currently the Iraqis and Afghanis will continue to die from a terrorist nuclear war of depleted uranium. Friends, a Tet Offensive is now taking place in Iraq and Afghanistan. Must even more of our troops die once again because of the predictable denial on the part of incompetent leadership? Must they die because our military and political leaders claim to have intelligence while having no wisdom?

No Shortage of Funds in California

May 3, 2004

Today we commemorate the 1886 Haymarket Demonstration in Chicago. A provocateur threw a bomb at that demonstration and this led to the trumped conviction and execution of four of the demonstrators: Albert Parsons, August Spies, Adolph Fischer and George Engel. After the execution, the new governor of Illinois, John Peter Altgeld, reviewed the facts of the case and immediately pardoned the three remaining prisoners. Today we are asking our governor to change his mind as well. Here are some thoughts we expressed this week together with the representatives of the Multi-Ethnic Immigrant Workers Organizing Network's Caravan for Justice. We spoke from the back of a truck used as a stage across from Governor Arnold Schwarzenegger's office.

There is no shortage of funds in the State of California. Actually we already have too much money. Our state is the sixth largest economic entity in the world. A tax representing a small percentage of the income of the top 1 percent of Californians (that's right, from our numerous billionaires and our myriad millionaires) would create an immediate surplus of funds to maintain all former state programs and to begin much needed new projects for social justice. No need to turn 200,000 students away from our community colleges, no need to reject students who have already been accepted to the University of California system, no need to close hospitals and to deny treatment to children with HIV/AIDS.

We are tired of hearing this state whine about how there is no money for these programs. Professors in the hard sciences like Paul O'Lague at UCLA have done the math. The only possible reason for any cutbacks in the budget is the endless patronizing of people who already have too much. California would be doing a favor to these people by working for distributive justice. A society with some level of economic equilibrium would greatly lessen crime.

We told Arnold that we thought he might be afraid of offending his friends at the Country Club and reminded him that the garment workers, janitors and farm workers that made up this caravan are not the servants. In our system of government he is to be the servant.

We also want the governor to know that he has a clear responsibility make demands on Washington, D.C.. As the leader of the largest state in the union he must demand that the Federal Government stop bankrupting the country by its endless counterproductive military adventures. Our fine young people, our future and millions of victims overseas are losing patience with this mindless foreign policy.

Was Arnold listening? We can only find that out by his performance.

Our Exports to Iraq

May 13, 2004

Tactics of our homeland prisons and the interrogation techniques of the School of the Americas have been exported to Iraq.

The physical, mental and sexual abuse of prisoners which has been documented in Iraq takes place in America's prisons and is codified in torture manuals from the School of the Americas at Ft. Benning, Georgia. Reports from Texas State prisons under the leadership of Governor George Bush are strikingly similar to those of Abu Ghraib prison.

Documentation of prison abuse in California is also clear. The recent abuse of children at the California Youth Authority was viewed by State Attorney General Lockyer and he refused to prosecute the perpetrators. It seems to me that the cause of the obviously feigned shock on the faces of our administration is related to the fact that they got caught.

There are no legal interrogation techniques of prisoners of war. Torture is simply a form of terrorism. Valuable information does not proceed from torture and even if it did it would be unacceptable.

The law is clear: prisoners of war are required to give their name, rank and serial number and their date of birth. That is all. Torture is conducted by morally defeated mindless functionaries. It is certainly not a sign of victory. It is a clear sign of defeat.

Was Governor Bush unaware of the conditions in his Texas prisons?

- Female prisoners were regularly kept in portable detention cells for hours in Texas summer heat with no water. Fear of more time in the cages led many women to submit sexually to their oppressors.

- Prison guards brutalizing inmates in the Brazoria County Detention Center in Angleton, Texas were taped beating prisoners (arrested on drug violations) and forcing them to crawl while kicking them and poking them with electric prods.

Did Governor Bush never see the tape?

Did the governor know nothing about the hunger strike at the notorious Terrell Unit facility in Livingston, Texas? where death-row prisoner Michael Sharp said before his execution, "Many guards think it is their patriotic duty to torture and brutalize prisoners."

Attorney Donna Brorby had described Texas' super-max prisons as "the worst in the country, where guards reportedly gas prisoners and throw them down on concrete floors while handcuffed."

And now we find the religious connection to torture and a possible Grand Inquisitor. Religious fanatic Lieutenant General William Boykin who believes we are fighting Satan as warriors of God gave instructions to a top Pentagon Official last summer on so-called interrogation techniques. Certainly no punishment is sufficient for the devil, is it?

What the Grand Inquisitors Found

May 21, 2004

And just what did the Grand Inquisitors find out by way of their high tech interrogation techniques, in other words, torture?

They found out that interrogation under torture is useless. They found out that even if they received any word of truth from their victim, they would be apt to disregard it as falsehood and that any falsehood they received might be considered true.

They found out that in spite of any accidental particle of truth they might uncover, it would never be worth the contagious and terminal moral leprosy they had contracted for life.

The Grand Inquisitors also found out that they began to believe their own lies and that they had the power to create a subversive out of an innocent by-stander. After all, they must be worthy of their hire.

They found out that their cult leaders were simply defeated frauds, Wizards of Oz and pathetic sadistic wimps.

They also found out that bombing is simply a method of collective torture. Oh yes, they uncovered the fact that torture is routine in our state and federal prisons, that torture was routine during our interventions in Vietnam, Guatemala, El Salvador and Nicaragua and that at least eight torture manuals have been issued by the Defense Department. They found out that we have a policy of knowingly sending people to countries like Syria and Egypt where they can easily be tortured to death. And now they witness the leader of the illegal gulag at Guantánamo being sent to oversee the Abu Ghraib prison in Iraq.

They found out that many of our techniques were taken from Israel, a country where torture was legal. And the inquisitors are beginning to discover that the infallible formula for creating suicide bombers is to break into the homes of families, brutalize their women and children, demonize their ethnicity, deny them food and water and kill them with impunity. It seems that the inquisitors have also found out that they have presided over the loss of another unnecessary war. After finding out all of these things we must ask if the inquisitors have learned anything. Perhaps they will learn that their policy of torture is actually collective suicide.

Prior to completing this bi-national suicide pact, it would be well to remind the U.S. and Israeli inquisitors that they can do penance, amend their lives and humanize their polities.

Contemporary Haiti

May 28, 2004

Please join us on Saturday, June 5 at Noon on the corner of Olympic and Broadway for a march to the Downtown Federal Building at 300 North Los Angeles Street . . . This march is to end the occupation of Iraq and Palestine, to restore the legal government of Haiti and to call attention to new threats to Colombia, Cuba and Venezuela as it connects the dots to our domestic needs of health care and education.

During the month of May we gathered in Washington, D.C. to discuss our role in the reestablishment of the legal government of Haiti. The Black Caucus of the U.S. House of Representatives took a strong stand against the visit to Washington of the illegally appointed Gerard Latortue. Congresswoman Maxine Waters said:

> Gerard Latortue is a mere puppet installed by the supporters of the coup d'etat that ousted the democratically elected President Jean Bertrand Aristide. Latortue is totally controlled by Assistant Secretary of State for Western Hemisphere Affairs, Roger Noriega.

This is the second time the United States was responsible for removing Jean Bertrand Aristide from Office. He had been elected by a landslide twice. The Haitian oligarchy knew it had no chance whatever of defeating Jean Bertrand Aristide at the polls so, with the direction of the United States, it reverted to its thirty-third coup.

At the Washington meeting we evaluated the best ways to get aid to the non-governmental organizations working on the ground in Haiti and arrived at a consensus that the Haiti Emergency Relief Fund of the Vanguard Public Foundation is the most effective instrument for immediate and direct aid to Haiti without going through the hands of the current illegal Haitian government.

Immediately after our meeting in Washington we received word of the catastrophic flooding on the border of Haiti and the Dominican Republic. These two countries share the Island of Hispaniola. The Dominican Republic has some ability to assist its people. However the government imposed on Haiti by the United States has no such potential for assisting its people. Assistance to Haiti at this time must be entirely from the outside.

Therefore I beg you to connect with the website <haitiaction.net> to find out more about contemporary Haiti and, if you will, to contribute directly through the non-profit Vanguard Public Foundation as directed by that website.

The Legacy of Ronald Reagan

June 10, 2004

Anyone's death helps us all to reflect on our tenuous hold on life. On a personal basis death is a tragedy for family and friends.

In politics and history, however, we must face the actual legacy of those who have gone before us. The legacy of the 40th President of the United States includes a foreign policy that declared war on international terrorism by approving rampant terror in Guatemala.

On the evening of his election, the government of Guatemala, together with its death squads, celebrated knowing that human rights would no longer be a component of U.S. policy. Labor leaders could be disappeared with impunity, unlimited arms would be sold and given to one of the most maniacal military establishments on earth.

There would be 662 rural villages annihilated in an effort to eliminate the indigenous people of Guatemala. The death squads would be praised.

An illegal war would be conducted against the people of Nicaragua. Targets in the war would be social workers, religious workers, teachers and torture would be routine as in Guatemala and El Salvador.

Our taxes paid for all of this but there is never enough money for slaughter so illegal fees from the sale of weapons to the Ayatollah Khomeini would be used to pay mercenaries who were instructed to torture and kill non-combatants. The 40th President referred to these rapists and murders as the moral equivalent of our founding fathers.

Thousands of regular U.S. troops would serve in El Salvador and later receive combat pay for training as 80,000 citizens of that small country were massacred.

Honduras was the command post for all of Central America. Over 75,000 U.S. troops were stationed there as a back up for the control of Guatemala, El Salvador and Nicaragua.

AIDs flourished among Honduras children who were victimized by our troops as U.S. Ambassador to Honduras John Negroponte presided over the Central American wars.

17

Unnecessary war is the legacy of the Reagan Administration. Just think of the absolute fraud which was called the "War" in Grenada. It was 1983 and our war mongering media told us that the troops, "Got there just in time." This was possibly the most unnecessary war in history.

What is the legacy of the smiles and jokes including the one about starting a nuclear war with the Soviet Union? The legacy is more unnecessary wars. More torture and summary execution, more unnecessary death of our excellent young people and innocent civilians.

The legacy of Reagan is Bush and the detritus of the Reagan Administration which surrounds him.

Prostitution

June 17, 2004

The world's oldest profession is alive and well. It is called "prostitution."

Some prostitutes sell their body and often it is to buy food for their children. Some prostitutes sell their soul. I am particularly concerned about this latter group.

There is an ancient story about Jacob and Esau and how Esau sold his birthright for a bowl of lentil soup.

Picture an Ivy League tenured professor who might be called to Washington to give expert advice to government. In this case the individual does not need the money to feed his or her children, the great hope is simply for more recognition and possibly a role in government. It becomes prostitution, however, the moment the professor begins to tell the government exactly what the government wants to hear. Gone is the value of decades of education. Gone is the integrity of academia.

Suppose such a person comes to Washington to huckster torture, knowing as did the Grand Inquisitors that torture is simply the terrorism of sadistic wimps and also knowing it will please the crown. That too is prostitution.

Some prostitutes also come from government itself, trying to use their current post to gain a higher post.

Picture an Assistant Attorney General signing a White House memo approving torture and stating that international laws against torture may be "unconstitutional." Consider how pleasing it might be to Mr. Bush to be told that it is his prerogative to torture or not to torture. A lifetime appointment to the U.S. 9th Circuit Court of Appeals becomes the prize for the babble of this fifty-page pro-torture memo. Do we have any right to judge the motives of Professor Alan Dershowitz or the new Federal Judge Jay S. Bybee. Perhaps not.

But we do have the right to say to them and others like them, that if the epithet fits, they should wear it.

Impeachment?

June 24, 2004

Why should we consider impeachment of the President when we are so close to an election? We must promote impeachment because in so doing we can clearly express the crimes of this government without any partisan consideration. Campaign talk is simply a form of advertising. In promoting impeachment we are stating facts of law, not advertising. What is more, should Bush be elected for the first time, we will have the foundation for immediate impeachment proceedings.

Here are some of the charges made by former Attorney General of the United States, Ramsey Clark:

President George W. Bush, Vice President Richard B. Cheney, Secretary of Defense Donald H. Rumsfeld, and Attorney General John David Ashcroft have committed violations and subversions of the Constitution of the United States of America in an attempt to carry out with impunity crimes against peace and humanity and war crimes and deprivations of civil rights of the people of the United States and other nations, by assuming powers of an imperial executive unaccountable to the law and usurping powers of Congress, the Judiciary and those reserved to the people of the United States by the following acts:

1. Seizing power to wage wars of aggression in defiance of the U.S. Constitution, the U.N. Charter and the rule of law, carrying out a massive assault on and occupation of Iraq, a country that is not threatening the United States, and resulting in the death and maiming of tens of thousands of Iraqis and hundreds of U.S. G.I.s.
2. Lying to the people of the United States, to Congress and to the United Nations, providing false and deceptive rationales for war, These are only two of the seventeen charges made by the former Attorney General.

In order to study this matter more thoroughly please go
http://www.impeachcentral.com.

The question of choosing impeachment over election is frequently asked. Both processes are essential to the health of the nation at this time of crisis. Elections are about voting for a preferred candidate; impeachment is about criminal wrongdoing.

To quote Dr. Martin Luther King, "The saving of our world from pending doom will come, not through the complacent adjustment of the conforming majority, but through the creative maladjustment of a non-conforming minority."

Independence Day

July 1, 2004

Let's talk about Independence Day, July 4th and our troops. Our troops have a right to question the legitimacy of their orders. The Uniform Code of Military Justice states that military personnel must obey the lawful command, of superior officers. The military also has an obligation to disobey unlawful orders including orders of the President that do not comply with the Uniform Code of Military Justice. And Principle 6 of the Nuremberg Charter states: The fact that a person acted pursuant to an order of the government or of a superior does not relieve the individual from responsibility under international law, provided a moral choice was in fact possible.

Now if our troops believe that the Commander in Chief is violating the United States Constitution and international law they are in a position to disobey unlawful orders.

This was the situation of Sergeant Camilo Mejia who remains the vanguard of legality in the face of illegal orders. He is behind bars as a free man because he did the right thing.

The right to disobey illegal orders is not simply a personal right, it is a collective right.

As larger numbers of troops make similar decisions it is up to our citizens to support their legal rights. They are not fighting a war against terrorists. They are fighting a war against Iraqi and Afghani people. They are fighting a war as invaders and occupiers. Let's stop the charade.

The new proconsul of empire is John Negroponte.

Yes, he was U.S. Ambassador to Honduras during the Reagan Administration and had the role of supervising the Contra Mercenaries together with 75,000 U.S. troops based there. He also supervised the deaths of tens of thousands of Nicaraguans who were tortured and assassinated in violation of international law. John Negroponte has proven himself as a war criminal. His record is a matter of history. The International Court of Justice condemned the very policy that Negroponte fostered. And now as he reigns as the de facto head of state in Iraq, we can expect the orders he gives as plenipotentiary representative of George Bush to be illegal orders. Following the Code of Military Justice, our troops have a right to disobey illegal orders coming from this war criminal and the one he represents.

Yes, troops are refusing to obey illegal orders. It is incumbent upon conscious citizens of the United States to support them individually and collectively in their quest for justice. Thank you Camilo Mejia and a Happy Independence Day to all.

Cuban Unity

July 8, 2004

Just as Washington's policy has succeeded in bringing the Sunni and Shi'a into a united resistance in Iraq, so has that policy united the Cubans in Miami together with the Cubans in the homeland. An outrageous plan from Washington has created a situation that is expected to turn many Florida voters away from supporting the first election of George Bush. Cuban Americans can now only visit their homeland for fourteen days once every three years.

On their return to the U.S. visitors cannot bring back any product purchased or acquired on the island. Remittances can now only be sent to parents, children or grandparents not to cousins, uncles or aunts.

The Washington proclamation has created a united opposition from the Cuban government, the Catholic Church in Cuba together with Cuban dissidents on the island and in Miami.

Aside from limiting the visits of Cuban Americans to their homeland, the new Washington policy is attempting to make it impossible for Cuba to deposit dollars obtained from tourism into foreign banks. This will make it impossible for Cuba to import needed food and medicines.

U.S. policy toward Cuba has been essentially vindictive and punitive for four decades but it has now reached the classic position of biting off its nose to spite its face.

Louisiana rice growers are anxious to sell their products to Cuba. Corporations throughout the United States have sent representatives to Cuba with a view to beginning commerce. But Washington is so stuck in its rigid ideological swamp it cannot even hear the voices of free enterprise.

Reverend Lucius Walker who has brought the methodology of Reverend Martin Luther King to an international level by his frequent nonviolent caravans to Cuba, refuses to seek licenses from the Treasury Department to bring aid to Cuba because humanitarian aid is exempt from such restrictions in international law. Walker as director of Pastor for Peace has led the way for hundreds of people to challenge the U.S. ban on travel to Cuba. Pastors for Peace will depart this month on its fifteenth Friendshipment to Cuba.

They will be joined by the Venceremos Brigade and The African Awareness Association.

The Wall

July 15, 2004

Well here comes the *New York Times* with crass disinformation. The headline states that the July 9 decision of the World Court is not binding. If we understand the framing of this decision as non-binding we will understand the entire approach of the United States and Israel before the rest of the world. Whatever element of international law the U.S. and Israeli governments do not approve of is declared non-binding. This is similar to organized crime stating that the judicial conviction of its leader is non-binding. But it is binding regardless of what organized crime says.

By using the term non-binding the U.S. and Israel are defying the United Nations Charter and the whole foundation of International Law together with humanitarian conventions and treaties. The U.N. Charter is a treaty and as such it becomes incarnate in the Constitution of the United States. Our Constitution, however, is the greatest obstacle for the current administration in Washington. We can expect it to continue to be trashed by crass illegality.

What word should be used rather than non-binding? The correct word is unenforceable.

The World Court's decision is unenforceable solely because of the military power of the United States and Israel. It is unenforceable solely because of the ideology of might makes right. It is unenforceable with the same logic that Stalin used when he asked how many divisions the Pope had. The one dissenting vote on the wall was U.S. Judge Thomas Buergenthal.

The fifty-six page opinion of the World Court stated that if Israel wanted to build the wall, it could do so entirely legally, on its own side of the green line. However it could not do so on illegally occupied territory. The court actually excluded the small section of the wall which is built within Israel.

The wall is a land grab. When completed it will represent the taking of a substantial portion of the West Bank by the Israeli government.

On October 21, 2003, in addition to the binding decision of the World Court, 144 nations of the General Assembly of the United Nations condemned the apartheid wall being built by Israel and demanded that it be torn down.

The wall is from 198–330 feet wide. This includes razor wire, two thirteen foot deep trenches, two frontage roads and more razor wire. At this time 500 bulldozers and earthmovers are carrying out the largest national project in Israel. Israel claims that this wall will deter suicide bombers. A substantial number of the Israeli people disagree, they think it will create more suicide bombers.

Mr. Sharon, tear down that wall!

Political Consciousness

August 5, 2004

What does it mean to be politically conscious?

A politically conscious human being must think in terms of the common good, the public good. It is clear, therefore, that many people who hold political office have no political consciousness. Some can only think in terms of what is good for them and their cronies. In short, they have no concept or understanding of the common good.

People who are walking political disasters can be nice, friendly, kind and thoughtful on a personal basis. They may love their mother, their children and their wife but they are not politically conscious. They live on a personal island. Political office for such people is simply part of their personal fortune. There is no relationship to distributive justice. To understand the harm done by the politically unconscious we need to look no further than the war profiteers of our current government. These are people who believe that business is business. Now if that is true and one has no moral compass and no sense of the common good, the only industry is the arms industry. The fact that their efforts lead to the unnecessary deaths of millions is of no concern. Without political consciousness the only concern is, "What is in it for me?" Three and four year old information is used to generate a terror alarm at the height of a political campaign? Tom Ridge gives the perfect quote for the occasion, "We don't do politics at the Department of Homeland Security." Aside from nationalistic and domestic concerns, one who is politically conscious in the twenty-first century must have an international perspective regarding the common good. As we endure the circus atmosphere of current political campaigns we must search for candidates who show some level of political consciousness and who can act on behalf of the international common good.

Unless candidates are conscious of the small and worn planet on which we live, unless they can work for a common good beyond our borders, I don't think they are fit for public office in 2004.

Without political consciousness of the international common good we will continue to have a large group of mindless politicians who love their mother and who will continue to unconsciously destroy the planet.

Don't Attack the Mosque

August 12, 2004

As the fighting and crisis intensifies in Najaf, and together with Voices in the Wilderness, we call for nonviolent acts demanding an end to the fighting.

Call your Congressional Representative, U.S. Senator and John Kerry's campaign headquarters to demand that they publicly call for an end to U.S. military actions in Najaf, both against its citizens as well as at the Imam Ali Mosque. If your Representatives don't respond positively, direct actions at their offices. Such nonviolent actions can include: a daily vigil outside of their office, a phone and fax campaign demanding they issue a statement on Najaf, or other creative acts like sitting in at their offices. You can also write letters to the editor of your local newspapers and hold vigils in your local community. The time to act is now.

Our military now declares preparations to attack the Shrine of Ali in the city of Najaf in Iraq. Our country stands on the precipice of declaring war on Islam. An attack on the Shrine of Ali is an attack on the heart of Islam and must be resisted in our country.

The U.S. military is urging civilians to leave Najaf. We take this as a signal that our country is preparing to turn Najaf into a free fire zone, in which all who move, civilian or not, are targeted for attack. A free fire zone and an attack on the Shrine would significantly escalate the violence throughout Iraq, increasing the danger for all Iraqis.

Together with Voices in the Wilderness, we call upon all U.S. government officials, elected or appointed to publicly declare their opposition. The Shrine of Ali is the holiest of shrines in Shi'a Islam. It is the burial place for Imam Ali, cousin and son-in-law of the Prophet Mohammed. The shrine is sacred to both Shi'a and Sunni Muslims. Attacking the Imam Ali Mosque is akin to bombing the burial site of Jesus for people of the Christian faith or the Western Wall for people of the Jewish faith.

An attack on the Mosque will simply manufacture more resistance. Such an attack also amounts to reckless endangerment of the people of the United States.

As U.S. citizens we must say "no" to this threatened attack on the heart of Islam and use all nonviolent means available to resist it.

Thank You Mordechai Vanunu

August 19, 2004

When an individual decides to commit suicide it is always a shock to be discovered before the act. Remember Mr. Loman in Death of a Salesman? And such is the case with those who heard the truth uttered by Mordechai Vanunu a nuclear technician working at Israel's secret nuclear installation in Dimona from 1976 to 1985. His leaders seemed to say, "Why don't you let us alone? If we want to commit suicide that is our business."

Amy Goodman had an exclusive interview with Mordechai this week. He has already spent eighteen years in prison, for trying to save his people from destruction and most of that time in solitary confinement. He continues his truth telling even if it should mean more prison time. A tiny state is quietly and illegally manufacturing not only conventional nuclear weapons of the type used on Hiroshima and Nagasaki, they are also manufacturing planet busting H bombs capable of killing tens of millions of people. Also in production are property saving and people killing neutron bombs. Mordechai considers Dimona to be a holocaust factory because wherever one of its weapons of mass destruction might be used an instantaneous holocaust will be created.

Certainly our intelligence agencies have known all about the production site in Dimona.

But they too remained silent because they are involved in the same suicidal project many times over. And as we openly create more and more models of nuclear annihilation we are hysterically pointing to other nations as the culprits. But what about the bargain basement nukes that have been sold by our ally Pakistan?

What about North Korea? What about Iran? Is it not clear that the only answer is to eliminate these weapons from the face of the earth. Yes, we have the technology to do it. No, we are not talking about unilateral disarmament, we are talking about an international and interdependent project.

Continuing the production of nuclear weapons in the United States or anywhere else is a sign of profound cynicism and despair. The greatest threat of nuclear disaster is by way of accident. There have been many nuclear accidents to date. Many Israelis and millions of the world's citizens thank you Mordechai for the sacrifice you have made to save your people and the planet. It is up to us to follow your example, speak the truth and awaken people who might prefer to sleep through their short life.

Criminal Indictment:
George W. Bush

August 26, 2004

Today former Attorney General Ramsey Clark will declare a criminal indictment charging: George W. Bush, Richard B. Cheney, Colin Powell, Donald H. Rumsfeld, John D. Ashcroft, Tommy Franks, and his successors as Commander of U.S. Forces in Iraq, George J. Tenet, L. Paul Bremer, III, John Negroponte and others to be named with Crimes Against Peace, War Crimes, Crimes Against Humanity and other criminal acts in violation of the Charter of the United Nations, International Law, the Constitution of the United States and Laws Made in Pursuance Thereof.

The Crimes Charged are:

1. Waging a War of Aggression against the sovereignty of Iraq and the rights of its people, resulting in tens of thousands of deaths and injuries among U.S. service people and the people of Iraq, mostly civilians. War of aggression is defined as "the Supreme international crime" in the Nuremberg Judgment.
2. Authorizing, encouraging and condoning the use of excessive force, including terror tactics called "Shock and Awe," targeting defenseless civilians and civilian facilities and indiscriminate bombing and assaults.
3. Authorizing and ordering the use of illegal weapons including super bombs, cluster bombs, depleted uranium enhanced bombs, missiles, shells and bullets and threatening the use of nuclear weapons.
4. Authorizing, ordering, concealing and condoning assassinations, summary executions, murders, disappearances, kidnappings and torture.

Friends, this tribunal led by an international legal scholar who served as Attorney General; of the United States, and which is taking place today at the Martin Luther King Auditorium in New York City, is not an exercise in futility. It is a statement for posterity that in this age when a war mongering media and an administration of war profiteers conducted the second massacre in Iraq, that knowledgeable people expressed their outrage, their dissent and their demand for impeachment.

Then our children and our grandchildren can say, "We always thought the American people were better than that." We had a government of thugs in 2004 and we will not tolerate any more. Never Again. Thanks Ramsey Clark.

For the full indictment against the Bush Administration,
http://www.iacenter.org/Iraq/iraq_wct-rc.htm

The Sidewalks of New York

September 1, 2004

The wisdom of the ages, the wisdom of the spirit is not conventional. It is unconventional.

What is happening this week on the streets of New York is one of the greatest outpourings of unconventional and spiritual wisdom.

People in the castle of Madison Square Gardens spoke the conventional wisdom, of personal wealth, of the rich and the famous. People on the street were there on behalf of the poor of the earth. That is the wisdom of the ages. It is unconventional and it is true wisdom.

People in the castle of Madison Square were there on behalf of continued mean spirited behavior and revenge . . . but the gentle of the earth were on the streets of New York completely vulnerable to the violence of the militarized police. That is the wisdom of the ages.

Conventional wisdom prefers to deny suffering, sickness and death; but those who understand true wisdom are on the sidewalks of New York on behalf of the suffering, the sick and the oppressed. This is true wisdom. The people in the castle of Madison Square Garden are speaking on behalf of those who hunger and thirst for wealth and power. But people on the streets of NY were hungering and thirsting after justice.

The people in the castle of the Madison Squares had access to the media of the world. But the people in the streets were there to be the voice of those without a voice. Political campaigns are full of duplicity but the wisdom of the spirit is single minded and sincere. What the people on the street were saying is precisely what they meant. they were not there for personal gain.

The people in the Madison Square Castle are there on behalf of a war system. The people on the streets were there on behalf of eternal wisdom echoing "Happy are you peacemakers . . . you shall be called the children of God."

And as Washington knows so well. No good deed will go unpunished.

Those in the streets were fearlessly speaking the truth to power and willing to accept severe and unwarranted punishment for their witness.

"Happy are those who are persecuted in the cause of justice, theirs is the castle of heaven."

The streets of New York were full of the wisdom of the ages this week. How proud we are of the sheer goodness they have demonstrated.

To Honor the Dead
and Fight for the Living

September 9, 2004

Today we commemorate the lives sacrificed on the filthy altar of war profiteers and pathological liars who are recklessly driving a ship of state they cannot steer.

Mr. Halliburton tells us that the losses are light and that is because the losses are light to him. They mean nothing to him. Mr. Halliburton also stated this week that if the democrats should win, "the danger is that we'll get hit again." Is that a threat Mr. Haliburton? He also said that our people might believe that "these terrorist attacks are just criminal acts." They were criminal acts, Mr. Haliburton. They were definitely not the acts of any one nation and no nation should have been attacked because of them. They rightfully should have been dealt with by international police science.

Friends, there are over forty vigils for peace taking place in the greater Los Angeles areas every week. And some people still say, "Where's the peace movement?" Join us tonight to commemorate the dead and wounded, primarily civilians, in this thirteen year old massacre which was originally called the "Gulf War." In view of the fact that there are over 700 vigils planned nationally on this occasion of the death of over 1,000 U.S. service people, not to mention the thousands of severely wounded together with and endless number of Iraqi women, men and children, go directly to http://www.moveon.org to find the vigil nearest you. Most of these vigils will be tonight, Thursday, September 9, and a few will be on Friday, September 10.

Think of all the plans and dreams that have been shattered by this unnecessary slaughter.

Think of all those who come home are who are declared normal who will take their own lives as in the wake of Vietnam. Almost 60,000 dead in battle and more than 60,000 suicides in the aftermath of that failed venture.

Friends it seems quite clear that our government is not capable of solving its addiction to war. Our lawless administration continues to bomb homes, kill whole families, lay seige to neighborhoods and shoot Iraqis day in and day out on their own streets, in their own land. This death making addiction pushed by war profiteers will only be solved by millions of citizens demanding a civil society marked by national and international legality.

The Likudization of the World

September 17, 2004

Naomi Klein has identified a serious policy problem as she writes in *The Globe* and *Mail*. Her title is "The Likudization of the World."

Here are some of her thoughts:

Common wisdom has it that after September 11, a new era of geo-politics was ushered in, defined by what is usually called "the Bush Doctrine": pre-emptive wars, attacks on "terrorist infrastructure" (read: entire countries), an insistence that all the enemy understands is force. In fact it would be more accurate to call this rigid world-view "The Likud Doctrine." What happened on September 11 2001 is that the Likud Doctrine, previously targeted against Palestinians, was picked up by the most powerful nation on Earth and applied on a global scale. Call it the Likudization of the world, the real legacy of 9/11.

. . . What I mean is that on September 11, George W Bush went looking for a political philosophy to guide him in his new role as "War President" . . . He found that philosophy in the Likud Doctrine, conveniently handed to him ready-made by the ardent Likudniks already ensconced in the White House. No thinking required. In the three years since, the Bush White House has applied this imported logic with chilling consistency to its global "war on terror"— complete with the pathologising and medicalising of the "Muslim mind". It was the guiding philosophy in Afghanistan and Iraq, and may well extend to Iran and Syria. It's not simply that Bush sees America's role as protecting Israel from a hostile Arab world. It's that he has cast the United States in the very same role in which Israel casts itself, facing the very same threat. In this narrative, the U.S. is fighting a never ending battle for its very survival against utterly irrational forces that seek nothing less than its total extermination.

. . . Mr. Sharon says terrorism is an epidemic that "has no borders, no fences" but this is not the case. Everywhere in the world, terrorism thrives within the illegitimate borders of occupation and dictatorship; it festers behind "security walls" put up by imperial powers; it crosses those borders and climbs over those fences to explode inside the countries responsible for, or complicit in, occupation and domination. Ariel Sharon is not the commander in chief of the war on terror; that dubious honour stays with George Bush. But on the third year anniversary of September 11, he deserves to be recognized as this disastrous campaign's spiritual/intellectual guru, a kind of trigger-happy Yoda for all the wannabe Luke Skywalkers out there, training for their epic battles in good vs. evil.

If we want to see the future of where the Likud Doctrine leads, we need only follow the guru home, to Israel — a country paralyzed by fear, embracing pariah policies of extrajudicial assassination and illegal settlement, and in furious denial about the brutality it commits daily.

For a free copy of the complete article by Naomi Klein visit
http://www.naomiklein.org/articles/2004/09/likud-doctrine

Defeat

September 23, 2004

William Rivers Pitt wrote an editorial for the website www.truthout.org in which he said:

> Every reason to go to Iraq has failed to retain even a semblance of credibility. Every bit of propaganda Osama bin Laden served up to the Muslim world for why America should be attacked and destroyed has been given credibility by what has taken place in Iraq. Victory in this "War on Terror," a propaganda war from the beginning, has been given to the September 11 attackers by the hand of George W. Bush, and by the hand of those who enabled his incomprehensible blundering.

Support for the position of William Rivers Pitt is also the position of many senior U.S. military officers who now believe the war in Iraq has turned into a disaster on an unprecedented scale. Sidney Blumenthal quotes the former head of the National Security Agency, General William Odom saying, "Right now, the course we're on, is achieving Bin Laden's ends."

Jeffrey Record, professor of strategy at the Air War College, said: "I see no ray of light on the horizon at all. The worst case has become true. . . . I see no exit. We've been down that road before. It's called Vietnamization."

W. Andrew Terrill, professor at the Army War College's strategic studies institute and Iraq specialist said, "I don't think you can kill the insurgency. We see larger and more coordinated military attacks. They are getting better and they self-regenerate. The idea there are x number of insurgents, and that when they're all dead we can get out is wrong. The insurgency has shown an ability to regenerate itself because there are people willing to fill the ranks of those who are killed. The political culture is even more hostile to U.S. presence. The longer we stay, the more they are confirmed in their view."

General Odom has concluded that the tension between the Bush Administration and the senior military officers over Iraq is worse than any he has ever seen with previous governments, including the years of the Vietnam War.

Friends we are not giving the statements of a hostile power. We are giving the views of the highest levels of our own military. Let the frauds who started this war give any excuse they want and let them get out of Iraq now.

The Whining Billionaires

September 30, 2004

Welcome to California, the state of the whining billionaires, the state of the pouting millionaires. Welcome to the state of corrupt judges. Certainly anyone who can give a sentence of twenty-five years to life for minor shoplifting is corrupt on the very face of the action.

What kind of humanoids are we growing in this fertile soil?

If we utilize potential tax revenues in this state, just what could we do? We could have: clean air, the finest schools and universities, full health coverage for every citizen, and a world class public transit system. We could even identify a new privileged class including children, together with the mentally and physically ill.

Instead of this we have one of the world's largest prison states designed especially for people of color.

We have the largest percentage of incarcerated children of any polity in the world.

Just as suicide bombers are created by unjust oppression so are delinquents created by a lack of public resources. So what is to be done? Actually it is not complicated. If the billionaires and millionaires were taxed at the same level as janitors and hotel workers we could easily accomplish all of the above. But the whining billionaires don't pay taxes at the same level as janitors and hotel workers. On the contrary they have created a nearly tax free environment for themselves.

Now one of these privileged people happens to be the governor of California and just look at what he did for the common good today.

He vetoed a bill designed to clear the air in the nation's largest port, Los Angeles.

This port also happens to be the largest air polluter in California. So our children get asthma and cancer because Arnold vetoes the clean air bill.

Now, if I should injure one person's lungs, I would be committing a felony. But a billionaire governor allows millions of people to suffer lung damage because he does not want to offend his class.

Friends, a powerful club of whining billionaires and pouting millionaires is making it impossible for California to be all that it can be. Don't blame the victims. This is class warfare conducted by the rich. It is up to us to remind this club that they can't take it with them and that when they die they will hold in their hands only that which they have given away.

Israeli Tragedy

October 17, 2004

There was a horrible tragedy at a luxury hotel in Egypt. Innocent people were killed, primarily Israelis.

But what is the context of this tragedy? The context is that for over four decades, one of the world's strongest military forces has continued the oppression of a people who have no army. The oppressed people continue to fight back attempting to defend themselves. Some fight with stones and sling-shots. Others fight as suicide bombers. We abhor the killing on both sides. Regardless of the intentions of combatants, innocent people die. The side with the overwhelming military apparatus, however, bears the greatest responsibility.

The entire world knows this but those responsible remain in denial.

This month the United States vetoed a resolution demanding an immediate end to Israeli military operations in Gaza. The United States cast the sole veto vote. Our country continues not only to give cart-blanche approval to Israeli oppression but also to pay for it with a minimum of $5 billion of our tax money every year.

This money is used to occupy, humiliate, torture and kill Palestinians. Can any rational human being wonder why there is resistance? Does anyone think this represents the will of the people of the United States? Have we forgotten our national cry of independence, "Live free or die!"

The refugee camps in Gaza are the most densely populated areas in the world. Jabaliya Camp has 90,000 people living in an area of three square kilometers. Large scale Israeli military operations with heavy and very imprecise weaponry have yielded catastrophic casualties this month, especially among children.

The international community which insists that Israel cease and desist its long standing oppression has not based its case on anti-Semitism. Opponents of Israel's tactics include both Israelis and members of the world-wide Jewish community. But the behavior of the Israeli government and especially of Ariel Sharon and the Likud Party are unfortunately apt to yield a tragic legacy for the Jewish State.

Formula For Destruction

October 24, 2004

What is the formula for destroying a small and weak country? Let's look at some political history. For over a century Republican and Democratic Administrations have used the following methodology of intervention. In most cases the victim country is populated by people of color:

1. Demonize the head of state. That is usually easy in the case of most heads of state.
2. Demonize the people and their culture.
3. Attack them to make them free.
4. Kill all resistance.
5. Impose a puppet head of state who speaks good English and who knows how to follow orders.
6. Build an indigenous military, well schooled in torture and summary execution.
7. Support that army with equipment and training.
8. Insist that the leadership be maintained by demonstration elections, that is elections for U.S. domestic consumption.
9. Have all political decisions of the new government reviewed by the U.S. Embassy which becomes the de facto capital of the country.
10. This formula has been used for over a century in more than 100 interventions.

It is tragic that our students have little or no education on the reality of such unnecessary interventions which have taken millions of innocent lives including those of our troops who have been unnecessarily sacrificed. As you see this methodology unfold in the current effort to subdue Iraq's people, please review the history of: Mexico, Guatemala, Nicaragua, El Salvador, Honduras, Brazil, Dominican Republic, Grenada, Chile, Bolivia, Vietnam, Cambodia, Iran, Greece, Korea, Indonesia, British Guiana, Laos, Haiti, Algeria, Peru, Zaire, Jamaica, Suriname, Panama, and Afghanistan to name a few.

Friends, we are incapable of being instruments of positive change unless we have some understanding of what has come before us.

Aside from our daily slaughter in Iraq and Afghanistan we are observing the thugs and murderers who have been placed in the leadership of Haiti by our government and having their lies reported with obedient and compliant exactitude by a servile media. The actual moral leadership of Haiti is with Father Gerard Jean-Just who remains in a stinking cell in Port a Prince with a strong possibility of soon joining the thousands of people assassinated for seeking self-determination.

The Time Has Come

October 31, 2004

Here is a suggested sequence for the days ahead. Please have a pen and paper at hand: On Monday, November 1, join the candle light vigil for War is Not the Answer. This will take place at Wilshire Blvd. and Veteran from 6:00 to 8:00 P.M. Please bring a candle, a sign and a paper cup.

On the following day, election day, cast your vote to remove one of the most destructive administrations in U.S. history. Let's not hear one word of cynicism. Let's hear intelligence, critical thinking and optimistic hope. You are invited to sign on to an urgent response network to be activated in the event of another stolen election. The website for this is www.nov3.us.

If there is serious voter disenfranchisement we ask you to join in protests beginning on Wednesday, November 3. You can both list events and find out where events are located by contacting the website www. unitedforpeace.org.

You are also invited to join us on Friday, November 5 at The Immanuel Presbyterian Church for an evening entitled "Peace is Possible." sponsored by KPFK and the Office of the Americas. The dinner reception starts at 5:30 P.M. and the program at 7:00 P.M.

On the following day, Saturday, November 6 at Noon there will be a march and rally beginning at Hollywood Blvd and Highland demanding and end to all occupations from Iraq to Haiti to Palestine.

Friends, the unnecessary, failed, illegal and immoral rape of Iraq has now gone on for fourteen years. I recall the eager students and the large number of women students and faculty at Al-Mustansiriya University in Baghdad. Today researchers at that university together with scholars from Johns Hopkins University and Columbia University have concluded that the U.S. invasion and occupation of Iraq has resulted in the deaths of at least 100,000 Iraqis. The study further reveals that most of the Iraqis who died were killed in violent deaths, primarily carried out by U.S. air strikes and that most of the individuals killed were women and children.

That's right Mr. Kerry. We may vote for you but please understand that we pledge absolutely no allegiance to your on-going war policy. Get out of Iraq now.

Veterans Day

November 11, 2004

Purported Prime Minister Ayad Allawi stated that the people were leaving the city of Fallujah because they were terrorized by terrorists. In his warped wisdom Allawi was talking about the citizens of Fallujah being afraid of the citizens of Fallujah. What was taking place, however, was something entirely different. Terror was raining down from AC-130 gun ships which circled the city all night long. This aircraft can put a high velocity slug into every square foot of a football field as it flies over. This is a totally dumb weapon. There is no precision to it. It is a weapon of indiscriminate killing. This monstrosity of death literally rained fire on Fallujah throughout an entire night. In the mindless babble of massacre, this is called "softening up" the target. Freely translate that to mean mass murder of civilians in Fallujah including many children.

But wait, this is holy murder, the Colonel told us so. Marine Colonel Gary Brandl commented: "The enemy has a face, it is Satan's. He is in Fallujah, and we are going to destroy him." Now exactly how does one distinguish Colonel Brandl from the Taliban?

Friends, crimes against humanity are being conducted on a daily basis in Iraq. Hospitals are under attack, mosques are defiled and ambulances are fired upon. The entire world looks on in disbelief and pledges resistance. After fourteen years of systematic destruction, we must leave Iraq now. In short we must repent.

A certain amount of repentance can be achieved by a presidential resignation. Remember Richard Nixon? He won his second term by a landslide in 1972 and he resigned the presidency in the summer of 1974. Because of the hard work of the legal community and informed citizenry, Mr. Nixon was forced to resign in the wake of the Watergate scandal. But Mr. Bush and his cohorts have dozens of scandals far worse than Watergate. For the sake of the world's people who are shocked and traumatized by our pursuit of endless war and our recent electoral circus, we must work vigorously for a Nixonian solution to our pathological problem presidency.

It's Time for Hearings

November 18, 2004

It is not simply one exhausted, angry and frightened Marine that shoots a wounded person. It is not simply a young woman rejected by Wal-Mart who tortures Iraqi prisoners. Napoleon said, "There are no bad soldiers, there are only bad officers."

Yes, it is the criminal directives of the commander in chief and his Faustian club of yes people. It is the illegal orders of the secretary of defense, It is the disingenuous demonization of the Iraqi people as high ranking officers prepare their troops for the killing fields. It is the buffoon opportunist Allawi who betrays his people by saying there were no civilian casualties in Fallujah. It is a media that has lost its credibility by placing profit above journalism. It is now it is up to us to bring this criminal administration to justice as the rest of the world looks at our country as a rogue and lawless state. (Note the Republican leadership changing the rules to exempt their leader from long standing norms of ethics).

Democrats might try to cop out by saying, "With a Republican House and Senate impeachment proceedings will fail." Do not let your Representative off the hook by such a weak comment. Any Representative and any Senator can call a hearing on the war crimes of our administration. It is our responsibility to demand that these hearings begin immediately in the House and in the Senate.

Call your Representatives at the congressional switchboard 202-225-3121 and demand that the hearings begin. Remind the Democrats of their rights as a minority party and how they can recover their missing backbone.

We want an accounting of the civilian casualties in Fallujah and the rest of that destroyed nation. Why are the Red Cross and the Red Crescent forbidden to operate? Why are hospitals taken over and why are Iraqi civilians denied access? Why are indiscriminate air attacks made on civilian targets? How many homes have been destroyed, how many schools? How many mosques? How many ambulances have been attacked? Who exempted the United States from the international prohibi-

49

tion on aggressive war? Such hearings are primarily a challenge to the Democrats in the House and Senate. After such hearings take place with or without impeachment we can begin our petition for a presidential resignation. Thanks for your wonderful example, Mr. Nixon.

Thanksgiving

November 25, 2004

Let us be thankful that Mr. Nixon had the brilliance to resign from the presidency in August of 1974. And remember, this resignation was over a little thing called the "Watergate Caper." Our current situation is many times worse that Watergate. We are also thankful that many Generals in the United States military have denounced the War in Iraq.

And we are thankful that torture is absolutely forbidden by the Universal Declaration of Human Rights and that those responsible must be punished.

Let us be thankful for the unembedded reporters who at great risk are practicing investigative journalism and identifying the terror practiced in our name.

And our thanks to the people of Spain who have removed their neofascist leader and replaced him with a brilliant progressive, Mr. Shoemaker (Zapatero).

And we must not forget the well organized and courageous people of Bolivia who removed their incompetent president by way of militant nonviolence.

And gratitude to the people of Ecuador who removed two presidents without access to the armed struggle.

And thanks to the people of Brazil who placed a life long labor leader into the leadership of one of the world's largest countries.

And congratulations to the people of Haiti for getting exactly the President they wanted elected by two landslide victories. His removal by our misguided leadership simply indicts them with one more criminal act.

And congratulations to those people in the United States and in the Ukraine who are demanding electoral justice.

And thanks to those citizens working to eliminate that ancient relic called the "Electoral College," which is a clear statement of the lack of trust our founders had in the common people. And thanks for stunning overreach of the Republican Congress as they try in vain to protect their leader from the demands of ethics. And thanks to the people of Venezuela who have chosen an African, Indian, Latino who represents the common good of that great country.

Oh yes, and thanks for those who want to allow someone not born in the USA to be president, for example Jean Bertrand Aristide.

Take heart America, the dawn is about to break, the dark days of state terror and the reign of the father of lies is waning.

———

Let the War Crimes Hearings Begin

December 1, 2004

International hearings on the criminality of the Bush administration have begun and continue vigorously.

The process began in Belgium but was muzzled by threats from the singular superpower.

And now, The Center for Constitutional Rights is filing a lawsuit in Germany against war crimes in Iraq. In a historic effort to hold high ranking U.S. officials accountable for brutal acts of torture including the widely publicized abuses carried out at Abu Ghraib, the Center for Constitutional Rights under the direction of Michael Ratner together with four Iraqi citizens will file a criminal complaint with the German Federal Prosecutor's Office at the Karsruhe Court in Germany. Under the doctrine of universal jurisdiction, suspected war criminals may be prosecuted regardless of where they are located.

And as Bush visited our northern neighbor, Canadian Lawyers charged him with torture under the Canadian Criminal Code. Attorney Gail Davidson stated the charges under provisions enacted pursuant to the United Nations Torture Convention.

Just yesterday, the United Nations panel on restructuring defined terrorism as:

> . . . any action that is intended to cause death or serious bodily harm to civilians or noncombatants, when the purpose of such act, by its nature or context, is to intimidate a population or to compel a government or an international organization to do or abstain from doing any act.

Using the new United Nations definition of terrorism, in the wake of Shock and Awe, it seems impossible to exempt the United States from that charge.

This United Nations definition of terrorism is quite different from the Bush definition which is, in short: "Terrorism is anything that differs with me." Friends, international rationality and the rule of law are going to overcome the rampant lies and arrogance which surrounds us.

As the international community gives the lead, please continue your efforts to awaken your sleepy members of Congress and demand that the hearings taking place internationally come home for fruition. I think our people are capable of finally recognizing the sham religiosity of murder, torture, rape and racism in the name of Jesus.

A Message from
the Gentle of the Earth

December 9, 2004

The Friends Committee on National Legislation evolved from the Quaker Church. Quakers have long understood and fostered the message of Peace on Earth. Please urge your church, synagogue or mosque to follow their lead.

At its annual meeting in Washington, D.C., the Friends Committee on National Legislation General Committee approved its legislative priorities for the 109th Congress. Included in its new priorities is:

> Remove all U.S. military forces and bases from Iraq, and fulfill U.S. moral and legal obligations to reconstruct Iraq through appropriate multinational, national, and Iraqi agencies.

The Friends Committee on National Legislation is urging members of Congress to initiate and support a sense of Congress resolution stating, as a principle of intent, that it is in the interest of the U.S. to remove all troops and bases from Iraq. In the meantime, urgent action is needed to address the spiraling violence.

Congress must demand an end to all U.S.-led offensive military operations in Iraq and an immediate U.S. initiated cease-fire. Congress must demand accountability for all violations of international law in Iraq.

Previous to this demand, the St. Louis Friends Meeting made a statement to the people of Iraq:

> As Quakers, and people of peace, we abhor and are deeply sorry for the acts of aggression, oppression, humiliation and torture committed by the United States Government in Iraq and elsewhere. We have opposed from the beginning the invasion and the ongoing occupation of Iraq by United States forces. And we humbly apologize for the death, injury, abuse and material destruction that have resulted from this use of force.

Rather than revel in broadside attacks on the religious community, it would be wise for many liberals to understand the radical simplicity of authentic spirituality.

Friends, we must understand that not every pulpit has been taken over by nationalistic fundamentalists, self righteous fools and blood thirsty war mongers.

Test your congregation to see if it has the sound spiritual integrity manifested by the Quakers and the Friends Committee on National Legislation.

Tyranny

December 17, 2004

Tyranny is the arbitrary or unrestrained exercise of power or the despotic abuse of authority by the government. During this time of year we recall the tyrant Herod and how he ordered the death of all of the children under the age of two in Bethlehem. They were called the "Holy Innocents."

The parents of Jesus were advised that they should get out of the country immediately so their son would not be killed. They became illegal aliens in Egypt until such time as it was possible to return quietly to their homeland.

And such it is today. Thousands of members of the armed services have fled, civilians are leaving the country as war crimes continue in Iraq. Tyrants lie because they believe they have a right to define truth. Washington says, "We think you have a nuclear bomb, therefore we are going to kill you. You ask why we can have thousands of nuclear bombs? Do you have a problem with that? Do you want to fight about it?" Far more would be accomplished by having tea with various world leaders. Now that the high powered hype of political campaigns is over we can actually get a handle on what the majority of our citizens want. Here are a few examples: The majority of people in the United States believe we should accept the jurisdiction of the International Criminal Court. The majority of the people in the United States believe that we should accept the Kyoto Accords on the environment. A large majority of our citizens believe that the United Nations and not the United States should take the lead in matters of security, reconstruction and political transition in Iraq. Overwhelming majorities of the public (some 80 percent) favor expansion of domestic programs, primarily health care, education and social security. As we might expect, the current claims that Social Security is bankrupt are classic administration falsehoods.

There are 80 percent that favor guaranteed health care even if it would raise taxes. Friends we use the word tyranny because the government is acting in direct opposition to the needs and desires of its citizens. We must continue our day to day efforts to have a functioning democratic culture in which the public plays a role in determining policy. As he grew into adulthood, Jesus referred to King Herod as a fox. Similarly we have a fox in our chicken coop.

Militarism and Christianity

December 23, 2004

Back in the first century A.D. there was an illegal, clandestine, community living in Rome. Its members were subject to the Roman Law which stated: *"Non licet esse Christianus,"* "It is not legal to be a Christian." The penalty was death.

The Romans were very good at logic and they determined that a member of this new sect could not possibly be a good citizen of empire. If you could not accept the emperor as a deity, you would not be a good citizen. Loyalty to the carpenter from Nazareth and loyalty to empire was clearly contradictory. After three centuries of being fed to the lions, Christianity was vindicated. Constantine the Great came forward with the Edict of Toleration and then went even further. He became a Christian.

The tragedy in the emperor's conversion was that he immediately imposed the culture of empire onto his newly selected church. He put the symbol of Jesus on the Roman Shield and began a period of muscular Christianity known as Christendom. The sword and the cross were joined in a political marriage of imperial conquest. I think that Islam was one of many responses to this form of militaristic Christianity. To be sure there were millions of Christians who rejected the violence of The Holy Roman Empire. Both in and out of the monastery Religious Orders were formed to promote and foster the lifestyle taught by Jesus. St Francis of Assisi even met with the Islamic leader Saladin to talk of peace in the midst of the Crusades. But sadly the political control of Christianity continued. There were six-hundred years of inquisition. There was the violence of the Conquistadores in this hemisphere. And there were Christian chaplains on both sides during the great wars of the twentieth century to imply that God was on both sides.

Many great people lived their Christian faith in the midst of these centuries in spite of the violence of political Christianity. Most U.S. Christians whether Protestant or Catholic were brought up with this very same imperial theology which joined their religion to state violence. Fortunately an international response began to this ongoing contradiction. What was called "Liberation Theology" became a major issue at the Puebla Conference in Mexico in 1979 and many followers of Jesus determined that it was indeed impossible to serve God and to serve empire. While they were too rigid in their punishments, the pre-Constantinian Roman Empire was correct in its logic. You just cannot serve God and serve empire.

Out with the Old Year

December 30, 2004

Congratulations to the world community as it responds to the worst natural disaster in two centuries. What a great reflection on just how small this planet is and what a moment to observe the oneness of the human race. All of our mindless separations based on color, creed, ethnicity and nation seem so silly in the wake of this calamity. We are in fact one family. There is but one tribe on this planet and it is the human race. But many remain paralyzed under a tsunami of division, a tidal wave of ignorance, greed violence and fear. Did someone say that the United States would contribute $35 million in aid? That is but the cost of one fancy house in Beverly Hills and that is less than will be spent on the coronation which is to take place in Washington, D.C. on January 20.

Friends, we cannot control the tectonic plates of this beautiful planet. We can however abolish a war system directed by mental pygmies, war profiteers and a sycophant media. If we want this planet to remain our home, we must put an end to the crimes for which we pay. Those responsible for such unnecessary slaughter are traitors to the planet, traitors to the human race and terrorists of the worst kind.

Once the war mongers are restrained we can begin to use our resources to heal the daily disasters of deaths from curable diseases and starvation. We might even be able to care for 20 percent of the children in Los Angeles who are malnourished. International cooperation could even put a tsunami warning system in the Indian Ocean. And please, don't bring out the tired old neo Malthusian myth about a population explosion. The explosions we must be concerned about are those of over 10,000 nuclear weapons here in the United States. Any one of these diabolical instruments could take far more lives than the current disaster.

There are easily a thousand people in Los Angeles who can contribute a million dollars or more to assist in the current international relief efforts. That's a billion from Los Angeles alone. With this as a norm, our nation could easily contribute $10 billion from the private sector in immediate disaster relief without anyone missing a single cocktail at the nineteenth hole.

Now is the time to wake from sleep and to put on the garments of sincerity and truth.

May this New Year be a happy one and lead us all into a new way of thinking.

One Senator Please

January 5, 2005

Do you remember that scene in Michael Moore's *Fahrenheit 9/11* when, in a joint session of Congress a group of Representatives begged for just one Senator to join them in a challenge to the Florida electoral college delegation? Well that scene might take place again tomorrow. The Constitution directs Congress to ratify the result of the Presidential Election in order to make it official. Congressman John Conyers has chaired hearings into Republican behavior in Ohio which include: inhibiting voter registration, inhibiting voting, misleading counts of the total vote, tampering with voting machines and local officials making up rules spontaneously about which votes will or wont be counted.

Please contact Senators Boxer and Feinstein immediately and urge them to stand up with the Members of the House of Representatives. After just one Senator stands up Congress will be compelled to debate the issues, which have been identified in Ohio.

An open debate would expose a clear destruction of voter's rights. The type of computer voting used in Ohio simply cannot be audited. Friends, what we are saying is that the election of November 2, 2004 was fundamentally flawed. Investigations of vote suppression are also taking place in New Hampshire, New Mexico, Florida and Nevada. While the internet and the international press have covered this extensively, the corporate media in our country has remained silent. Personally I would hope to see a new election conducted with a voter verified permanent record. Regardless of whether my wish succeeds we can all support House Resolution 2239, The Voter Confidence and Increased Accessibility Act which has been introduced into the House of Representatives by Congressman Holt. A voter verified permanent record or hard copy of each ballot would be required. There will be a rally at 10:00 A.M. tomorrow in Lafayette Park across from the White House, this rally will be followed by a march to the Capitol at Noon.

What is at stake here is our right to vote. That right has not been protected in the years 2000 and 2004. Electronic voting machine fraud, and partisan discriminatory decisions by state officials must cease. Call

Senator Boxer and Senator Feinstein now and leave a message insisting that they both stand up tomorrow to join with the members of the House of Representatives to expose the failed election in Ohio.

The Salvador Option

January 12, 2005

After four years of lies about weapons of mass destruction, about Saddam's links with September 11, and about our motives for this war, after the denial and ignoring of civilian casualties, after the refusal to even photograph our returning dead and wounded, after the ugliest and brutal routine practice of torture as a scandal to the world, after the destruction of numerous holy sites including the complete destruction of one of Iraq's largest cities and after listening to the imposed Iraqi head of state fortify the previous lies and add to them by saying there were no civilian casualties in Fallujah, our policy and our objectives are in complete disarray, flawed, counterproductive and failed. So what are the pathological liars going to do now? According to *Newsweek* magazine they are going to install the Salvador option which is the Central American option.

Many of us witnessed that option personally for more than a decade. Quite simply this so-called option means torturing and killing anyone that might be suspected of possibly favoring the resistance in any way. This is the option of killing every man woman and child in the town of El Mozote, El Salvador because they were suspected of possibly supporting some rebels. This is the option of raping and murdering religious women who may not cherish the corrupt Salvadoran government, this is the option of murdering the Archbishop because he told the troops to stop the oppression.

Indeed the Salvador or Central American option is to hire mercenaries to torture and kill social workers, teachers, coop members, land tenure experts. In short the so-called Salvador option is to add war crime to war crime after a hideous record of aggression.

What is to be done?

- An immediate cease fire and halt to all military actions.
- A withdrawal of all U.S. bases and forces from Iraq.
- Assuring the territorial integrity and sovereignty of Iraq.

- Funding Iraqi efforts to re-employ ministry staff, train new police and security forces.
- Terminating contracts with U.S. corporations and giving Iraqis control over reconstruction funds.
- In short to stabilize Iraq by committing to long-term U.S. financial support for Iraqi-led reconstruction.

To continue our ongoing Iraq massacre or even worse, to engage in the Salvador option is the formula for the moral destruction of the United States of America.

Inauguration Day

January 19, 2005

Time Magazine's Man of the Year will be inaugurated tomorrow.

I read the puff piece in *Time* and was reminded of the Irish lady at her husband's funeral.

The priest went on and on about what a great man her husband was and after fifteen minutes of this his wife looked at her daughter and said, "Would you go up to the altar and see who is in the box?"

What we now have in Washington is a political cult. In place of Jim Jones we have a leader who has surrounded himself with yes people. He has selected no one to serve in his cabinet who is willing to offer a critical thought. Bush condones torture. His selection for Attorney General condones torture. Bush wants to take out Iran, his selection for Secretary of State will say, "Me too."

As every cult leader, Bush is a fear monger.

Iraq was going to attack us. No it was not. He did that one for the war profiteers. Social Security is running on empty! No it is not. Just remove the cap on wealthy recipients who do not pay one cent more into Social Security than people earning half as much as they do. He is doing this one for Wall Street Medical malpractice suits are hurting the economy. No they are not. They are keeping the medical profession on its toes. He did this one for the insurance companies.

We are fighting terrorists called "al-Qaeda"? If such a group exists Bush has done everything possible to make it grow.

Our punishment for Iraq is simply ongoing terror.

We celebrated the life of the great Martin Luther King this week. What a shame that some of the organizers did not want expressions from the peace movement. Apparently the organizers were not aware of Dr. King's militant opposition to the Indo China War.

Actually Dr. King has the program for us. We must take to the streets as never before. We do not want to be led by a cult leader who accepts no criticism and who, as every cult leader thinks he speaks for God. Join us on Counter-Inauguration Day, Thursday, January 20 at the Westwood Federal Building on the corner of Wilshire and Veteran at 6:00 P.M. This will be the beginning of demonstrations to continue as long as this individual is in office. We are demonstrating for the lives of our troops, the rights of the Iraqi people, the rights of the people in this country who are trying to live on maxed out credit cards.

We want Mr. Bush to follow the excellent example of Richard Nixon and to resign as soon as possible.

Freedoms We Don't Want

January 26, 2005

We heard a great deal about freedom in the recent inaugural address. Have you ever thought about the freedoms that you don't want?

Here are a few I don't want:

The freedom to die of malnutrition.
The freedom to die of curable diseases.
The freedom for children to become sex slaves.
The freedom to be illiterate.
The freedom to be cluster bombed.
The freedom from all international law.
The freedom to tell lies that take lives.
The freedom to violate the sovereignty of any nation for any reason.
The freedom to renew the Divine Right of Kings as a national policy.
The freedom of the conquistadores to enslave, oppress and impose religion.
The freedom to torture.
The freedom to practice state terror.
The freedom to reduce cities to rubble.
The freedom to depose popular and peace loving leaders in places like Haiti and Venezuela.

And I don't want the corporations to have freedom to destroy the sacred atmosphere that surrounds our planet.

And while corporate criminals and their servants in politics continue a rampage of global destruction they are destroying our youth, robbing our treasury, and trashing our nation.

This orgy of mass murder is now opposed by the gaia, by the planet itself. Dr. Rajendra Pachauri, head of the United Nations Intergovernmental Panel on Climate Change, a man who was strongly backed by Bush for the position, now echoes the finding of many climate scientists who say it might now be too late to avert environmental disasters. While

69

our out of control administration believes it has the freedom to resist any references to climate change at the global conference on disaster preparation, the dollar is in an international freefall and our mindless leadership is planning to blow up Iran.

A world organized around markets and profits, forgetting nature and people, is ill-equipped to deal either with tsunamis or the degradation of our precious atmosphere. We must understand, as states Vandana Shiva, that we are earth beings, compassion, not money is the currency of our oneness.

Humane Economics

February 3, 2005

They call it the dismal science. But economics would no longer have to be dismal if it brought in the human equation.

What makes economics dismal is the fact that the gauges it uses are outdated.

It is like having the instrument panel of a Ford Tri-motor Aircraft on a giant 757. Gauges like the gross national product are not meaningful as regards human development.

If there are two people in the society and one person has $1 million and the other has nothing, the average income is $500,000. In spite of this average one of the two can be living in misery.

What is to be done? Create new and meaningful gauges. The most meaningful economic gauge is the Gross Social Product. Such a gauge does not measure income averages, on the contrary it measures the quality of life.

The gross social product would graph:

What is air quality this year as compared with last year?

What is the quality of water this year as compared to last year?

And we would similarly compare the quality of public transit?

What is the health care delivery this year as compared with last year? Who is still left out? How many homeless this year?

What about dentistry? Are half of the people in the United States still unable to go to a dentist?

What is the quality of public education?

What is the level of diplomacy practiced by the nation? How well does it cooperate with international agencies? How generous are we with international disaster relief?

What have we done this year to maintain international peace?

You see those who want to privatize the state of our union only deal platitudes and flights of fancy. Without a doubt privatization will increase the Gross National Product, and war will increase the Gross National Product. The only problem is that the gross national product has nothing to do with the quality of life in our country or the planet. In short, economic growth is not the measure of quality of life. the way to measure quality of life is to install the new gauge, the Gross Social Product. This gauge will identify war as bankruptcy. This gauge will lead us to distributive justice and thereby curtail crime. This gauge will take the word "dismal" out of the science of economics and make its professionals something more than a group of hired guns trying to protect individual corporations by every form of chicanery. This gauge, the gross social product, will identify the current state of the union as an ongoing fraud against the people who live here.

The Budget

February 9, 2005

When you call your members of Congress today and the rest of the week, please consider the following recommendations. Remind them that there is not one cent in this new and massive budget to pay for endless wars in Iraq and Afghanistan. Therefore when they receive the new request for $80 billion more as a supplemental appropriation request they should:

1. Oppose any new funds: No supplemental $80 billion for endless war. Any new funds should be allocated solely for troop withdrawal and interim troop protection.
2. End the occupation: Halt U.S. military actions immediately, shift U.S. troops to the borders of Iraq and leave no U.S. bases behind. Support Congresswoman Lynn Woolsey's (D-CA) resolution calling on the President to begin the immediate withdrawal of U.S. troops from Iraq.
3. Support Iraqi sovereignty: Give Iraqis full control over reconstruction funds including Iraqi ministries, new police and security forces. Terminate contracts with U.S. companies and turn projects over to Iraqis while providing transparent accounting of all U.S. contracts.
4. Stabilize Iraq: Commit to long-term U.S. financial support for Iraqi-led reconstruction and allow the U.N. and other international agencies to support an Iraq democracy free from U.S. intervention.
5. Provide real support for our troops: End the "stop-loss" policies that keep troops on active duty far beyond their contracts. Provide thorough psychological counseling, health care, and benefits to returning Iraq war veterans and their families. Bring our troops home!

And while we hypocritically turn our sights on Iran accusing that country of having an incipient nuclear weapons program, U.S. nuclear weapons spending has grown by 84 percent since 1995. The total cost of our nuclear forces is $40 billion annually. This includes 10,000 nuclear warheads with some 2,000 on hair-trigger alert. By what warped logic do we think we have a right to these genocidal instruments? And we are the only power that has used them.

The proposed budget is an immoral document. Anyone concerned about moral values in or out of government should simply reject it. Where your treasure is, there your heart will be.

The True Faith

February 16, 2005

Why is religion such an area for hatred, political conflict and war? Mahatma Gandhi dealt with this problem on a daily basis. Gandhi saw no distinction between the City of God and the City of Man. He insisted that there be a political consciousness in religion and a religious consciousness in politics. In short he saw them as the same. If spiritual people reject ahimsa or non-harm they will approve of every form of violence to attain their objectives. Saints, he thought, could be more murderous than sinners. In short, he saw the trap of fundamentalisms.

Religion must rid itself of dogmatic certainty. Shedding dogma intellectually is required in order to practice non-harm in the physical world. In a parallel to the Hippocratic oath of doctors, the religionists must agree to do no harm and thus open their minds to the validity of other faiths. The proof of faith is not doctrinal purity. That should be obvious from centuries of inquisition conducted according to Dostoevsky by people who had no faith at all. Instead of the impossible task of trying to define God, the person of faith defines a life-style of total dedication, sacrifice and love. This is the "proof of faith."

This is how Satyagraha or truth force can become the motor force of religion and politics. Satyagraha is direct action without violence. It is the true act of faith. It includes refusal to cooperate with laws that are unjust joined with the willingness to suffer the consequences. Yes, we are speaking of non-violent law-breaking. At a meeting in South Africa in 1906, 3,000 Indian citizens met at the Empire Theatre in Johannesburg. On the agenda was an item resolving that the members of the Indian community would go to jail rather than to submit to an ordinance requiring them to carry a residency permit under pain of deportation or prison. At first it was to be decided by majority vote. But then Gandhi suggested that each person should decide for themselves whether to take a vow before God to break this law. A vow was different from a majority vote. By taking a vow each person has an obligation to keep it. "A person who lightly pledges their word and then breaks it is a person of straw," said Gandhi. All present rose and took the vow. In the case of the Indian community in Transvaal it meant deliberate violation of a government ordinance and a commitment to fill the local jails.

Regardless of our religious or non-religious background, as we rid ourselves of dogmatic certainty, as we accept non-harm and a dedication to truth force, we will become spiritually capable of the non-cooperation which is required to end corrupt government.

Coalition of
Justice and Peace Groups

March 3, 2005

It was a privilege to participate in a massive gathering of some five hundred peace and justice organizations in St. Louis last month. We were struck by the maturity of the assembly and the harmony demonstrated by so many autonomous communities working together under the banner of United for Peace and Justice.

One key action, which we should all support, is coming up shortly. I am speaking of the International Day of Protest against the War in Iraq which is planned for Saturday, March. We ask all groups to endorse and support this day of protest in Los Angeles which is called by the Answer Coalition. For information call 323-464-1636.

We demand an end to the occupation of Iraq and denounce it as one of history's great war crimes.

Some thoughts on how to do it:

- Any supplemental budgetary funds granted by Congress must include expenditures for immediate withdrawal of U.S. troops from Iraq. This means ending the occupation and removal of U.S. bases. This position is in support of Congresswoman Lynn Woolsey's recent resolution.
- Support Iraqi sovereignty by giving them control over reconstruction. Support international agencies assisting in reconstruction.
- Provide real support for our troops by ending the "stop loss" policy, which keeps troops on active duty far beyond their contract agreements. Provide psychological counseling, health care and benefits to returning Iraq veterans and their families.

The art of making a moral revolution is the art of uniting forces. We look for the unification of all progressive forces in opposition to the on-going criminality of the Iraq War. We will accomplish this by identifying our strategic points of unity. Clearly there are many things to be done and it is logical to have a division of labor among these hundreds of grass roots organizations.

We will gather at noon on Saturday, March 19 on the famous corner of Hollywood and Vine to recall the infamous day when this on-going disaster began. The Iraq War is spiritually bankrupting the United States, killing its youth and massacring innocent civilians.

Torture

March 9, 2005

Jonathan Schell has referred to the media as the obfuscation industry. Let us cut through that obfuscation regarding the matter of torture. The President of the United States, the Attorney General and the Secretary of State and the Secretary of Defense have made themselves perfectly clear. They all approve torture. They support torture and they promote torture. There is absolutely no question about it. They know it goes on in our domestic prisons, they know it goes on in our military behavior. They know that through a foul process called "rendition" we are also sending suspects to torture and death in foreign lands without due process.

The mealy mouthed comments, the weasel words and the flat out double talk of these four officials have made their approval of torture transparent.

The entire torture industry, much of which is conducted by corporate mercenaries, represents the face of evil. First and foremost, it is immorality at its lowest and most stinking level. It is wrong, unforgivable and self-condemning on the face.

Secondly torture endangers our personnel overseas. Instead of the Geneva Accords which instruct all combatants that they are to give only their name rank and serial number, they now can expect torture treatment in kind.

As the Grand Inquisitor showed him the instruments of torture, Galileo was content to say that the sun goes around the earth. No one should be expected to say anything true under torture. Torture is simply the pristine form of terrorism. It is nothing less than extreme rape.

Those who conduct torture the are living dead. They are shallow, banal, obedient zombies. It would be better for them if they had never been born. The statements of top officials demonstrate the dictionary definition of mealy mouthed. What they say about torture amounts to either avoiding the question or flat out lies. Torture is also unconstitutional and illegal. A functional Congress would begin impeachment proceedings immediately.

In the centuries of history of this abomination, nothing of value has been learned. Nothing but the inhumanity of the torturers.

Universal Declaration of Human Rights states in Article Five: No one shall be subjected to torture or to cruel, inhuman or degrading treatment or punishment.

Demand an end to this disgrace to the United States of America.

Terri Schiavo

March 23, 2005

The sheer opportunism of the President and the Congress has been made clear to the world. They have taken advantage of a woman who has lived in a vegetative condition for fifteen years in order to promote their deadly agenda.

"It is wisest to always err on the side of life," says the President in a historic statement of hypocrisy. Did he err on the side of life by sending thousands of healthy young Americans to death, serious injury and mental illness in an unnecessary war in Iraq?

Did he err on the side of life by massacring endless thousands of healthy Iraqi children and other non-combatants?

Congress holds a special session, Bush jets back to the nation's capital. Dr. Quentin Young (http://www.pnhp.org) who chairs the Department of Medicine at Chicago's Cook County Hospital says:

> It is stunning how little regard this president has for human life. His interest seems to extend to only one tragic brain-damaged woman. The U.S. is the only industrialized country to lack health care coverage for all citizens. Over 18,000 Americans perish every year because they lack health insurance. A lack of health insurance increases the chances a fifty-five-year-old will die before they turn sixty-four by 40 percent. If the President wanted to save lives he would call for an emergency session to make Congress vote to extend Medicare to every American.

Jesuit Father Simon Harak (http://www.warresisters.org) says:

> The more universal your ethical principles are, the more moral force they will have. I hear of Bush's flying back to D.C. to sign the Schiavo bill, and I think of him flying back from his first presidential campaign to sign the death warrants of Texas prisoners. I think of Bush signing a bill in Texas to cut off funds for life support for people who want their children to live, but can't afford it. I hear of the government's concern for this individual, tragic case, and I think of the hundreds of thousands

of Iraqi children whom we diseased and starved to death during sanctions, and now the hundred thousand more Iraqis who have died in this invasion and occupation.

Friends, if our minds are clear, we will acknowledge that we have witnessed this administration conduct one great act of self condemnation. May Terri Schiavo rest in peace and may there be reconciliation between her husband and her parents. Neither Pope nor President have authority over her future.

The Words of Camilo Mejia

March 30, 2005

My words today are taken from some of the comments made by Camilo Mejia who has recently completed a year in prison for refusing to return to fight in Iraq as he sought the status of conscientious objector.

I was deployed to Iraq in April 2003 and returned home for a two-week leave in October. Going home gave me the opportunity to put my thoughts in order and to listen to what my conscience had to say. People would ask me about my war experiences and answering them took me back to all the horrors-the firefights, the ambushes, the time I saw a young Iraqi dragged by his shoulders through a pool of his own blood or an innocent man was decapitated by our machine gun fire. The time I saw a soldier broken down inside because he killed a child, or an old man on his knees, crying with his arms raised to the sky, perhaps asking God why we had taken the life of his son.

I thought of the suffering of a people whose country was in ruins and who were further humiliated by the raids, patrols and curfews of an occupying army.

And I realized that none of the reasons we were told about why we were in Iraq turned out to be true. I couldn't find a single good reason for having been there, for having shot at people and for having been shot at.

I realized that I was part of a war that I believed was immoral and criminal, a war of aggression, a war of imperial domination. I realized that acting upon my principles became incompatible with my role in the military, and I decided that I could not return to Iraq.

By putting my weapon down, I chose to reassert myself as a human being.

I have not deserted the military or been disloyal to the men and women of the military. I have not been disloyal to a country. I have only been loyal to my principles.

When I turned myself in, with all my fears and doubts, I did it not only for myself. I did it for the people of Iraq, even for those who fired upon me. They were just on the other side of a battleground where war itself was the only enemy. I did it for the Iraqi children, who are victims of mines and depleted uranium. I did it for the thousands of unknown civilians killed in war. My time in prison is a small price compared to the price Iraqis and Americans have paid with their lives.

I say that I don't believe in heroes, but I believe that ordinary people can do extraordinary things.

Camilo's web site is: www.freecamilo.org

Conscience

There seems to be some differences about the place of conscience in the Catholic Church. And there ought to be. Some Catholics thought that conscience was only for Protestants and they certainly could have received this impression from various Popes.

The Vatican Council of 1962–1965 was a liberating moment for millions of Catholics.

Here is the statement on conscience:

> The human person sees and recognizes the demands of the divine law through conscience. All are bound to follow their conscience faithfully in every sphere of activity. Therefore the individual must not be forced to act against conscience nor be prevented from acting according to conscience, especially in religious matters.
>
> —*Declaration on Religious Liberty*
> Second Vatican Council, 1965

It was conscience that led me to defy a gag order from the Church regarding U.S. military intervention in Guatemala. It was conscience that led Theresa to leave her convent post in southern Chile and become a Social Worker in Los Angeles.

Thanks to this clear understanding of conscience Theresa and I have been married for thirty-five years. We would like to be the change that we desire. We are grateful for following our conscience, having children and becoming grandparents.

The removal of conscience as the ultimate norm of action is one definition of a cult.

And sadly, many people have a cultish relationship to their faith. It is at this transition moment in history that we must urge people to listen to their inner voice and to remove all cultish and mindless behavior from their spiritual formation.

The key to an enlightened conscience is critical thinking. I thank my father for his instruction on this matter. As a prominent attorney and later Judge of the Superior Court his critical mind was always in gear even as he sat at Mass on Sunday and listened to the sermon. On one occasion, the priest was ranting and raving and gesticulating about some esoteric issue, Dad wrote a note on a church envelope and handed it me. I must have been ten years old at the time. His note said, "The Father has gone hopelessly insane."

I laughed but I never forgot his point. A critical mind will develop a healthy spirituality. An unquestioning mind will create a robot.

It is critical thinking and an active conscience that has led millions of people to work for the abolition of the war system together with the development of an international system of justice and peace.

Iniquity Lying to Itself

April 13, 2005

The Holy Week Liturgy has a recurrent theme of "Iniquity Lying to Itself." And such were the hearings this week.

The most candid comment I heard at the Negroponte hearing was the voice of Andres Thomas Conteris.

Conteris is a Latin America human rights activist. He spoke out during John Negroponte's Senate confirmation hearing today (and was handcuffed and detained.) He said, "I spoke up at the hearing just as they were talking about rendition. Rendition is equal to U.S. support for torture. It's our government sending people to other countries where they can be tortured."

Conteris added:

> John Negroponte is an expert at covering up for torture. He did it while he was ambassador to Honduras, he did it as torture in Abu Ghraib and elsewhere continued while he was ambassador to Iraq. Now, if he is confirmed he will be in charge of the most massive intelligence apparatus in the world. It's an apparatus that produces torture manuals and engages in torture—that trains people from other countries on how to torture, as we have seen from the School of the Americas.
>
> Negroponte is a death squad diplomat. He is associated, rightly, around the world with human rights violations. He supported death squads in Honduras, like Battalion 316. I lived in Honduras for five years, I know the impact Negroponte's policies had there in the early 1980s.

Conteris worked as a producer for *Hidden in Plain Sight*, a feature-length documentary that looks at the nature of U.S. policy in Latin America through the prism of the School of the Americas (renamed, in January of 2001, the Western Hemisphere Institute for Security Cooperation), the controversial military school that trains Latin American soldiers in the USA.

Friends, we can't be a little bit for torture any more than we can be a little bit for rape. Torture is immoral, illegal and unconstitutional.

What we saw in Washington this week was unqualified approval for torture in the form of a love feast for John Negroponte.

Silence is approval. Negroponte's silence speaks volumes as does the silence of the Senate. We must begin a national and international protest against torture as U.S. policy. What we have sowed, we will reap; Iniquity Lying to Itself!

Faith

How do progressive people in religion respond to the election of Pope Benedict XVI? Exactly the way that thinking people respond to any authority. In the field of logic the argument, "I am the Boss." is simply a classic example of a fallacy. "I am the Boss" has no relation to the validity or the truth of any argument. Therefore people who have their mind in gear continue to move forward regardless of who is the boss.

St Thomas Aquinas continued with his use of the methodology of Aristotle in spite of the accusation that he was glorifying a "pagan" philosopher. Dante made it clear in his Commedia that the Pope should not rule the world. Michelangelo painted high Church leaders in hell as he followed the example of Dante.

Galileo would not bury the telescope he had created. And Joan of Arc was canonized by Pope Benedict the XV after years of denunciation.

And look at the numbers: 75 percent of U.S. Catholics understand that their conscience is the ultimate norm of morality even when they differ with the Pope. What should come into focus during this papacy is an understanding that imperial religion has gone too far. It has said too much. It has lacked reverence and respect. It has even equated faith with a formula rather than a life style. Dictators and murderers can recite a formula but this does not make them people of faith. People of faith are marked by the fruits of their life.

Marla Ruzicka is a beautiful example of faith. She constantly returned to the most deadly parts of Iraq. She knew that our government refused to dignify its victims by even counting or acknowledging them. Therefore she created a census of Iraqi civilian casualties. And Marla Ruzicka petitioned tens of million of dollars from our government to aid the survivors. Marla spoke to us at length about her project called, "The Campaign for Innocent Victims in Conflict," or CIVIC. She gave us a big hug when she departed for Iraq.

Marla was killed on April 16 in Baghdad by a car bomb. A medic on the scene said her last words were, "I'm alive." Nothing could be more true! Marla Ruzicka, PRESENTE! Faith is present in this kind of life style. The name of one's religion tells us little or nothing.

The Party of God

May 4, 2005

I am very touched by the evangelism of Senator Frist. After years of seeking I have now seen the light.

Here are some purported qualities of people of faith:

- People of faith just love wars, especially unnecessary wars because we know we are killing the devil. The Generals told us so.
- God loves but one nation, our nation. God does not love other nations and wants to help us destroy them. Actually the United Nations is the Anti-Christ.
- God is in favor of racism, as people of faith we must choose people of color as our enemy. We do not regularly bomb England.
- God loves the rich and as a matter of fact the poor are pre-destined to hell so we must remind them of this with endless punishments.
- The poor should go to prison for life for stealing a pizza. The Enrons of the world should be gently chastised. Class justice is God's way.
- Corporations are the friends of God and therefore corporations should not be taxed.
- After all, they live forever and ordinary people fade out after a few years.
- The public sector must be destroyed because it would give some aid to bad people and we believe that salvation is private enterprise.
- Seeking the common good of the people of the earth is communistic and therefore it must not be tolerated.
- If we allow everyone to have medical care we are simply delaying their right to go to heaven.
- If we allow education for everyone they might just lose this perspective.

- Women should be submissive, indeed everyone should be submissive to the voice of God which is actually the voice of our President. The Divine Right of Kings was established for a reason.

So friends, here is the faith of the Party of God, The Taliban West. If you find someone who does not agree with this assessment, please call Senator Frist immediately.

That anyone would believe this sham in the eighteenth century is truly shocking. But to have this as a mainstream current in twenty-first century United States is a sign that theocracy is on the way and many people have become delusional as they attempt to justify the behavior of their corrupt leadership.

Pablo Paredes

May 13, 2005

Troops refusing to serve in Iraq are the vanguard of the Peace Movement.

This week in San Diego these veterans led the charge to put the Iraq War on trial as they gave courageous statements to protest the Court Marshall hearing of Pablo Paredes.

And yesterday while he was undergoing the sentencing phase of his trial, a play written by Pablo Paredes was taking place in the park adjacent to the military base. We were expecting Pablo to receive at least a year in prison. And just as this mock trial, which put the war on trial, was concluding, word came from the base that Pablo had received no prison time at all. He will serve three months of hard labor without incarceration, he will have two months of restriction to the military base, and reduction to the rank of a recruit. He is also eligible for an honorable discharge.

This decision appears to be unique. In fact we can say the military court did something that civilian Federal Courts have refused to do. This military court allowed the accused to give a motive for his conduct. It may seem unbelievable but in the most famous civilian cases regarding civil disobedience in the peace movement, cases like the Catonsville Nine, the accused have been admonished that if they cite the war as the motive for their actions they will be removed from the courtroom and put in jail for contempt of court. And I recall witnessing accused peace people being dragged from the courtroom and jailed precisely because they would not stop saying that their action was in protest to the war. It now appears that a military court is giving a message to our civilian courts. Yes, the accused can and should explain their motive for civil disobedience. Accused murderers have always been allowed to explain why they committed their alleged crime while thousands of members of the peace movement have been denied that right.

Pablo Paredes, thanks for your courage as you refused to set sail to Iraq on the USS Bonhomme Richard. And thanks for putting this illegal, immoral and disgusting rape of Iraq on trial while sending a message to our civilian Federal Courts that peacemakers must always be allowed to explain the motive for their anti-war actions. U.S. Navy Judge Robert Klant made it precisely clear that every service person can reasonably question the legality of a particular war and retains the right to speak out and to follow their conscience.

The Iraq War was put on trial yesterday in San Diego. The Iraq War was convicted and condemned by military patriot, Pablo Paredes.

Impeachment

May 18, 2005

While the commercial media exploits the alleged sexual misconduct of Michael Jackson on a 24/7 basis, the criminality of our international behavior becomes commonplace.

What criminality? Let me count the ways.

The endless carnage in Iraq, the people we kill are referred to as terrorists. What a wonderful situation for the imbedded media. Who among the dead is going to prove that he or she was not a terrorist? Every dictatorship has played this game. The ones we kill are the evil ones. If they happen to be innocent, for example children, they are simply collateral damage.

Then we have the case of the Prime Minister of Haiti Yvon Neptune, jailed for ten months with no charges against him. Neptune is on a prison fast unto death seeking justice for his people. The policy that overthrew his government has been routine behavior for Washington since the days of Thomas Jefferson. To the horror of our founders, Haiti abolished slavery in 1804.

And then there is the case of the Colombian paramilitary which our country has supported for decades. This enormous death squad is holding one of the largest inventories of cocaine ever identified. These drugs are for sale in the United States and the income serves to continue the rape and plunder of the Colombian people.

Yes, it is the same pattern that took place in Nicaragua in the 1980s. Gary Webb's book, *Dark Alliance* explains the method in detail. Gary's good work was punished by the same media that endlessly feeds us Michael Jackson.

The Bush approval ratings are dropping but not fast enough. Every member of Congress now knows that in April of 2002, at the Crawford Ranch in Texas, George Bush and Prime Minister Tony Blair agreed to wage an unprovoked and illegal war against Iraq. Eighty-nine House Democrats have expressed their outrage in a letter to the President, which says in part: "While the president of the United States was telling the citizens and the congress that they had no intention to start a war with

Iraq, they were working very close with Tony Blair and the British leadership at making this a foregone conclusion."

Former Attorney General of the United States, Ramsey Clark commented, "Impeachment now is the only way we, the American people, can promise ourselves and the world that we will not tolerate crimes against peace and humanity by our government. Knowing what we know, to wait longer is to condone what has been done and risk more."

Friends, to make this impeachment a reality, all we need is a handful of Democrats with a spine, Republicans with a conscience and people with hope and conviction. Let's make it happen.

What Might Have Been

May 27, 2005

The saddest words ever spoken were, "It might have been."

Our powerful nation might have led the world into abolishing nuclear weapons. We have all the necessary technology. We simply do not have the will. And don't let anyone say this is not realistic. The realists of the world know that nuclear weapons will either be abolished or used. There is no room for debate on this issue. It is our lack of leadership which is unrealistic. The entire world can see our duplicity in presuming that we can have tens of thousands of nukes as we point the finger at other nations who might possibly have one nuke.

Our powerful nation might have led the world in humanitarian law. With a leadership vacuum we have torture as an official policy. Torture is an international crime and the very definition of terrorism. Torture has never been a source of information, on the contrary it is conducted to obtain false confessions, to terrorize those who have not yet been tortured or as a source of "entertainment" for psychotics. Some rebel groups in Latin America discovered the wisdom of treating their captives well. In some cases the captives not only spoke the truth but also changed sides.

Our powerful nation might have led the world in restraining the sale of weapons. On the contrary we continue to sell arms to every possible dictatorship on the planet.

What might have been is America as a beacon to the world. On the contrary we have become the disgust of the world by our lawless, mean spirited, violent, small minded, racist and stupid policies.

Amnesty International referred to the atrocious human rights violations of the Bush administration which diminish the moral authority of the United States and sets a global example encouraging abuse by other nations. The list of accusations which introduced Amnesty International's annual report in London mentioned crimes by the United States including: torture of detainees in Iraq, torture of prisoners at Guantánamo Bay in Cuba, and rendition of prisoners to country known to practice torture.

Amnesty further stated that the United States "thumbs its nose at the rule of law and human rights."

Rather than what might have been a light to the world, this group of war criminals has no legitimate claim to the tax money of our hard working citizens.

We don't have to focus on what might have been. But we must focus our attention on what is going to be and that means humane leadership for a humane future.

Gwangju

June 1, 2005

On May 18, 1980 the people of Gwangju, in South Korea, initiated their resistance to the second military coup and dictatorship, which had toppled their long awaited civilian government. The city was liberated by its citizens and ten days of civil society followed. After this brief victory elite South Korean troops under U.S. command were deployed from the demilitarized zone and brutally crushed the liberation movement. More than 2,000 children, students, men and women were killed, thousands of others were tortured and imprisoned.

The uprising in Gwangju was the beginning of a struggle for democracy and self-determination that continues to reverberate to the present moment. 2005 must be the year of the reunification of Korea. One culture, one language, one people who remain divided by a foreign power.

As citizens of the United States, we have much to regret. It was not enough that our military participated in Gwangju massacre but at the very same time our troops were engaged militarily in similar oppressive actions in Honduras, El Salvador, Guatemala and Nicaragua. And all of this took place after a destructive war in Vietnam which took the lives of 3,000,000 people. None of these military actions represented victory for the United States. After each failure the same policy was repeated with the same lies, the same massacres and the same ignorance.

Conscious citizens of the United States are outraged as an endless and destructive militarism increases with new threats against North Korea. The Korean peninsula is known as the world's most heavily militarized zone. Before this beautiful planet is destroyed by mindless militarism, we must enter into solidarity with the people of South Korea as they celebrate resistance which began at Kwangju in 1980 and continues to the present day.

Koreans look to the reunification of their country and the removal of millions of insidious land mines which are specifically designed to maim rather than to kill. Why? Because the wounded require time and effort not needed by the dead. How few citizens of the United States know that one of the reasons for hunger in North Korea is U.S. imposed economic sanctions and the use of food as a weapon. Food and agricultural aid combined with diplomacy seeking the reunification of Korea would be much more effective than ongoing threats to once again use nuclear weapons as we did in Hiroshima and Nagasaki. Our continuing punishment of North Korea simply demonstrates the urgent need to abolish nuclear weapons internationally.

The technology for this task is available. All we need is the will.

Heresy

June 8, 2005

There have been trials for heresy, there have been executions for heresy and there have been endless ecclesiastical denunciations of heresy.

Heresy is false doctrine and has frequently been associated with people who have deviated from official church doctrine.

It is curious that heresy has rarely, if ever, been applied to conduct. It seems to me that conduct, which emanates from mutilated, manipulated and cult oriented religiosity should be identified.

Here in my opinion are a few examples of what I consider heresy.

It is heresy to believe that religion should bless war.

It is heresy to believe that nationalism has a role in religion. It is heresy to fail to show reverence for a diversity of religious experience.

It is heresy to accept inquisition and torture as policy.

It is heresy to demonize any ethnic or racial group.

It is heresy to demonize any nation.

It is heresy to judge whole nations as worthy of destruction.

It is heresy to claim to be the voice of God for the world.

It is heresy to claim that God is on the side of any nation state.

It is heresy to practice hate.

It is heresy to lack compassion and mercy.

It is heresy to lie as personal or collective policy.

It is heresy to rob from the poor by the massive production of unnecessary and counterproductive armaments.

It is heresy to produce and conspire to use nuclear weapons.

It is heresy to fail to communicate with others through respectful exchange.

It is heresy to take innocent lives.

It is heresy to order people to kill.

It is heresy to make war instead of peace.

It is heresy to use religion as a cloak for malice.

It is heresy to use religion as a cloak for racism.

It is heresy to physically threaten individuals or groups.
It is heresy not to respect free will.

Friends, it appears we are governed by a group of heretics.
We must direct them out of their errant ways.

The Devil's Language

June 15, 2005

Regardless of whether you believe in devils as persons or simply as black holes of negativity, we must attempt to identify such forces. In scripture the native tongue of the devil is identified as the lie. When the devil lies it speaks its native language. Knowing the truth is one of life's constant struggles. But it is the truth that sets us free and liberates us from the power of the lie.

The lie has become institutionalized in government. The first casualty in any war is the truth. So we hear lies from the executive branch, from the Department of Defense and from the State Department. The commercial media reveres most every false statement made by these powers. Some truth speakers are crucified whether their name is Jesus or Gary Webb. If you read Webb's lucid book, *The Dark Alliance*, there is little or no room for doubt about how the major U.S. papers attacked his data and his integrity. The book is a must read for anyone who aspires to be a journalist. Cocaine arrived in the United States on the same planes that brought arms to Nicaragua for the illegal Contra War.

Those drugs were distributed nationally by the contras with full knowledge of our intelligence agencies. Weapons went down to Nicaragua to kill the innocent, drugs came back to addict our citizens and much of the profit was used as an illegal war chest. The truth can make us free from the tragedy of sending our youth to once again be killed for a lie. The simple truth will also spare the lives of many innocent Iraqis, Iranians and Koreans.

Like most wars, the Iraq conflict was started by a contrivance . . . that is by a lie. The governmental liars are responsible for every single death, for every single injury, for every single case of delayed traumatic stress syndrome and for all who have been poisoned by depleted uranium. By the way, the very name depleted uranium is a lie. It is not depleted, it is highly radioactive and toxic.

There must be no impunity for the host of criminals who have presided over the lies regarding the twin towers and the lies regarding the

Downing Street Memo. Such negative powers and principalities are destroying the United States of America.

The lie is the native tongue of the forces of death.

Only the truth will liberate us.

Somebody Spoke to Fort Bragg

June 29, 2005

Someone spoke to the troops at Fort Bragg last night. Whoever spoke was not in touch with recent history. The speaker seemed to think the war in Iraq was related to the attacks on the twin towers on September 11, 2001. It was not. The war in Iraq was started to grab power in the Middle East. Those who planned it were among the most deceitful and immoral individuals who have ever served in government. Their arrogance, mediocrity and shamelessness simply mark seeking power at any price.

The speaker lied saying that Iraq had to be rebuilt because of the tyrant who previously ruled there. No, that was not true. As in the case of many tyrants, for example Mussolini, the physical conditions in Iraq under the tyrant Saddam Hussein were some of the best in the Arab world. The speaker knows very well that Iraq has to be rebuilt because 88,000 tons of bombs were dropped on that nation by the order of his father.

Last night's speaker knew and relished the fact that Iraq has been under unceasing attacks for fourteen years. It has been bombed, it has been starved out, it has been denied any medical assistance under the individual who served as president after the reign of the father of last night's speaker. Iraq does not have to be rebuilt because of a former tyrant. It has to be rebuilt because we have destroyed it. The Shock and Awe attack simply broke the back of a country that was attempting to dig its way out of the ashes.

Someone should attempt to get across to last night's speaker that after you blow the Iraqi children to pieces with pretty cluster bombs, after you routinely torture their sons and daughters, after you abolish their sacred shrines and their sacred cities, after you define them as devils, after you poison their bodies and their soil with highly toxic radio active dust, you might just expect them to resist. There is no ethic in the world which identifies self defense as terrorism. All rational human beings will defend their families and their personal and spiritual integrity. Insurgency is one thing, terrorism is another. And in the process of their rage a few people will unfortunately become terrorists.

Criminals are often thought to be delusional and uninformed but they frequently know exactly what they are doing and why. Should his view of the War in Iraq remain as policy, the utter devastation of that country together with the current and rapid deterioration of the United States will continue concomitantly.

Mr. Bush, please do a favor to the world's people, please step down together with your arrogant, mediocre and war mongering cronies.

Thank you.

Subversive Literature

July 6, 2005

Just suppose you are one of the newly elected members of Iraq's new client government. Just suppose you are reading a political science book and you come across a subversive document. You hope and pray that your U.S. handlers do not discover your reading material.

The document says:

That to secure these rights, governments are instituted among men, deriving their just powers from the consent of the governed.

That whenever any form of government becomes destructive of these ends, it is the right of the people to alter or to abolish it, and to institute new government.

You furtively read on discovering that the subversives who wrote this were speaking of a foreign head of state by the name of George. They directly confronted George with the following indictments: He has affected to render the military independent of and superior to the civil power. He has combined with others to subject us to jurisdiction foreign to our constitution, and unacknowledged by our laws; giving assent to their acts of pretended legislation:

For quartering large bodies of armed troops among us;

For protecting them, by a mock trial from punishment for any murders which they should commit on the inhabitants of these states;

For imposing taxes on us without our consent;

For depriving us in many cases, of the benefit of trial by jury;

For transporting us beyond seas to be tried for pretended offenses;

He is at this time transporting large armies of foreign mercenaries to complete the works of death, desolation and tyranny, already begun with circumstances of cruelty and perfidy scarcely paralleled in the most barbarous ages, and totally unworthy the head of a civilized nation.

Just picture the member of the new Iraqi client state gathering his or her colleagues together to approve of this subversive document and to pledge their allegiance to it by stating:

> And for the support of this Declaration, with a firm reliance on the protection of divine providence, we mutually pledge to each other our lives, our fortunes and our sacred honor.

Immorality and Malice
at the Service of Ignorance

July 13, 2005

Just think of the horror of sending your kids off to school and shortly thereafter finding out that they had been killed by a bomb. People throughout the world have been experiencing this terror whether they live in England, Iraq, Israel, Palestine or the United States. Our condolences to the endless number of victims and families. Such strategies are immoral and mindless. In the past fourteen years in Iraq, however, over 5,000 times the civilian casualties of the recent London bombing have occurred. Has there been the slightest expression of grief for these Iraqi civilians?

Now after receiving the equivalent of over 5,000 London bombings would it not be expected that some people might just respond in anger, in rage and in terror? We are stunned when the Blair/Bush response states that this is because they hate our way of life. But wait a minute, if our way of life includes the routine killing hundreds of thousands of people, both Blair and Bush have a point.

All rational beings on the planet can now see the futility of one nation bankrupting its people to purchase self-destructive armaments. We assert our power over weak and defenseless states, some of them respond with rage. Then we ask why they don't love us. The policy to date has been one of immorality at the service of ignorance.

Friends, the point here is that the war system is a suicide system. We are shocked by suicide bombers but we have become the international suicide bombers. Our bombings result in the death of our people as well as the intended victims.

We need a realignment. By that I do not mean a change of political parties. A realignment implies an entirely new perspective on the part of a majority.

Our realignment must include a global view. There are mindless voices from highly trained and poorly educated media pundits who are saying that the Muslims of the world want to destroy us. These must be the ghosts of those who thought the Vietnamese Buddhists wanted to destroy us or the Central American Christians wanted to destroy us.

Quite simply, all we have to do is reflect on the fundamental right to self defense while knowing that some people will respond by making their own rules.

Those who repeat the past do not respect the past. The past is marked by violence, racism and ignorance. Respect for the past implies change, realignment and wisdom.

The planet cannot be sustained by arrogant power. The planet can only be sustained by rational people building a system of justice and peace.

Logic

July 20, 2005

In the study of logic, an argument based solely on authority is considered a classic fallacy. The logic of, "I'm in charge here," has absolutely no reference to the truth or validity of the argument. Oh, yes, it may be translated as, I can fire you, I can punish you or even I can kill you but it has absolutely no reference to the truth of what is being said. We are taught to respect authority and that is a serious mistake. Authority must demonstrate the validity and the truth of its position in order to be respected. This problem is especially great with children, they are taught to respect their elders but they may not be warned how to recognize a child molester. And it gets worse with schooling. See how they learn to repeat what the teacher wants. The very history books they study are warped with the triumphalism of state sponsored texts. They repeat the drill not because of the validity or truth which it contains but simply because it is the drill.

Reflect on General Westmoreland. He believed that the enemy did not respect human life as much as we did. Well he learned that myth at West Point as it was handed down from the time of the Spanish American War. Did the statement have any truth? Of course not. But he learned it from authority without understanding that an argument based on authority only is a false argument. He spent his days in Vietnam begging for more troops as he presided over the massacre of 3 million people. They simply do not respect human life as much as we do? The value of General Westmoreland's logic was zero. But he did have authority.

And friends that is the situation with our current leadership. Our administration uses its authority to denounce the terrorism of others as it refuses to denounce its constant practice of state terrorism world wide. Our authorities denounce torture conducted by others but they deny the torture which they practice as official policy.

Our authorities denounce the assassinations committed by others but they continue to practice assassinations. There are two cases where this abuse should be self-evident. Israel as related to Palestine and United States as related to Iraq. In both cases the weaker state has clearly been the victim of institutionalized violence. In both cases the stronger state refuses to acknowledge its responsibility for having created the problem.

When you see that bumper sticker which simply states QUESTION AUTHORITY please realize that the great political powers of the earth certainly have a monopoly on the violence they can create. Unfortunately their power demonstrates absolutely no claim to any truth or validity in their endless babble of propaganda. Without critical thinking and conscience we become mindless robots and automatons.

It is our moral responsibility to question authority and to rectify the evils created by mindless authority.

How to Stop Terrorism

July 27, 2005

Have you ever noticed how careful the media is to tell us what happened in various cases of terrorism against us or our allies?

Actually the media is quite thorough on this.

One small problem, they rarely if ever get into the question of why it happened. Attempts on the part of our political leaders to explain the WHY of terrorism are the very definition of the word asinine. The entire world admires the constructive achievements of the people of the United States. But they have no admiration at all for our terrorism. Comments from our political leaders on this matter would be ludicrous if they were not so tragic.

So how do we stop terrorism? We stop terrorism by stopping our long standing terrorism. This is a good time to reflect on the terror of Hiroshima where hundreds of thousands of civilians were incinerated unnecessarily. Sorry folks but the judgment of history does not support the military propaganda that claims the bombs were necessary to stop the war. The war was over. And there is even less support for any claim that the incineration of Nagasaki was necessary some three days later. This was terror, sheer terror. And yes, it was a message to our ally, the Soviet Union that they would get no credit for ending the Second World War.

Terror and torture marked our interventions in Central America, terror and torture marked the brutal Christmas attack on Panama in 1989. And now terror and torture mark our killing of Iraqis together with our support for the terrorist occupation of Palestine. Our international terrorism has held the entire world hostage with nuclear weapons as our message clearly states that we can have as many nuclear weapons as we want but we will abolish any state that we judge should not have them. What logic!

The presence of over eight-hundred military bases around the globe terrorizes people everywhere. Indeed we are addicted to terror. And as any addict we are striking out at everyone rather than acknowledging our addiction.

We will accomplish nothing until we acknowledge why people are striking at us.

And now we are ready to put an individual on the Supreme Court who does not believe that prisoners of war are entitled to hear the charges against them, to have due process of law and who supports kangaroo military tribunals. What a set-up for continued terror.

Please take note of our addictive behavior regarding the destruction of Fallujah. No photos have been tolerated. The media forgot to mention that half of the Iraqi soldiers who were assigned to that mission deserted and that 20 percent were in open mutiny against us.

So we should look in the mirror and acknowledge our role as the world's greatest manufacturer of terror. Our ill advised and brutal behavior will continue to create terror until we cease and desist from our terrorism. The truth hurts, doesn't it?

Cindy Sheehan

August 13, 2005

Cindy Sheehan has left her home in Vacaville, California to cover the nation and the world on behalf of her son, Casey, who was killed in Iraq. She is currently near Crawford, Texas petitioning an interview with George Bush. George is, of course, too busy during his vacation to speak to her. Much commercial media is there to report on this valiant action.

Cindy plans to stay at her post in a tent near the Bush Ranch until the end of August. People interested in justice and peace are arriving to join Cindy in solidarity to end this unnecessary and immoral war.

Every possible lie, every act of hypocrisy has been used. Every journalistic hack has been recruited to throw fuel on this hellish fire. In spite of advice from our intelligence agencies warning the President that the war would result in even more attacks here at home, the President continues to recklessly endanger the people of the United States by his rampant acts of terror in Iraq.

All those responsible for this holocaust in Iraq must be brought to justice. This war began in 1991. Fifteen years of bombing, brutal sanctions and invasions have resulted in millions of civilian deaths.

There are hundreds of crosses around Cindy's tent in the Crawford countryside. These represent just some of the women and men from the United States who have died in Iraq for a lie. It will take years to measure all the lives that have been ruined by Bush, father and son.

We must count all those who are now mentally ill from trauma. And we must begin to count the uncounted dead who have died on their way to hospitals in Germany.

It all cries to heaven for national repentance as we denounce the crimes committed in our name.

You are welcome to go to Crawford now to join Cindy or to follow her to Washington, D.C. in September as the struggle goes on. Cindy, may your brilliant action be the occasion of the mobilization of our citizens. And Casey Sheehan, may you rest in peace and may your mother be recognized as a national hero.

Truth Telling

August 17, 2005

Sixty years after the greatest act of terrorism in world history we continue to engage in nuclear war. Uranium 238 should never have been called "depleted." It is highly radioactive. It was used with fury in the Gulf War with Iraq which began in 1991 and its continued use has contaminated our troops and the Iraqi people ever since.

The Christian Science Monitor reports that radiation levels in downtown Baghdad are 1,900 times higher than normal. The radioactivity from our weapons using Uranium 238 has penetrated the entire area. It is in the blood of our troops who have come home sick. It is shared by their wives and children. It has also led to gross abnormalities in the children of Iraq. And now, 250,000 of the troops that served at the outset of this endless war are permanently disabled. Our troops and purported enemies in Afghanistan are equally endangered. And yes, this nuclear weapon, Uranium 238 was also used in the recent war in Yugoslavia. President Clinton is not absolved from the war crimes of nuclearism nor the terror of international sanctions.

But Uranium 238 is not the only cause of Gulf War Illness. President Clinton also signed Executive Order 13139, which ordered our troops to receive a variety of untested vaccines. Isn't it ironic that the pharmaceutical industry and the war machine are so closely joined at the hip. Just think what a boon Bill Clinton's executive order was to the pharmaceutical industry. Perhaps this will help us to understand how the drug companies were able to take over television advertising with their endless drug pushing.

So what is the point?

There is no indication that a change of party will stop our run-away militarism and lawlessness. And the facade of nationalistic pseudo Christianity is not going to help us either. The only way out of this mess is to see ourselves primarily as citizens of the planet which has only one people called the "human race." The atavistic views of our sick leadership require political illiteracy and moral unconsciousness. A moral revolution is required to end the slavery of militarism. Yes, we need the spiritual conversion that will lead to reverence for others as brothers and sisters in fact. We must look in the mirror and acknowledge that from the atom bombs to Uranium 238 we are and the have been the greatest purveyor of violence on earth. Should we acknowledge our addiction and repent we will quickly find that we are in far greater danger from obesity than we are from foreign terrorists.

Pat Robertson

Reverend Pat Robertson has become the personification of nationalistic pseudo Christianity. During his television program, *The 700 Club*, he proposed an act of sheer terrorism in calling for the assassination of Hugo Chavez, the President of Venezuela. This is the Christianity of anyone who makes an idol out of the state. This is the Christianity that was popular in the Third Reich as Adolph manipulated Catholics and Lutherans to the Nazi cause.

This is the Christianity of Christendom, the Crusades, the Inquisition and the Conquistadores. This is the Christianity for which Pope John Paul II apologized.

Pat Robertson previously supported the sheer terrorism of our illegal Contra War in Nicaragua which was clearly one of the greatest scandals in United States history.

And now he joins the mob that shouted, "We have no king but Caesar!"

It takes a warped and putrefied conscience to call for the murder of President Hugo Chavez of Venezuela. And what might be the motive for this murder? The motive is that the empire does not approve of Hugo Chavez. This servant of empire represents everything that Jesus distained. Here are some words from Jesus on this matter which might be directed to Pat Robertson:

Hypocrites! It was you Isaiah meant when he so rightly prophesied: These people honors me with their lips, while their hearts are far from me. Their worship of me is worthless; and their doctrines are mere human rules. (Matt. 15.7–9)

Ignore them—they are blind people leading other blind people. And when the blind lead the blind, they all will fall into a ditch. (Matt. 15.14)

Woe to you religious scholars, you frauds! You travel over land and over sea to make a single convert, and once that person is converted, you create a proselyte twice as wicked as yourselves. (Matt. 23.15)

118

Serpents, brood of vipers . . . (Matt. 23.33)

The ministry of Pat Robertson has been to betray the one he claims to serve. Remember what Jesus said of the traitor in his midst: "It would be better for him had he not been born."

There are thirty pieces of silver waiting for you, Pat.

Distributive Justice

Here is an offer that our listeners cannot refuse. The Wall Street Journal tell us that the Yellowstone Club is offering membership to the super rich for an introductory fee of only $10 million. Naturally there will be annual fees as well. But just think of the prestige?

Just how much of a moral justification is there for such a Club? According to the principle of distributive justice the right to such organized greed is near zero. Why? In a humane economic system we might study a graph which looks like a archery target.

The center bulls eye would represent our needs for survival. Such needs would be called "rights" in a developed society. For example the rights to housing, food, clothing, education and medical care. There are concentric circles beyond the bulls eye but each one represents things we have less of a right to until the needs at the center are met. As the central needs are met, a society based on the common good would permit its citizens to expand its vision to lesser rights. In any analysis of distributive justice the right to join a $10 million a year club would never exist until all of the homeless were housed, all of the sick cared for and all of the hungry fed. In short, our hearts could stop bleeding for people who take in millions of dollars per year.

Now the odd part of our culture is that many people who earn $30,000 per year or less might seriously object to the principle of distributive justice. Why? Because they have been socialized to dream of billions. Some would even say that such limitations would hinder the incentive for excellence. But the incentive for excellence can be easily seen in scores of Nobel Prize winners who have achieved international fame and who live on a fixed university salary. This gives the lie to the concept that we must have the potential to be billionaires or we won't strive for excellence.

The principle of distributive justice is not based on the concept that everyone should receive the same income. That is not part of the program. On the contrary, it is It is based on the concept that excessive wealth is the cause of poverty. This principle has not yet reached the political economy of the United States. However, it must go beyond all national borders and become part of the international political economy of the planet's people. May students in the future intelligently study the fact that $10 million membership clubs and the arms merchants who joined them were the reason that millions of people lived on garbage dumps in 2005.

No Finger Pointing

September 7, 2005

Now let's not have any finger pointing!

That's what the accused says when the prosecutor presents the evidence. In this case the prosecutor is represented by the people of the world and the accused have overwhelming evidence against them.

The destruction of the great city of New Orleans together with much of the Gulf Coast is simply a part of the price of the Iraq War. Every year efforts have been made by informed people requesting more federal funding for the levies and infrastructure of that great city on the Mississippi River. And these requests have been denied in order to pay for an unnecessary, illegal and immoral war. The denial of these necessary funds is also part of a larger ideology which has been festering for three decades. The ideology is called "privatization." This ideology is based on a religion of profit for the few. As a result the entire public infrastructure of the United States is deteriorating. The public sector has been under ceaseless attack. We have only to look at the efforts to defund public utilities, social security, public schools, public parks, public highways, public sewer systems, public libraries, public universities and public hospitals. What is even more horrific is that this rigid and useless ideology of private greed has been extended internationally by way of so-called globalization or, neo-liberalism which is simply a reversion to the worst of nineteenth century laissez faire capitalism.

It is the public sector that has made life livable in the United States. It is the lack of public sector infrastructure, which has made New Orleans and the Gulf Coast unlivable. Let the troops from Louisiana, Mississippi and Alabama be the first to return from Iraq. And may they be followed immediately by the rest of our troops to come home and save their country from the terrorism generated by privatization.

But friends let's not just point the finger, let's prosecute the malfeasance of office of those who have systematically defunded the public sector of the United States of America, let us prosecute those who have created endless unnecessary wars and who have extended our military outreach to over eight hundred foreign enclaves which the local people are begging us to leave. And this is being done as the infrastructure of the United States rots out. New Orleans represents a clear example of privatization and unregulated capitalism. The poor stand on their roofs and beg for help while the President flies over to give them a feigned blessing while FEMA lists Pat Robertson's Operation Blessing as a serious source of legitimate aid. Add to this the fact that our corrupt leadership cares so little about poor people of color that we have just refused aid from fifty-five countries who are anxious to help.

May the thousands of dead in this unnecessary disaster be the occasion of our demanding an end to the unnecessary wars in Afghanistan and Iraq. And may we begin to use the tax money of the United States for the common good of the people of the United States instead of for destruction of innocent people abroad.

Collateral Damage

September 14, 2005

Well friends, here is the collateral damage from the wars of Afghanistan and Iraq. Do you remember when Dr. King said that every bomb that fell on Vietnam also fell on the United States. Do we get it now? Will we ever get it? The war in the Persian Gulf has destroyed the Gulf Coast of the United States.

Our schools have been bombed into test preparation centers in an attempt to make robotized and standardized students who are highly trained and very poorly educated.

The most common visitors to our schools are military public relations people who give candy to the students. This reminds me of the Guatemalan Military who would give candy to the children one day and burn the village to the ground on the following day.

Our students are seduced into militarism in the following ways:

Would you like some money for college? It would be good for you to know that seven out of ten students can receive financial aid without going into the military. The vast majority of veterans actually receive NO educational benefits from the military, not one cent.

And now the military is invading our schools with The Armed Services Vocational Aptitude Battery (ASVAB) a test developed by the Department of Defense for military recruiters to determine the abilities of a student for military occupational specialties. This test is administered without parents permission and test results are released to the military without parents permission.

Students who take the test often don't even know that it is a military test.

Students who appear to have an aptitude for military service are heavily recruited after the test is taken.

The Junior Reserve Officer Training Corps (JROTC) is currently replacing Physical Education Classes in many of our schools.

The flat out lying of recruiters has been exposed endlessly. One of the most common comments of boot camp drill sergeants is, "Forget everything the recruiters told you!" Occasionally parents believe that mili-

124

tary discipline will be good for their kids. But the discipline of keep your mouth shut, do what you are told and follow orders is entirely external and designed to make a thoughtless killing machine out of a human being. The only authentic discipline is self discipline which is capable of critical thinking and application of conscience.

Our militarism has destroyed New Orleans and the Gulf Coast. It has also rotted out the entire infrastructure of the United States. It is also a cancer on our educational system. Indeed every bomb which has fallen in Afghanistan and Iraq has fallen on our country as well.

Concern for Humanity

September 21, 2005

The Defense Department has revised its program for the use of nuclear weapons. This revision empowers military commanders to request presidential approval to engage in a preventive attack with nuclear weapons on a nation or an alleged terrorist group which might use weapons of mass destruction.

The previous policy which was stated in 1995 contained no mention of using nuclear weapons preemptively.

But the new doctrine makes it clear that nuclear weapons can be used against an enemy that is using or intending to use weapons of mass destruction. Now just consider for a moment if this had been the policy before the current war in Iraq, we could have eliminated tens of millions of Iraqi civilians by now because of the presidential lie stating that they had weapons of mass destruction. Knowing that the truth is the first casualty in any war, this new policy gives us self approval to eliminate any government, any nation, any group of people at any time. The fact that preventive war was the policy of the Third Reich and that this type of behavior has been condemned by all international law was not given any consideration in the new proposal.

What most people don't know is that the greatest weapon of mass destruction on the planet is the assault rifle. Yes, this is the weapon that kills more people each year than any other. The arms merchants are an international club. Their allegiance is to profit only. Some are U.S. citizens and some are not. They have fostered, promoted and celebrated the wars in Afghanistan and Iraq and are in the same club as the creators of African genocide as they sell their wares to war lords interested in diamonds and oil.

Whether we are talking about nuclear weapons of mass destruction or about assault rifles, the need for international disarmament is clear. Our unilateral approach to this policy is unsustainable and suicidal. It is our responsibility to denounce the these reckless war policy and to build a future of compliance with international law. One good way to begin the task is to join us on Saturday, September 24 as we gather at Noon at the corner of Olympic and Broadway to march to the Downtown Federal Building. We are marching to end the out of control militarism which is destroying the world. We are marching to end the occupation of Iraq, Palestine, and Haiti. We are marching to get military recruiters out of our schools, we are marching to stop the bloodthirsty threats against Iran, Cuba, Venezuela and North Korea. We are marching so that our grandchildren will not be vaporized by a nuclear mistake.

The Demonstrations

September 28, 2005

Congratulations to everyone who participated last Saturday in history making gatherings in Los Angeles, San Francisco, Washington, D.C., Seattle and throughout the world. We were overjoyed with the international response. But please understand that we need you every day. We need you to help remove the criminals who are driving our ship of state on to the rocks. We need you to demand the restoration of the public sector of the United States. We need you to stop the looting of funds designated for the repair of the Gulf Coast as our government has become the world's largest center of organized crime. We can be soft on crime no longer. Could our criminal justice system be any worse if it had been designed by the KKK?

We need you to bring our troops home now. We need you to impeach and imprison those responsible for the deaths of our young men and women in Iraq and Afghanistan. We need you to be a voice of repentance for the innocents who have been massacred in our name.

We need you to join the international quest for an authentic spiritual and moral revolution to achieve a universal common good. We need you to end divisive sectarianism and to bring that unity which is found in the struggle for justice, peace, love, joy, courage, compassion and endurance.

As we demand restitution for the crimes of this corrupt era, let the word go forth: We will not tolerate the violation of the public trust which some voters have mistakenly placed in our president and other officials as they blatantly conduct malfeasance of office.

Pay attention:

1. You don't privatize the Public Sector to funnel government funds to your corrupt cronies.
2. You don't loot funds which have been designated for widows and orphans.

3. You don't let third rate religious charlatans canonize and demonize other faiths nor ask for assassinations.

Yes, we have been entirely too soft on organized crime!

Our hard earned tax money has been used to kill millions of innocent people.

Our hard earned tax money has been looted by Halliburton and Bechtel.

Our hard earned tax money has been used to hire international thugs for mercenary warfare.

Our hard earned tax money has been used as part of an international lying machine.

Our sycophant commercial media is creating a nation of political illiterates.

Yes, we need you to help us in building an international system of peace. The nation state is too small for our total allegiance. Let us pledge allegiance to this beautiful planet with justice and peace for all.

BRING THE TROOPS HOME NOW.

Testimony of the Generals

October 5, 2005

The U.S. generals running the war in Iraq presented a new assessment of the military situation with some sworn testimony this week. They testified to the fact that 149,000 U.S. troops in Iraq are increasingly part of the problem rather than the solution.

The generals said the U.S. occupation was fueling the insurgency, making the Iraqi troops more dependent and expanding terrorism. They insisted that the withdrawal of American troops is imperative.

On the home front, there are only some 32 percent of our citizens who approve of the Iraq War. Now that the sworn testimony of the generals has been heard, just what is going on in Iraq? Moving northwest up the Euphrates River we find serial massacres that will be long remembered as war crimes. Fallujah, Ramadi, Haqlaniyah, Haditha and Karbala. Suspected insurgents are being massacred. And who are the suspected insurgents? Anyone who is in the area. And for each suspected insurgent that is massacred, ten new insurgents are created. The generals gave their testimony in Washington but our tactics and strategies in Iraq have not changed. Reuters global managing editor states that the conduct of American forces toward journalists in Iraq is, "spiraling out of control." 66 journalists and media workers have been killed in Iraq since March of 2003.

Human Rights Watch has received testimony from members of the 82nd Airborne Division that prisoners were tortured as a form of stress relief or for sport. Aside from creating thousands more insurgents, we can expect such forms of stress relief and sport to come home.

Congratulations to Federal District Judge Alvin Hellerstein who ordered the Defense Department to release additional torture photos and videos which were provided by Sergeant Joseph Darby. Kill them all, let God divide them up! seems to be the logo.

So let's get it clear. In Washington the generals tell us we are creating more insurgents by virtue of our out of control slaughter. In Iraq, however, we are continuing and expanding our out of control slaughter which absolutely and logically multiplies the resistance. A military spokesperson said that the goal of these offensives is to help the Iraqi authorities set up polling places so people can vote. But since when did bombing and strafing become the road to the ballot box?

Last week the peace movement put twice as many people in Washington as there are troops in Iraq. It seems to me that the time has come for our citizens to simply go on strike until the government starts to represent us.

Fixing the Poor

October 12, 2005

Well, friends, what is a hurricane for? For some the real purpose of a hurricane is to promote an irrational, selfish and unforgivable looting by the rich.

Here is the drill:

1. Suspend the requirement that federal contractors have affirmative action plans and the requirement to pay locally prevailing wages.
2. Cut Medicaid and food stamp programs.
3. Reduce taxes for the wealthy. Congressman Mike Pense of Indiana says this is how you fight poverty.

So Mr. Bush suspended the Davis Bacon Act, a 1931 law that prohibits federally funded construction jobs from paying wages less than the local average.

And he also suspends rules requiring federal contractors to file affirmative action plans which his allies called "cumbersome." If justice is so cumbersome perhaps they think we ought to eliminate it altogether, right?

Our majority members of the House of Representatives are suggesting a $370 billion cut in domestic spending over the next five years as they push for school vouchers in New Orleans.

So friends, as New Orleans reopens, the same people are being left behind who were left behind during the hurricane. Public schools are closed, public housing is closed, access to public health care is closed, and avenues to justice are closed.

There are 28,000 people still living in shelters in Louisiana. But there are 38,000 public housing apartments in New Orleans and none have been reopened in spite of the fact that many are in good condition. The National Low Income Housing Coalition estimated that 112,000 low income homes were damaged by the hurricane in New Orleans but local state and federal authorities are not committed to reopening public housing. Public Schools enrolled 60,000 children before the hurricane. But the school board president now estimates that no schools on the city's east bank, where the majority of the people live, will reopen during this academic year.

Attorney William Quigley, who is a professor of law at Loyola University in New Orleans, says:

> When those in power close the public schools, close public housing, fire people from their jobs, refuse to provide access to affordable public healthcare, and close off all avenues for justice, it is not necessary to erect a sign outside of New Orleans saying, "Poor People Not Allowed to Return." People cannot come back in these circumstances and that is exactly what is happening.

Public vs Private Murder

October 26, 2005

And now we have over 2,000 dead, tens of thousands of seriously wounded and from the actual beginning of this war in 1991, over 1 million Iraqi deaths, most of them civilians together with countless people traumatized for life. Mark Goldman has written a piece called "Public vs. Private Murder," I would like to share some of his thoughts with you.

If one day George W. Bush had opened up a drawer to his desk and pulled out a six shooter and shot Colin Powell in the heart . . . presumably that would have resulted in a national scandal . . . Bush would have been impeached and eventually tried for murder.

But as it turns out, Bush did not pull out a gun and shoot Colin Powell dead, or anyone else. Instead he pulled out a pen and signed his name to a number of executive orders which resulted in the murder or dismemberment of many tens of thousands of innocent men, women, and children. In addition, his orders destroyed the infrastructure of an entire country, made hundreds of thousands of people homeless and created endless pain and sorrow. And he did all this without any legitimate authority. He simply created this disaster by using lies, deceit, bribery, trickery, secrecy, propaganda and every kind of unconscionable human behavior that he and his cronies could devise.

Every step along the way, Bush and his cabal trampled on the rule of law, corrupting the morals of an entire nation while reeking havoc beyond anyone's imagination. All of this was set in motion by the illegal and unauthorized whims of a few ideologues. But now, his crimes have become our crimes.

These are the ultimate crime against peace and against humanity. All of his lies were not enough to gain the required authorization from the United Nations. He should have known that to break the Charter of the United Nations is to break the Constitution of the United States because treaties become part of the Constitution. But Bush went ahead anyway and no one stopped him.

How can this happen? It can happen when people are willing to compromise their integrity, are willing to lie to themselves and others for convenience, are willing to rationalize their behavior in order to conform or to gain money, power or prestige, assuage fear, or refuse to acknowledge uncomfortable truths. It can also happen when people are betrayed by those they trust.

Mass murder has been committed here and so far we are afraid to face up to it and take responsibility for it. All it takes is for citizens to ignore their responsibilities just a little bit, that's all it takes for a nation to betray itself.

We must now stir up the courage to indict, convict and punish the murderers.

Thanks Mark Goldman.

People's Summit of the Americas

November 9, 2005

Congratulations to the People's Summit of the Americas which took place simultaneously with the Summit of the Americas in Mar del Plata, Argentina.

A constant theme has come from the poor of the Americas. "The struggle itself is the victory." This is how Latin America is showing leadership and refuses to be overcome by the stench of violence, ignorance, hypocrisy, falsehood and ersatz religion in which we live.

They know that efforts to control the global economy by eight powerful nations has been a huge failure. The precious air we breathe requires international action and regulation, the oceans which are over one third dead require international action and regulation. But our nation has become an international factory of terror. Shock and Awe was terror.

Our military policy is terror. Our domestic policy is also terror as we see essential programs for our people trashed as incompetent, and apolitical cronies divide up endless billions of our tax money for their self interests.

The movement for justice and peace, however, is truly world-wide. We believe that the world is ready and eager for a major realignment.

Here is what we mean:

- Among the vast majority of the globe there is virtually no opposition to accepting the Universal Declaration of Human Rights. This means that the world's people soundly denounce the existing warfare system.
- In the new global and interdependent community, indeed in any developed society, health care must be a right. In the new global and interdependent community, education must be a right. * In the new global and interdependent community reverence for the planet will be understood. The air, the water, the soil and most of all, the people will be treated with reverence and respect.

136

- As we look to the decline and fall of corporate dictatorship, the bottom line of profit must never again be the bottom line.
- The new bottom line must be the felt needs of humanity. We all know what they are: adequate nutrition, housing, medical care, education and environmental sustainability. The outlay required to accomplish these things is far less than what we are spending on a corrupt warfare state.

Please don't ask others what you can do. Ask yourself what you are going to do. Ask yourself how you are going to join in with like minded people to build new organic structures which grow from the base of society.

The voice for justice and peace is now a majority. Please follow the lead of the People's Summit of the Americas and enter into the struggle which is itself a victory.

Office of The Americas
Twenty-second Anniversary

November 18, 2005

The Office of the Americas will honor Cindy Sheehan this Saturday, November 19. Cindy has galvanized the world with her demand to know for what noble cause her son Casey died.

We will also honor Daniel Ellsberg who remains an international voice of conscience. Dan risked 115 years in prison by releasing 7,000 pages of Pentagon policy papers to the Senate Foreign Relations Committee and later to the *New York Times*.

We will honor Dolores Huerta who co-founded the United Farm Workers Union together with Cesar Chavez and is bringing to farm workers the benefits enjoyed by members of other unions. In addition to her great work with farm workers, Dolores has become a world wide spokesperson for justice and peace.

We will honor Jodie Evans who co-founded Code Pink with Medea Benjamin. Major media have been unable to ignore the courageous actions of Code Pink as these women intervene at high level government meetings to demand an end to an unnecessary war.

Speaking on behalf of these great people, I am certain they don't want us to put them on a pedestal and then to regress into admiring bystanders. On the contrary, what they have done in their way we can do in our way. Every conscious human being in our society must be mobilized to overcome the international disgrace created by our administration as it conducts an illegal and immoral war, while seeking new conflicts, threatening nuclear disaster and dedicating itself to the promotion of torture. Such behavior has led international resistance which will continue until we cease and desist from our belligerence.

We simply cannot be spectators watching life go by. We cannot leave the work of justice and peace solely to these four wonderful people. We must join with like-minded people to expand on what these honorees have done; demanding truth in government, identifying and punishing criminal behavior and denouncing the war mongering crony capitalism and greed which has infected our government.

Government Logic

November 23, 2005

The logic of the administration is the logic of Advertising 101. If you have taken Advertising 101 you know that one of the key principles is to take the weakest point in the product and put it up front as if it were a strong point. If the truck you are trying to sell falls apart in one year, your ad will say, "Our Trucks last longer." If your cigarette gives cancer of the lungs, it will be advertised as . . . springtime.

Another example; many of our troops did not want to go to Iraq. They went to Iraq against their will. But they either went to Iraq or they had the option of going to a military prison. And how does the government propaganda advertise this? It says, SUPPORT OUR TROOPS with the clear implication that those troops are exactly where they want to be. The full sentence would be, "Support our troops because they want to be in Iraq and they went there of their own will." And this propaganda continues as thousands of our troops have defected and many heroic veterans have come home to denounce the torture, the killing of civilians, the destruction of an entire nation.

Just think about the phrase, "We must stay in Iraq so that our troops will not have died in vain." In other words, "Let's have more young people and more Iraqis die so that no one will think that those who preceded them died in vain.

As in advertising, our leaders have shown a reckless contempt for truth. Cheney refers to people who have his number as dishonest, cowardly, reprehensible and unpatriotic. I think he is looking in a mirror.

The tragedy is that many fine young people died cruelly and unnecessarily in Vietnam together with millions of civilians. Fine young people have died in Iraq together with yes, millions of Iraqis if we start the count in January of 1991 when the war actually began. Yes, they died because of a mendacious government which is lost in its own hubris.

Those who seek the truth are seeking a spiritual value. Those who create the lies are adversaries of the truth. They are not free. Let's clarify the point. These shortened lives were not in vain. These lives as all lives

139

are an ongoing miracle. But their death was too soon and also unnecessary. Those responsible for these unnecessary deaths must be brought to
justice as quickly as possible.

Let's junk Advertising 101 and all that it implies.

Victory

November 30, 2005

Historians will eventually reach an accurate consensus on our warfare state. I think it will go something like this: The Korean War has never ended. There was a cease fire but no peace treaty. Some 3 million Koreans and Chinese were killed together with 50,000 of our citizens. Our country did not win that war and it is not over.

The War in Vietnam? Yes, this long war had an end. The United States lost the war together with some 60,000 of our finest young people while 3 million Vietnamese perished, mostly civilians. U.S. attacks included the carpet bombing of civilians and chemical warfare by way of dioxin (agent orange).

Then there was a war in El Salvador, where our country supported the dictatorship and spent billions on munitions and on command and control of counter-insurgency. No, we did not win in El Salvador but the very same people who trained the Salvadoran death squads are now in Iraq training death squads. And the rebels we fought in El Salvador now make up a major political party known as the FMLN.

Then there was the Contra War in Nicaragua where the United States spent billions to pay and arm mercenaries to attack exclusively civilian targets, teachers, social workers, religious people and farmers. It was sheer terrorism against Nicaraguan civilians. 40,000 Nicaraguans were slaughtered. What did we win in Nicaragua? Nothing. The Sandinistas are the largest political party in the country today. When the secret war was running out of money the United States illegally sold arms to the Ayatollah Khomeini to get funds for more mercenaries and more arms. The same aircraft from the United States that shipped arms to Nicaragua for the Contras were used to bring cocaine back to this country on the return trips. The Contra mercenaries evolved into the private military corporations who are fighting and torturing people in Iraq today and who remain exempt from the Code of Military Justice.

And what did we win in Guatemala after supporting one of the most brutal and bestial military forces on earth for four decades? After spending billions of dollars which resulted in the killing of 200,000 Guatemalans, the very rebel force we fought is now a respected political party.

Need we mention the on-going Plan Colombia which is actually a U.S. Plan for Colombia which includes each and every one of the errors we have made in past wars.

Did our country have no victories? Well its seems we did win the war in Grenada in 1983. The island has a population the size of Santa Monica has no military and, of course there was absolutely no reason for war.

This endless and failed militarism should help us to understand why the United States cannot deliver health care, education and a vibrant public infrastructure to our population. To repeat the same action again and again and to expect different results is a sure sign of insanity.

The Supreme Court

December 7, 2005

The smallest and most powerful branch of our government is the Supreme Court. Citizens generally only think about the Supreme Court when a vacancy needs to be filled. But there is something much deeper at this time. The Supreme Court is simply not doing what it was designed to do. If we had a truly functional Supreme Court the nine would understand that they have the privilege of judicial review. The court would indicate by its performance that it understands the key decision supported by Chief Justice John Marshall in 1803; Marbury vs. Madison. This decision established the power of judicial review, that is the power of the courts to decide whether a governmental official or institution has acted within the limits of the constitution, and if not, to declare its action null and void. This decision applies to the performance of both the president and the congress.

The court has the power to declare presidential decisions as unconstitutional. The court has the power to declare an act of congress unconstitutional. It is up to an informed citizenry to instruct the court on the proper use of its power.

A functional and conscious Supreme Court would proceed with the following decisions immediately:

1. The court would order the President to cease and desist in his war making because the President has no constitutional right to start any war.
2. Major portions of The Patriot Act would be declared null and void as unconstitutional.
3. Major portions of the No Child Left Behind legislation would be declared unconstitutional.
4. A conscious court would immediately repent of its long practice of class justice. We have one form of justice for the majority and another form of justice for the minority for people of color, for the poor. Any justice of the Supreme Court would have to be sociologically illiterate not to see this. This is

143

known as the tyranny of the majority. The death penalty which was unconstitutional in our country and later declared constitutional would immediately take its place with the trash of history where it belongs.

5. A conscious court would declare such various secret governments including the CIA to be unconstitutional. Their structures are foreign to United States government.

6. A Supreme Court that was alive and conscious would immediately inform Mr. Cheney and Mr. Bush that their love and promotion of torture is illegal and contemptible.

It is our responsibility as citizens to demand that the life long appointees on the Supreme Court protect us from the incompetence of the executive and legislative branches of government.

Time to Leave the Box

December 14, 2005

Are you ready to leave the box now?

If you are, you will find a whole new world waiting for you.

The box is necrophilia, or love of death. The box is bound by the cardboard of fear, ignorance, moral illiteracy, vengeance, and stupidity. But the box feels comfortable.

Before we go on, please try to identify one instructive comment you might have heard from the spokespeople for the box. For example, Mr. Charles Krauthammer is playing parlor games with us about the usefulness of torture. He is in the box and its dark in there. But well paid opportunists are going to tell us that just everyone agrees with Mr. Krauthammer.

Unconscious spokespeople are telling us that the death penalty is effective. Actually it is so effective that we now have one of the highest murder rates in the world to say nothing of the highest rates of incarceration. What is inside the box is death and a love of death generated by induced fear. The death people even say that we are winning in Iraq.

On the contrary, we are simply restructuring a torturing dictatorship similar to what we created in Nicaragua under Somoza or in Guatemala or El Salvador under a military facade of democracy. Friends, there is no life in the box. It is full of dead people's bones.

As we leave the box and do our homework, we find that an imposter is in the presidency. This individual was not elected in 2000 and was not elected again in the year 2004. The data is now in and documented in the book *Censored 2006* by Peter Phillips and Project Censored, Seven Stories Press.

Yes, friends as you leave the box you will rise from the dead and join the global group of truth seekers. No more adoration of the nation state, no more acceptance of the state cult of cold blooded murder by execution and war.

Stanley "Tookie" Williams has just been murdered by the state of California, and many others await this cold blooded state homicide. They are to be killed as victims of class justice. In the box there is one system

145

of justice for the poor, for people of color and another system for people who have substantial amounts of money. It is only out of the box that we find what redemption means, what rehabilitation means, what reform means. To deny that these things are possible is to be spiritually dead.

Come on friends, it is time to leave the box and to say as Stanley Williams might have regarding those still in darkness, "Father, forgive them for they have absolutely no idea what they are doing!"

Christmas

December 21, 2005

So now both businesses and individuals must be chided for saying, Happy Holidays. They are to be forced into religious correctness by zealots demanding that they say, "A Blessed Christmas." Now that is a lovely phrase and I have no opposition to it. But to impose the greeting as a proselytizing moment is really sick.The only religion Jesus ever had was Judaism. He never converted to any other faith. Many Jews revere Jesus, but not as Messiah. In his Judaism, Jesus was a sharp and critical thinker and he directed his ire toward religious leaders like the Fallwells and Robertsons of his day. Yes, it was the gentle Jesus who called these people hypocrites, frauds, serpents, and a brood of vipers and saying, "You travel over land and over sea to make a single convert, and once that person is converted, you create a proselyte twice as wicked as yourself."

Jesus spoke with great reverence of those outside of his fold, the Samaritans, the Sidonians, the Syrians and those wise men from the east, my God, were they Arabs?

It should be clear to all, the message of Jesus was not sectarian, was not parochial, was not exclusive. It was universal, and inclusive.

So if thoughtful people out of respect for those who are not sectarian Christians choose to say "Happy Holidays," we should accept that as civility and reverence for many religious and cultural traditions. As we study Jesus' narrations about those outside his personal religion, it is clear that he was praising the compassion of the Samaritan, and the reception of God's grace by Naaman the Syrian. He was not promoting a sect, on the contrary, he was promoting humane behavior which is the electricity of authentic spirituality: justice, compassion, peace, joy, courage, endurance and love.

Can anyone picture Jesus running around buying everything in sight, sitting on Santa's lap and boycotting stores that say, Happy Holidays? And there is another celebration in the wings, that of the New Year. While I don't want to impose it on you, I would suggest one resolution for 2006: "I will resolve to make this the year that I will double my efforts to work for justice and peace. Authentic religion will never bless war. May peace be with us all."

Reasons to Intervene

January 11, 2006

It is unfortunate that the only way Latin America can have relative peace is when the United States is busy with other wars. Way back in 1938 Mexico succeeded in nationalizing its oil because our country was preparing for WW II and we wanted Mexico an ally. Fascism was very popular in Mexico and the U.S. was afraid that Mexico would go with the Axis powers so we did not intervene when Lázaro Cárdenas nationalized Mexican oil.

We did intervene, however, in Iran when they insisted on nationalizing their oil. That gave us the dictatorship of the Shah of Iran. And we did intervene when Iraq would not agree to privatize their oil. That is how the current fifteen year old war began in Iraq.

In spite of our brutal and unnecessary war in the Middle East, we are currently intervening in Colombia with both mercenary corporate troops as well as with our military. We have also kidnapped the popular president of Haiti and exiled him to South Africa leaving Haiti in shambles. But we simply can't intervene everywhere that our pathetic leadership would desire.

Currently our failed administration would like to intervene in Syria, Iran, Venezuela and North Korea. Actually, I think were it not for other pending wars we would certainly attempt to invade the rest of Latin America as well. Why? The Aymara and Quechua people of Bolivia have run the water and gas privatizers out of their country and have chosen an indigenous president, Evo Morales. Isn't that an affront to the Conquistadores from the north?

And what about Uruguay? There are socialists in high places. Isn't that a cause for intervention? And what about Argentina, where workers are actually taking over the management of industry?

There is a good reason to intervene. And Brazil has a president from the Workers Party. Goodness, we don't even have a workers party. That must be a reason to intervene. Why don't these people love us? Could it be that for every dollar we have invested in Latin America during the past century, we have taken out $3.00 of profit? And when our president recently went to Argentina for the Mar del Plata Summit, he was unable to dictate the rules of the game. The opposition to the methods of the World Trade Organization was powerful and effective.

And in Chile a fellow physician and disciple of Salvador Allende is making her way into power. Can't we dust off Henry Kissinger to locate a dictator like Augusto Pinochet to supplant her?

Friends, representative democracy was designed so that the literate few might rule the illiterate many. But times have changed. The Latin American people are demanding participatory democracy, economic democracy and substantive democracy.

Perhaps we can learn something from them.

A Standardized Test For Aspirants To Serve As
Justices On The Supreme Court

January 18, 2006

Here is a standardized test for anyone who would aspire to be a justice on the Supreme Court of the United States.

I have even answered the questions as I think Judge Alito might answer them.

1. Are you in favor of the death penalty? *Yes*.
2. Is the President allowed to start a war? *Yes*.
3. Do we have liberty and justice for all in the United States? *Yes*.
4. Would you send an innocent person to death because of a procedural impasse? *Yes*.
5. The United States is a classless society? *Yes*.
6. Do you believe that torture is legal? *Yes*.
7. Do you think that the Supreme Court is less powerful than the President? *Yes*.
8. Do you think that the power of judicial review must exclude foreign policy decisions? *Yes*.
9. Regardless of your religion, do you think that less harm would be done if abortion were illegal? *Yes*.
10. Do you think our prison system is just? *Yes*.
11. It is best to keep the Constitution the way it is and NOT to amend it to declare health care as a right for all. *Yes*.
12. It is best to keep the Constitution the way it is and NOT to amend it to declare education a right for all citizens. *Yes*.
13. Are the CIA and NSA structured in accord with the Constitution of the United States? *Yes*.
14. Is rendition of captives for torture in foreign lands legal? *Yes*.

Were I the examiner, I would then say, "Thank you for your participation, Judge, but you have failed every question. Sorry, we have no further questions. Please look for some other employment."

It seems to me that the spiritual death process is well underway when a majority of the Supreme Court Justices can concur on the death penalty. They obviously are out of touch with the civilized world which has denounced the death penalty. They obviously have made the war, death, gun, military industrial culture into a suicidal cult. THE SUPREME CULT.

"Yes" men have been drafted into our administration with a vengeance. Their yes is to power; their no is to the sovereignty of the people.

Liberty and Justice for All

January 25, 2006

You be the judge. Here comes a Chief Warrant Officer to take charge of a prisoner, Iraqi Major General Abed Hamed Mowhoush. First the general is beaten for thirty minutes, then he is held down and water is poured in his face, then the general was stuffed into a sleeping bag by the Chief Warrant Officer who then wraps the bag with electrical wire and sits on his chest for twenty minutes. The general dies.

The case is heard at Fort Carson, Colorado by a military court. There is no jail time for the Warrant Officer but he must spend the next sixty days on vacation at his home, his office or his church. Now on the same day, Daniel Burns, a non-violent protester was sentenced to six months in prison for spattering some of his blood at a military recruiting center to oppose the outset of the looming disastrous war in Iraq.

Three more of these St. Patrick's Four who poured blood at the recruiting center on March 17, 2003, will be sentenced this week. We expect them to receive the same six month sentence.

Just what is the message here? Let our children understand. If you are a good robot, follow orders, and torture one of our enemies to death, you will receive no jail time. If, on the other hand, you face an approaching evil and attempt to identify it by classic non-violent and prophetic action, you will be declared an enemy of the state and given a severe prison sentence.

The St. Patrick Four have made a very important statement to the people of the United States. They made a necessary statement of opposition to a war that is now known to be both illegal and immoral. It is a war which represents a major moral and political defeat for the United States.

And our lying administration continues to say, "We don't torture."

The same anti-intellectual and ahistorical elements that freed the warrant officer who was "just following orders" are now involved in a campaign to demonize Islam as an evil religion. Opportunists clothed as intellectuals from all over the country are quickly jumping on this lucrative band wagon.

So now do you understand that we are really torturing the devil? Please repeat after me, "We are torturing the devil!" And if you refuse to repeat that, we have approved ways of dealing with you.

Why We Can't Wait

February 1, 2006

Why were we out in the streets last night?

Because the man giving the speech and the realities of 2006 had little or nothing in common. The state of the Union was a clap fest for the wealthy. It was not real.

Why can't we wait for this regime to depart? Because those of us who teach can't accept material from our students if the White House is cited as a source. Why? Because the White House is currently not a credible source. Why can't we wait? Because the President and his cabal of ideological cronies have led our young people to the death in an unnecessary war.

He actually restarted a war begun by his father, continued by Bill Clinton and escalated once again by flat out lies. The war is now in its fifteenth year of terror on the people of Iraq.

Why can't we wait for the Bush regime to depart? Because they have approved of torture and then denied it. Torture has no place in a civilized society. We do not currently have a civilized administration. Members of the military who have tortured their victims to death now have virtual impunity from prosecution. In order to avoid embarrassment they have rendered some victims to foreign countries to be tortured.

Why can't we wait for the Bush regime to depart? Because they have disappeared people living in the United States. They have abolished the great writ of habeas corpus. What due process of law has been used for prisoners illegally held at Guantánamo?

What due process of law has been administered to the prisoners at Abu Ghraib? In some cases they have punished the lowest level of enlisted personnel and ignored the high ranking individuals who gave the orders, Mr. Rumsfeld for example.

Why can't we wait? Because the administration is now sending pilotless planes to bomb probable suspects in foreign countries as they randomly kill scores of innocent civilians in the process. Threats of slaughter are delivered to Iran, Syria, North Korea and Palestine.

154

Why can't we wait? Because the administration has approved rampant terror of invading civilian homes, killing and torturing the civilian occupants, destroying whole cities like Fallujah in illegal acts of collective punishment while using illegal weapons such as cluster bombs, white phosphorus and depleted uranium.

This out-of-control militarism has created international resistance and is recklessly endangering the people of the United States. The man who spoke so eloquently last night apparently does not have a clue about how he has trashed our country as he trashed our purported enemies.

The most noble act of Mr. Nixon's political career was his resignation from the presidency. Mr. Bush, we respectfully ask you to follow this excellent example.

Yes People

February 8, 2006

Where do the people who surround George Bush come from? They are actually a very conventional breed.

Many of these folks learned how to respect authority at an early age.

- Give the teacher the answer the teacher wants.
- Agree with whatever the authority figure says.
- Consider any intelligent question to be negative, indeed, to be a threat.
- Consider compliance with all commands to be positive.
- Just ask where the power is and yield to that power.

At a certain age this attitude petrifies and you have the perfect company person. This person now has no identity except to the company, to the firm, or to the political administration. Unfortunately this kind of formation leaves the individual with no moral compass.

Take the Attorney General for example, after observing his conduct under questioning it seems like he had this kind of formation. I think he just might conform to any opportunity without losing his smirk. "We have no king but Caesar." And if another king comes along, we will have no king but that one.

The only variable therefore, depends on who is in power. The soul then belongs wherever power resides. And such is the sadness of an unconscious life.

Exactly what place does authority have in framing a logical decision? Centuries of study in the field of Logic have given us a clear consensus. Authority has no part at all in framing a logical decision. The argument from authority has long been regarded as a classic fallacy. Authority can threaten to punish with a club; that is called an *argumentum ad baculum*. Yes, authority can punish and even torture, but authority is never a valid step in sound reasoning. This is why studying the behavior of military commanders is a study in sheer madness. General Westmoreland believed that he could have marched on to victory in Viet-

156

nam if he just had 750,000 troops on the ground. This in spite of the fact that most of the Vietnamese and most of our troops knew that the war was definitively lost. And last night we heard our Vice Commander in Chief, Dick Cheney speak of victory in Iraq. Now do we understand that military intelligence is an oxymoron?

Friends, to have a human life rather than the life of a cog in a machine we must question authority and when necessary we must defy authority. The phrase. "I'm in charge here," has never meant that I am correct.

Friendly Fire

February 15, 2006

If we are gentle in our judgment we can say, it was surely an accident that Dick Cheney shot his good friend in the face and in the heart. Yes, it was "friendly fire."

Unfortunately, however, it is no accident that in Cheney's role as the chief handler of George Bush, he has invited . . . no not invited, but forced many other people to be shot in the face or in the heart, to be maimed, to be tortured and to be murdered.

Some have died as a result of accidents, some have died from chemical warfare, some have died by suicide bombings, some have died from fragmentation bombs, some have died from our own white phosphorous. Many have also been hit by friendly fire, just as Mr. Harry M. Whittington was hit by friendly fire. Many have gone to hospitals to be told that they are paralyzed for life. Some have lost their mental balance. But what do these people have in common? Whether they are U.S. troops, British troops or Iraqi civilians, they are all victims; they are victims of an ill planned hunting trip to Iraq. These people must not be divided up as us and them. Whether they are identified as our own military or as Iraqi civilians makes little difference. When you have been shot in the face your commonality is in your victimhood. The most tragic victims are the children. They are not flown to Germany to have their wounds tended. When they suffer a wound they die. Their hospitals have been destroyed. How they loved to pick up those bright colored bomblets in search of a toy.

How quickly they are blown to pieces! Our stand-up comics have had a great time with Cheney hunting quail but his actual legacy far from humorous. His legacy is that of a mindless military-industrial-congressional-prison-gun complex which exists by the promotion of torture, terrorism and murder. For God's sake Mr. Cheney, please remove yourself from office and take your shotgun with you before you kill again.

Proposal for Departure

February 22, 2006

For years prior to our defeat in the Vietnam War, North Vietnam proposed a series of dialogical peace accords. And at that time our administration insisted that dialogue was impossible. During this period of intransigence both our casualties and those of the Vietnamese people escalated dramatically.

And now the Iraqi National Resistance is offering a similar dialogical plan for ending the current conflict. The lives of our service people and the lives of innocent Iraqis depend on our government's response. Here is the substance of what the Iraqi National Resistance is asking:

The U.S. must set a date for withdrawal. This withdrawal should be complete within six months. Iraqi resistance units will commit to a ceasefire during that time.

A new interim transitional government should take over until internationally-supervised elections are conducted.

A peacekeeping force is allowable but only from countries that have not been part of the occupation. The U.S. and U.K. should pay $20 to $50 billion in compensation and reconstruction costs. U.S. corporations will not be excluded from postwar contracts. A commission on human rights violations is to be constituted by the new government.

This document does not reflect the so-called Zarqawi forces. However, adoption of this approach would reduce the Zarqawi base radically and leave them even more isolated than they are at present.

According to recent surveys, nearly half of all Iraqis are supportive of the armed national resistance against occupation, and some 80 percent want the U.S. government to set a timetable.

It seems to me that our government, the media and the people of the United States must do everything possible to publicize the existence of this offer from the Iraqi National Resistance as we approach the third anniversary of this disastrous, illegal, unnecessary and failed military venture.

Considering the civility of this Iraqi Resistance proposal for the departure of the United States, why do our military-industrial forces insist on expanding our bases in that devastated land?

What Do We Want?

March 1, 2006

What do we want? The same thing the Palestinians want, the occupation must end.

This is also what 82 percent of all Iraqis want. And this is why 47 percent of all Iraqis support armed resistance to the occupation. In the rage that followed the bombing of the Askariya shrine both Sunnis and Shi'as blamed the U.S. occupation. If we were in Basra we would have witnessed a large Sunni-Shi'a protest rally on behalf of Iraqi unity and the departure of the United States. The chant was, "No to America!"

We must call for the complete withdrawal of all U.S. and coalition troops, together with our foreign mercenaries and our military bases. And by the way, what do our troops want? The Zogby poll says that 72 percent of them want us to get out of Iraq.

Meanwhile the Israeli Defense Minister Shaul Mofaz declares Palestine part of the axis of evil together with Syria and Iran and declares that more punitive measures will be taken by Israeli forces against the Palestinian people.

Meanwhile, according to highly credible sources, Israel and the United States are prepared to let their people die together in a nuclear holocaust. Their sights appear to be set on the use of nuclear weapons in Iran. A criminal act of such magnitude would undoubtedly lead to severe blowback in Israel and the United States. Such an Israeli/U.S. attack on Iran would thereby become the world's largest suicide mission. Some of the fanatics involved are apparently so ignorant that they speak of using nukes against the Palestinians as well.

Indeed U.S. foreign policy and its culture of violence is becoming a toxic brew to the entire planet. Does anyone think that increased nuclearism, ongoing wars and the ignoring of international laws are going to make the world a safer place?

So the United States and Israel both of whom have weapons of mass destruction are liable to attack Iran which has no such weapons. We have been down this filthy road before. This is the road that our government has strewn with hundreds of thousands of murdered victims in the wake of pathological lying.

As a result of lawless militarism the United States has become a failed state, a feared state and a terrorist state. As citizens we are required to resist the takeover of our government by organized crime.

The President Goes to India

March 8, 2006

Here is a free translation of the President's comments as he returned from his triumphant trip to India and Pakistan.

My fellow Americans, I want to give great big nuclear bombs to the Indian government so India can protect itself from Pakistan. I want Pakistan to maintain its great big nuclear bombs so that Pakistan can protect itself from India.

As you know many people in India are hungry, especially the children, so I am going to sell Martin F-16's and Boeing F-18 fighter jets to India so they can fight to feed their children.

Now I have already forgiven Mr. Khan in Pakistan for smuggling nuclear weapons equipment to anyone in the world because we are friends with his boss, General Pervez Musharraf. Of course we used to be friends with Manuel Noriega, Saddam Hussein and Osama Bin Laden but I am sure we will not have such problems in the future. Furthermore, Pervez Musharraf has given us permission to bomb any part of his country as long as we think we are bombing bad people, especially people who used to be our friends like the Taliban. Musharraf has been so gracious that we are also allowed to massacre people who are in the vicinity of these bombings. After all, why were they standing so close to known terrorists?

Oh, yes, we are worried about China because they are so big and they are still communists you know. So India is free now to fire nuclear warheads at China. Oh, yes, China can respond but then we can fire at China and China not knowing the origin of the nuclear attack can fire at Russia. Then Russia, not knowing the origin of the attack can fire at Britain and then France, confused by the whole issue, can fire its nukes at Israel. Then Israel can launch a nuclear attack on Iran. Then of course the United States could easily lose Chicago by accident after it destroys North Korea.

Friends, the combination of irrationality, incompetence, ignorance, arrogance and greed has reached an intolerable level. This entire administration must do us the favor of stepping down before they destroy the planet. This is why we can't wait.

Rational people have structured a Nuclear Non-Proliferation Treaty with a view to abolishing nuclear weapons entirely. But our so-called leaders have created a rogue state acting in opposition to all common sense while endangering our future, the future of our children and the future of the planet.

Welcoming the Wounded

March 15, 2006

Last night we welcomed Alaa' Khalid Hamdan and her father Khalid Hamdan Abd at the Venice Methodist Church. Cole Miller brought them to the United States to represent the millions of Iraqis who have suffered under sixteen years of war from Washington. Her brother and her three cousins could not attend because they are dead. This is the collateral damage described by General Tommy Franks when he said, "We don't do body counts." In other words, these people don't count.

As citizens of this country we must take immediate action to remove this criminal administration. Mr. Bush and his personal falange of organized crime must step down. How do we do that? First we take to the streets. Saturday, March 18 at noon, we will meet at Hollywood and Vine to denounce three years of preventative war, illegal weapons, occupation, torture and summary execution.

On the following day, Sunday March 19 at 12:30 PM the peace movement will meet at the Westwood Federal Building at Wilshire and Veteran to march together with Fernando Suarez del Solar, Pablo Paredes, Aidan Delgado and Camilo Mejia to the Santa Monica Pier and the Arlington West Memorial. The veterans and their supporters will continue that march to La Paz, California, the burial place of Cesar Chavez and on to San Francisco.

In addition to the marches we recommend three legislative actions for impeachment:

The State of Vermont is in process of following rule 603 for the impeachment of the President by way of state legislatures. That rule written by then Vice President Thomas Jefferson speaks of removal of the President by way of charges from the state legislatures. The rule still stands in our House of Representatives.

We must insist that our California legislators follow the good example of Vermont. There is also Congressman John Conyers' House Resolution 635 which calls for the impeachment of the President. All Citizens are invited to sign on to this one.

164

And in the Senate of the United States we have the Russ Feingold Resolution to censure the President for breaking the law. A censure of this kind is looked upon as the first step toward impeachment.

This is not only a federal and state issue. The San Francisco City Council has just passed a resolution to impeach Bush and Cheney.

Friends, the greatest myth in our midst is that of powerlessness. We are not powerless.

Economics 101

II

March 22, 2006

To understand our economic system you must comprehend the following: If you have money, you will be paid money for having money. If you do not have money you must pay money to get money. This is called "interest." Our ancestors called it "usury." It was known as a sin in both Islam and Christianity. Actually this system of injustice is one of the prime generators of war.

So it is not at all surprising that one of the supreme architects of the rape of Iraq is now head of the World Bank.

Now do you understand why credit card companies are begging you to borrow money? They know they can get 25 percent interest on the money they lend you. If you don't have money you must pay money to get it. And these friendly credit card companies are delighted to come after anything you do own if you can't find the money to pay them for not having the money you need.

This simple economic reality is one of the key reasons for international poverty. Actually, anyone making over $25,000 per year is in the top 1 percent of the globe's income.

The World Bank is anxious to lend money to small countries. Loans develop dependency. The loans lead to control of the small country and its assets just as your assets are in danger every time you request a loan. The problem is systemic. It can only be solved by observing the practical currents of change coming from places like Venezuela where Hugo Chavez is using income from oil for programs of social justice. Conventional mythology will say, "But there will be no incentive if there is no profit."

Friends, some of the most effective and incentive driven people on this planet are living on fixed incomes. Consider the physicists, chemists, economists, academics and perpetrators of justice and peace who win Nobel prizes. Their incentive is not profit, it is excellence. And such is the case as well for those who do not win such prizes but are driven and sustained by the pursuit of justice and peace. Excellence can also be motivated by cooperation rather than by profit driven competition.

We will build a peace system as we abolish a system, which is based on squeezing the life out of the world's poorest people.

Can You Top This?

March 29, 2006

The Third Reich conducted an evil holocaust of innocent people. This was a nightmarish attempt to destroy the Jewish people while including Gypsies, gays, communists and other non-Arians.

Having learned nothing at all from history, our current administration is on the verge of starting another horrific holocaust. With no ethics and no morality Washington is plotting, planning and conspiring to commit nuclear devastation. This time the ovens will be airborne and indiscriminate. But military double speak refers to these new models of tactical nuclear weapons as if they were both harmless and helpful.

The scientific community differs with the mindless perpetrators of a nuclear holocaust. The current models can do as much or more devastation as did the ovens that vaporized Hiroshima and Nagasaki.

The King of Jordan warned this week that any such attack on Iran by either the U.S. or Israel will send the Middle East into flames.

But the United States has just issued a strategic doctrine paper announcing that it will use nuclear weapons in any future conflicts when and how it wishes. This doctrine has gone beyond the limits of the Third Reich in its cynical disregard for the human race.

If we considered Hitler's methods as crass examples of social psychosis, exactly how shall we categorize the current plans of the Bush Administration?

Of course it is our duty to demand opposition to this murderous policy from the Congress that is supposed to represent us and we must do that.

But friends, at this critical moment in history, we must do something else. We must contact each and every member of the Supreme Court and remind them that the power of Judicial Review applies to foreign as well as domestic policy. That's right, the Supreme Court has the power to declare any act of the President unconstitutional. It seems to me that even a right wing batch of justices can understand that the current irrational, illegal, immoral and suicidal plans of this failed administration must be curtailed.

Demand that the Supreme Court initiate the process of denunciation of the Executive. Let the censure, impeachment and conviction begin before millions of our own citizens and our neighbors on the planet die unnecessarily in an international holocaust.

Veterans Speak Out

April 5, 2006

The veterans from the everlasting Iraq War have recently completed a march through Alabama, Mississippi and on to New Orleans in Louisiana.

Here are some of their comments as they marched:

"I ran over a little kid and I killed him."

"I know the war was wrong and I am sorry."

"When any explosive device went off we were told to shoot anything that moved."

"This war is not about freedom."

"We were told these are not people, they are animals."

"If you look at them as human, how can you kill them?"

"I went up to an Iraqi, hugged him and said I was sorry. He told me it was OK."

"I keep taking sleeping pills every day, I don't want to wake up."

"This is a total disregard for humanity."

"We know it was wrong and we are sorry . . . I mean killing civilians and indiscriminately."

"These people in Washington are a greater threat than the terrorists."

"I did not fight for freedom in Iraq."

These are just some words from the Iraq Veterans as they marched to New Orleans.

Hundreds of thousands of these "uninjured" veterans are coming home to join the tens of thousands of those severely wounded physically or mentally and to reflect on the endless number of innocent victims in Iraq who are flippantly dismissed by the obscene word, "collateral damage."

From the United Kingdom we have Sean Rayment's article in *The Telegraph* where he speaks of secret talks by the dogs of war in a plan attack Iran. In the absolute spiritual void and darkness of military planning, warped minds are discussing an attack on Iran with Tactical Toma-hawk cruise missiles fired from U.S. Navy ships and submarines.

Further attacks would include B-2 stealth bombers equipped with eight 4,500 pound enhanced BLU-28 satellite-guided bombs flying from the Island of Diego Garcia in the Indian Ocean. The intent of this evil concept is to eliminate nuclear weapons which Iran does not have. The effect of this evil concept will be to tear thousands of children and civilians to pieces while convincing over a billion people that war has been declared on Islam. Aside from being a crime against humanity, such an attack on Iran will profoundly endanger the security of our citizens as well as the rest of this endangered planet.

Captain Ahab Has Lost It

April 12, 2006

Last week I spoke of how the British Press released material on a plot for a U.S. attack on Iran.

And now Seymour Hirsch writing in the *New Yorker* issue for April 17, 2006 has identified another component to this outrage. He writes that this plot is not simply an attack by conventional bombs like the mass murder weapon called "BLU-28." This is a clear plan to use genocidal B61-11 nuclear bombs. And of course all of this will be directed at a nation that does not have nuclear weapons. Has there ever been a dictator who has acted in a more unilateral fashion than George Bush? I don't think so. This person is armed and dangerous. History teaches us that it is commonplace for a failing dictator to attempt to cover his scandals by directing the population's attention to some imagined exterior foe. And George might just see this massacre as a way to divert attention from his other crimes. The plan as described by Seymour Hirsch in this week's *New Yorker* is simply unacceptable by any sane person. Whether president or peon, every individual involved in such a genocidal conspiracy against Iran should be in prison.

What to do? The marches of immigrants are leading the way. They will conduct a major work stoppage on May 1 to remind our government of their essential role in the economy of the United States. Rather than joining in the plot to murder the children of Iran I would suggest that we plan a similar work stoppage or General Strike. Such a direct action is the essence of democracy. One person, one vote. By withholding our labor we make it clear to this den of thieves that they had better start working for us. We don't work for them.

Unfortunately we do pay taxes to them. We give them our hard earned money in good faith and they use it to murder people. They have done nothing to fix Iraq and they have shown scant will to fix New Orleans or the rest of the rotting infrastructure of the United States.

A national strike or refusal to work would be a clear message to Washington that this administration must cease and desist its mindless militarism and stop being a threat to the existence of this planet.

Regardless of what Washington thinks, a nuclear attack on Iran conducted by the United States or by Israel will be considered a declaration of war on Islam and will be in fact a declaration of war on the human race.

A Vital Sign in Congress

April 19, 2006

It has been so hard find any living thing in Congress. But here is a vital sign and I hope there will be many more. Congressman and former presidential candidate Dennis Kucinich, who is also the Ranking Democrat on the House Government Reform Subcommittee on National Security, Emerging Threats and International Relations sent the following letter to George Bush about the current presence of U.S. troops in Iran:

Dear President Bush:
   Recently, it has been reported that U.S. troops are conducting military operations in Iran. If true, it appears that you have already made the decision to commit U.S. military forces to a unilateral conflict with Iran, even before direct or indirect negotiations with the government of Iran had been attempted, without U.N. support and without authorization from the U.S. Congress.
   The presence of U.S. troops in Iran constitutes a hostile act against that country. At a time when diplomacy is urgently needed, it escalates an international crisis. It undermines any attempt to negotiate with the government of Iran. And it will undermine U.S. diplomatic efforts at the U.N.
   Furthermore, it places U.S. troops occupying neighboring Iraq in greater danger. The achievement of stability and a transition to Iraqi security control will be compromised, reversing any progress that has been cited by the Administration.
   It would be hard to believe that such an imprudent decision had been taken, but for the number and variety of sources confirming it. In the last week, the national media have reported that you have in fact commenced a military operation in Iran. Today, retired Air Force Col. Sam Gardiner related on CNN that the Iranian Ambassador to the IAEA, Aliasghar Soltaniyeh, reported to him that the Iranians have captured dissident forces who have confessed to working with U.S. troops in Iran. Earlier in the week, Seymour Hersh reported that a U.S. source had told him that U.S. marines were operating in the Baluchi, Azeri and Kurdish

regions of Iran. Any military deployment to Iran would constitute an urgent matter of national significance. I urge you to report immediately to Congress on all activities involving American forces in Iran. I look forward to a prompt response.

Sincerely,
Dennis J. Kucinich
Member of Congress

Discernment

April 26, 2006

Discernment is important when buying groceries or buying a spiritual path.

Are you about to buy a chemical feast of cancer causing garbage, or are you buying healthy food? Sometimes it is difficult to discern, but for our benefit and that of our family, discern we must.

And think how important discernment is as we pursue authentic spirituality.

Here are a few litmus tests for authenticity:

Does the message bless war?
If it does, don't buy it.

Does the message imply that your country represents the will of God?
If it does, don't buy it.

Does the message identify a single sect as God's exclusive voice?
If it does, don't buy it.

Does the message claim to know everything about God?
If it does, don't buy it.

Indeed such messages are made by people who create God in their personal image and likeness.

On the contrary.

Discernment can lead to acceptance of the following: How about a message saying that the direction of history is in our hands and that there can be different futures depending on our struggles.

I buy that one.

How about a message that speaks about compassion and love for all?

Oh yes, we can compassionately incarcerate those who are a danger to public safety.

Love and compassion do not exclude sound reason. I can buy that.

How about a message that looks upon this miraculous planet as an object of reverence?

I can buy that.

How about a message that looks with awe and respect at the work of science and technology knowing that all research must be directed to humane goals?

And how about a message that observes that each species repeats its evolutionary history in the course of its gestation? I can buy that. How about a message that stands in awe of the universe and may wish to express that awe in music, poetry, ritual, and the anthropology of religion.

Friends, this approach is quite different from the cancer causing garbage that is currently huckstered by self-seeking religionists.

Spiritual discernment demands that we exclude messages which are based on nationalism, war, exclusivity, vindictiveness, and separation of the earth's people into artificial sub-groups. Discernment is necessary at our grocery store and in our quest for authentic spirituality.

A Day Without an Immigrant

May 3, 2006

It was a joy to participate in the two Los Angeles gatherings last Monday. The early march terminated at City Hall and the later march terminated at La Brea and Wilshire. These two May Day marches were the largest in a historic national outpouring of immigrants and those in solidarity with them.

The great democratic power of the General Strike and boycott represented by the Noon March was profoundly instructive. It was organized from the base by people who believed in these powerful tools in the arsenal of non-violence. Dr. Martin Luther King had also used these tools effectively. Indeed the General Strike and Boycott can bring participatory democracy to the United States. The Noon March was conducted with joy and dignity. It represented the vanguard of immigrant power.

The Afternoon March was also successful and actually was an even larger gathering. Certainly there was tension between the two actions, but it was intelligent and peaceful tension. The Church, the Unions and the City Government were in complete support of the afternoon March. Students were urged to attend after school and employees who could not leave their jobs were encouraged to attend after work. Some observers considered this second march to be divisive.

But regardless of the intentions of the organizers, the second march gave an opportunity to those who were not ready to support a general strike and boycott.

Rather than demeaning the people who went to the second and larger march, it is important to understand that for many it was a huge step in the struggle for justice.

And it seems to me that everyone should oppose the so-called Guest Worker Program. It is simply a repetition of the old Bracero Program which divided families and exploited workers. We do not need a program that creates second class citizens.

In recent decades we have witnessed the globalization of capital. These immigrant marches help us to understand that there is a second component to this phenomenon and that is the globalization of labor. If capital can go anywhere in the world without restriction, it is only logical that those who create capital, namely workers, should also be able to travel freely. I consider the people who come to our country to be refugees, not illegal aliens. The military and economic terror that drove them here is often created by United States policy.

The President Writes a Letter

II

May 10, 2006

President Mahmoud Ahmadinejad writes a letter to President Bush. The Iranian president said many things that were in accord with his Persian culture.

But really would it not be easier to start a nuclear war rather than to do some homework on Persian culture? We are completely set up for the nuclear war but we are not set up to ask a group of Persian experts to analyze the letter and to respond in a respectful manner. But you see, intelligent letter writing is difficult and nuclear war is so easy.

All Bush needs is a button for the war. But to respond to the letter he would need an education on the matter or to ask someone who has had an education to be of assistance.

The rape of Iraq has gone on for fifteen years now. The first Bush Administration, the Clinton Administration and the Lesser Bush Administration consistently demonstrated near absolute zero understanding of the cultures of Iraq. Some dialogue, some honesty and some humanity would have avoided the Iraq disaster. But dialogue, honesty and humanity require some spiritual substance.

Regardless of the personal failings on the part of President Mahmoud Ahmadinejad and regardless of his pietistic approach to our pietistic President, why would we not answer the Iranian's question? "Are you pleased with the current condition of the world? Do you think present policies can continue?" This is an excellent question and could be the beginning of a substantive dialogue and a peaceful future.

Friends, we are talking about the first direct contact between an Iranian head of state and an American president since the revolution of 1979. We are talking about a risk that was taken by the Iranian president who could be called a traitor by some of his own people for even writing such a letter.

President Ahmadinejad was clearly looking for common ground for an ongoing dialogue. Our Secretary of State should be sent to Iran with a respectful response to this important letter. There is no need at all for our response to agree with Mahmoud Ahmadinejad.

180

The only requirement is that the response be educated, respectful, thoughtful and dialogical. Diplomacy has been the rarest component in the Bush Administration. Here is an opportunity that must not be missed. Here is an opportunity for our country to give some indication that it might accept a peaceful solution to this unnecessary crisis.

Divine Strake

May 17, 2006

What is a strake? A strake is a device for controlling airflow over an aircraft or the flow of water under a ship. But the Divine Strake is a 700 ton bomb made of ammonium nitrate and fuel oil. This monstrosity is to be detonated in the atmosphere in lieu of the Robust Nuclear Earth Penetrator and will have a force similar to that nuclear weapon. The test is planned for June 23rd in the Nevada desert close to the sites where hundreds of nuclear tests were conducted between 1950 and 1992.

Scientists who have retained their sanity believe that the Divine Strake will stir up nuclear contamination from forty-two years of nuclear bombing on the lands of the Western Shoshone. Yes it was the Western Shoshone who had the intelligence to file a lawsuit declaring that this planned atmospheric explosion would disturb contaminants left from previous nuclear tests. The original blast date of June 2 was pushed back because of their lawsuit.

But this is where the word divine comes in. The planners of this mega explosion seem to think they are divine, they are playing god and even the courts give way to their gods of metal.

Citizens of the city of St. George, Utah, not far from the site, identify thousands of people who are now suffering from cancer as a result of radiation released from those previous nuclear bombs.

And the cancer patients are supposed to believe it when the National Nuclear Security Administration and the Defense Threat Reduction Agency say that the detonation of Divine Strake is perfectly safe. In view of the lack of credibility of the current Administration, it seems that the people of northern Nevada and Utah should make their peace with God and prepare to die of cancer.

Those who have planned this upcoming crime should be tried and convicted.

Divine Strake is an act of terrorism against the land and the people of the United States of America. Many of our citizens have taken an oath to protect this country from enemies foreign and domestic. It seems that the demise of this land will be the work of domestic enemies who think they are divine.

Rational human beings will conduct a protest to the abomination of Divine Strake on May 28 in Nevada.

Palestinian Anti-Terrorist Act
of 2006 HR 4681

May 24, 2006

Prime Minister Golda Meir told us, "There is no such thing as Palestinians; they never existed." Then we see them thrown off their land, their homes bulldozed, their militants jailed and tortured. Then Israel refuses to recognize or negotiate with their leadership. And all of this happened long before Hamas was elected. As normal human beings, Palestinians have resisted.

The Israeli peace movement has recognized this reality for decades. The government of Israel is the aggressor. Aggressors are opposed by people all over the globe.

And this is similar to what is happening in Iraq. The U.S. government is the aggressor. The Iraqis are fighting back. Should anyone be surprised?

And now our pathetic banana republic House of Representatives has passed House Resolution 4681. This bill restricts humanitarian aid to Palestine. It also threatens to withhold portions of the U.S. dues to the United Nations if Palestine continues to demand Israel's compliance with existing international law.

This vile piece of legislation designates territory controlled by the Palestinian Authority as a terrorist sanctuary and refuses visas to members of the Palestinian Legislative Council and Palestinian Mission to the United Nations. It also instructs the U.S. Representative to the World Bank to oppose the continuation of humanitarian aid to Palestine.

Representative Betty McCollum has banned the Israeli Lobby AIPAC from her office until she receives a formal apology from this powerful "wag the dog" group for saying she is supporting terrorists.

Here is what Representative Jim McDermott of Washington State has to say about this bill:

> The World Health Organization sees a rapid decline of the public health system in Palestine. This bill will only make the already dire situation even worse. As a doctor I took an oath to heal. Allowing innocent Palestinians to go hungry, while denying them medical treatment cannot possibly correct injustice, or lead to peace.

Join Rabbi Arthur Waskow in his efforts to assist the Palestinian people as the Israeli government stops international aid, freezes Palestinian tax revenues and creates an acute shortage of medical and food aid. Palestinian children are already suffering dire physical and mental damage from this outrage.

Massacre

May 31, 2006

This age will be remembered for its love of fiction. The Left Behind Series sells tens of millions of copies fostering a nineteenth century mythology about the end of days. Many readers fanatically grasp on to the myth as if it were reality. Dan Brown writes a book called the *Da Vinci Code* and people are saying, "See I told you so."

Both books are legitimate, that is legitimate fiction. The fascinating element is how so many people have absorbed these writings as non-fiction.

I think we can understand what is happening here. Many people are so terrorized by reality that they want to live happily in fantasy land forever.

Just think how many hard fact, heavily researched books have come out regarding the war crimes our administration commits each day. Fear of the truth and the desire to say, "Oh, I didn't know that," seems to lead the way in this quest for fantasy.

And now Time Magazine uncovers a massacre in Iraq. We are grateful for this legitimate journalism. But we must watch for the spin. We can't let this go with a few privates and sergeants condemned as bad apples. The Haditha Massacre includes a series of flat out denials and cover-ups by the military, just as the My Lai Massacre in Vietnam or the Abu Ghraib torture scandal. These are not isolated incidents, on the contrary, these acts personify our policy. The atrocity was not simply My Lai, it was the sheer evil of killing 3 million people in Vietnam. The atrocity is not simply Abu Ghraib, it is the fact that torture was routine then and has continued to be routine now.

The atrocity is not simply Haditha, it is fifteen years of butchering innocent people in Iraq. The invasion of homes and massacre of civilian inhabitants is a daily occurrence in Iraq. Many of these massacres are punitive actions like the punitive attacks on the people who lived in Fallujah, Some 6,000 civilians were killed during that November 2004 assault. This was simply not news until unimbedded reporters, at great personal risk went for the facts and not the fantasy.

As we lost the war in Vietnam every massacre was declared to be an attack on insurgents. And the same is happening in Iraq. A massacre of civilians is reported by the military as an Iraqi offensive. That is why we continue to identify dead insurgents who are two and three years old.

We definitively lost in Vietnam and now our behavior in Iraq mirrors the deception, deceit and treachery that is leading to our absolute failure there. Fiction continues to be popular. But only non-fiction can make us free.

The Button

June 7, 2006

Certainly we have become numb to the reality of nuclear destruction. This shadow has been over the human race for sixty years and now the danger of its use is greater than ever. One single individual in Washington has the future of this planet in his hands. There are no checks and balances, there is no judicial review, there is no advice and consent of the Congress. Friends, we are living in a nuclear dictatorship. The President can eliminate hundreds of millions of people in a host of countries simply by pushing the button. This should never be the prerogative of one individual. Actually, it should never be the prerogative of any individual or of any group.

Suppose a nuclear explosion takes place in the United States. Will the President strike back at a nation that had no part in the attack as he did after 9/11? After striking the wrong nation and having deadly radiation flow into surrounding countries, should we be surprised if they retaliate? The President's button represents a suicide attack on all of us.

Even if we had the most brilliant and humane president imaginable, she or he should never have authority over such a button.

This is not a matter of brilliance of an individual, it is a matter of the future of this miracle planet. And if you don't believe it is a miracle planet, please show me one like it.

Nationalism is killing us. It is archaic, fossilized, irrelevant and destructive. What does it take to awaken people to this reality? At this moment in history our every thought and plan must be made with the planet in mind.

Global warming is a reality but the greed for short term profit together with a failed and catastrophic war has Washington trying to divert our attention to issues that should not even be in the sphere of the Federal Government.

Unfortunately what is good for profit is very bad for the globe.

Fully electric cars were manufactured and running well in the 1920s. But they were abolished by the oil industry. If this were not the case don't you think we would have made some progress with electric vehicles in the last eighty-six years?

We must take the quest for profit out of the world's drivers seat. We must take the button out of the hands of the President. And how do we do that? We do it by planetary thinking, the only kind of thinking that will make life possible for our grandchildren.

And we must turn our thinking into action by with a new Declaration of Peace.

The worn out eighteenth century nationalism in which we are currently living assures us that our grandchildren will have neither life, nor liberty nor the pursuit of happiness.

The South Central Farmers

June 14, 2006

June 13, 2006, a day of infamy in the history of Los Angeles. Sheriffs and LAPD arrive in the middle of the night to attack peaceful people who have created a paradise in what was a trash heap. It was a quasi-military action and it was entirely unnecessary. These people were given ten minutes to get out after years of hard work and development of the area.

Exactly what threat to public safety were these peaceful urban farmers? Why were their trees cut down? Why were their plots bulldozed?

This beautiful oasis was developed fourteen years ago in the wake of the uprising of 1992.

Land was offered to the South Central Community by the City of Los Angeles. The land was broken, scarred, paved over. There were abandoned refrigerators, shards of glass, old tires, piles of rags and discarded furniture. The South Central Farmers took away the trash, cut down the weeds and got rid of the rats. They turned the soil and found that it could live again and it provided food for 350 families.

What a putrid example of class justice. The poor are those selected to receive the death penalty. The poor are those selected to die in unnecessary wars. The poor are those who fill our prisons with 2 million inmates as part of the military, industrial, prison, gun and warfare state complex. And now the poor are evicted in an act of treachery by the City of Los Angeles.

There is only one solution and that includes restitution. First that this land be immediately set aside as the property of The South Central Farmers.

Second we must begin plans for many similar farms in the City of Los Angeles. We want these farms so that talented people will continue to grow crops that we will never see in a super-market. Precious seeds were brought in to produce crops that heal and nourish. Los Angeles will remain with a broken heart until restitution is achieved.

Call Mayor Villaraigosa and demand that the pledge made by the City of Los Angeles be respected. Call City Council Member Jan Perry and demand that she represent the people of her district. Call Mr. Ralph Horowitz the developer who initiated the eviction and insist that he negotiate with The Trust for Public Land and the Annenberg Foundation to make the South Central Farm a permanent symbol of the greatness of those who created it.

The South Central Farmers' web site is: www.southcentralfarmers.org.

The Twins

July 5, 2006

The most powerful military force in the history of the world continues its fifteen year assault on a weak and devastated nation called "Iraq." The methodology includes collective punishment of civilians by indiscriminate bombing, house to house massacres, imprisonment without trial and routine torture. When our forces suffer a defeat such collective punishments have led to increased premeditated killing of countless civilians.

The people of Iraq are fighting to defend themselves and they are also fighting their fellow citizens who have submitted to the rule of a foreign empire. Citizens of Iraq who are doing what our United States citizens would do if we were invaded are called "terrorists." Indeed, Iraqis are frequently referred to as members of an outside force known as al-Qaeda.

We are reminded of France when it was occupied by the Third Reich and how the French Resistance fought the French who submitted to the German occupation. A handful of our troops, generally the lowest level of enlisted personnel, are brought before military justice on charges of torture, murder and rape. Actually the entire fifteen years has been nothing but torture murder and rape.

Not far from Iraq we can observe parallel behavior as the fourth largest military in the world continues its brutal attacks on Palestine. Collective punishment is and has been the rule for decades. One Israeli prisoner leads to the shelling of civilians and the willful destruction of and entire electrical system. Palestinian civilians suffer from direct bombardment, a cut off of food, medical aid and the withholding of economic assistance.

The government elected by the Palestinians is rejected with the same charges that were leveled at previous regimes. Thousands of Palestinians have been held captive, tortured and killed. Their homes have been bulldozed and their country divided into Bantustans of separation. The wall is the message.

For decades now, the long standing exceptionalism practiced by the United States has been granted to Israel. We can have 10,000 nukes but you can't have one. We can attack you but if you resist we will massacre your people. No one is more aware of this crisis than the Israeli people and the Israeli Press. As one visiting Israeli scholar said, "You Americans are going to fight to the last drop of Israeli blood." Our nation, with Israel in its shadow, seems suicidally determined to create an international tsunami of resistance.

A Declaration of Peace

July 12, 2006

Yes, it is true. Hundreds of organizations and many thousands of people have declared peace and have signed a declaration of peace. The puppet government created by the United States in Iraq is a total loss. The Iraqi security forces are in complete disarray. Some are working for the other side, some are involved in organized crime, and according to the *Los Angeles Times*, the new 268,610 member Iraqi Interior Ministry has a far larger security force than all of the troops from the United States which are currently in Iraq. These Iraqi forces are clearly marked by brutality, bribery, summary execution, and rape. There are kidnapping rings in this new Iraqi ministry. Iraqis do not trust them. Payroll fraud is rampant. Large amounts of communications equipment is missing. Female detainees are sexually assaulted. The Ministry of the Interior is a counterproductive and broken department of the new Iraqi government imposed by our administration. Actually the Iraqi security forces in Iraq have all the characteristics of the forces that the United States paid for during the Somoza Dynasty in Nicaragua, during the Duvalier rule in Haiti, or the forces of South Vietnam during that endless war.

Respect from the rest of the world has been lost. Dedicated young service people from the United States are becoming conscious of how they have been lied to, used and discarded together with endless numbers of innocent Iraqis.

Services justly due to our citizens have been denied while billions in our hard earned taxes have been tossed helter skelter to war profiteers with zero accountability.

These are some of the reasons that the peace movement has produced The Declaration of Peace. We have signed that declaration together with hundreds of organizations and hundreds of thousands of individuals. We call on the Congress and the Administration to end the war.

The ancient and powerful spiritual weapon of fasting is now deployed. This is called the Troops Home Fast which thousands have already begun. Some will fast on liquids only, some will fast completely for a day, a week or as long as their conscience dictates.

194

Up to a September 21 deadline, we will participate in marches, vigils and lobbying for immediate withdrawal of our troops. From September 21–28 there will be direct actions in Washington, D.C. and throughout the nation. In the spirit of Mohandas Gandhi and Dr. Martin Luther King some signers will be led by conscience to engage in non-violent civil disobedience and risk arrest to express their principled opposition to the U.S. War in Iraq. These nonviolent activities will continue until the United States withdraws from Iraq. You can sign on to this pledge by going to: www.declarationofpeace.org

Our Newspaper

July 19, 2006

Here begins the lead editorial in the *Los Angeles Times* on Monday, July 17, 2006:

> Make no mistake about it: Responsibility for the escalating carnage in Lebanon and northern Israel lies with one side and one side only. And that is Hezbollah . . .

Substantial numbers of Israelis disagree with the *Los Angeles Times*. They are demonstrating in Central Tel Aviv to protest Israel's attacks on Lebanon and the continued offensive of the Israeli Defense Forces in the Gaza Strip. The protesters called the Israeli Defense Force operations an unnecessary war and demanded that the Israeli government hold negotiations on an exchange of prisoners.

Contrary to the *Los Angeles Times* editorial many Israelis understand that the escalating carnage is also related to the oppression of Palestinians.

For example:

- There are some 9,000 routinely tortured Palestinian prisoners held in Israel without trial.
- There are some 400 routinely tortured Palestinian children held in Israel without trial.
- Hundreds of Palestinians have had their homes destroyed without a charge or a hearing.
- Targeted assassinations of Palestinians are also routine. These are cold blooded murders of suspects without evidence or trial.
- Significant numbers of the elected Palestinian government have been captured and are now being held without trial.
- Collective punishment has been the rule. Food, medicine and funds have been withheld from Palestine.

History makes it clear that resistance can be expected from any occupied country. This is why Israeli citizens are demonstrating in Tel Aviv for peace and this is why hundreds of Israeli Officers have refused to serve in occupied Palestine. They seem to know that the ancient and vengeful and useless axiom of an eye for an eye and a tooth for a tooth has been replaced by, "Two thousand eyes for an eye and one thousand jaws for a tooth."

Sadly, many people select denial as a way of mindless life. So we must praise Israelis who at this moment of crisis know from long experience that war itself is the evil, war is the problem, war is the mistake and war is the enemy. Instead of the absolutist statement about, "one side, and one side only," it would have been far better for the *Los Angeles Times* to acknowledge that the obstructionist policy of our nation has blocked literally scores of United Nations resolutions which could have brought peace to Israel and its neighbors.

God Speaks

July 26, 2006

Have you ever wondered how to define blasphemy? Blasphemy is to speak irreverently about God or sacred things.

Blasphemy takes place when a president says that God speaks through him. Just think, God told Mr. Bush to speed up the delivery of bombs to Israel. Does Mr. Bush think that these bombs only kill bad children? Such gifts from heaven would never kill good children, would they? Did God tell Mr. Bush to also send the cluster bombs which are an international crime? Did God tell him to send the white phosphorous, another international crime?

Now the reason these bombs must be delivered in great haste is that according to the *New York Times*, Israel has a long list of targets in Lebanon which it is anxious to strike.

But wait, did God tell Mr. Bush to send a message to Israel to stop the bombing of Lebanon while Condi Rice was there? Did God say, "OK Condi has left, you can resume the slaughter?" Did God speak through Mr. Bush telling him to send the GBU-28 bombs which are now on their way? These terrorist weapons only weigh 5,000 pounds each. And all of this murderous and valueless trash including the U.S. F-16 jets is paid for by you and me. Now do you understand why we can't deliver health care to our citizens? That's right, it's because we are stupidly promoting international chaos.

In the meantime conscious Israelis are demonstrating against the war. Thousands marched in Tel Aviv to protest Israel's dropping twenty-three tons of bombs on Lebanon in a single night. Hundreds of civilians, one third of them children, are dead, thousands are maimed.

The Israeli demonstrators are wisely demanding a prisoner exchange with Hezbollah and Hamas. They also urged their soldiers not to fight. And the numbers of Israeli officers refusing to serve now include over 100 pilots.

The principal slogans of the Israeli peace demonstrations have been:
"The occupation is a disaster, leave Lebanon now,"
"Children in Beirut and Haifa want to go on living."

"We will not die and not kill in the service of the United States."

In both Israel and the United States we have heard these intelligent cries for justice and peace. We must continue the protests before our incompetent, ignorant, violent and blaspheming leadership destroys itself together with the children. Hezbollah and Hamas were born from the previous invasion of Lebanon and the occupation of Palestine. Just as the number of Iraqi insurgents increases every day as a result of our occupation of Iraq, so Hezbollah and Hamas will expand dramatically as a result of Israel massive attacks on civilians. The Israeli demonstrators know that. But in the U.S. and Israel, military intelligence remains an oxymoron.

Resistance is Real

August 2, 2006

Where did Hamas come from? It rose up as a response to fifty years of oppression and humiliation of the Palestinian people. Where did Hezbollah come from? It was formed as a defense against Israel's invasion of Lebanon in 1982 which left 22,000 people dead.

Where did the Iraqi resistance come from? It was born as a result of the U.S. occupation of Iraq.

Why don't Hezbollah, Hamas and the Iraqi resistance just sit still? Didn't Jesus say, "When someone strikes you on the right cheek, turn and offer the other."

Well, that is good advice and certainly may apply to random insults. But Jesus did not say, "Just ignore it when your children are held and tortured by a foreign power." He did not say, "Just be quiet when your home is bulldozed." He did not say, "It is OK to allow your mother, your grandmother and your sick to be bombed to pieces."

How could any sane person not expect resistance from oppressed people? Indeed it is the pathology of militarists that they just never get it. What happened? These people are fighting back? They aren't supposed to do that . . . are they? Why don't they get the message? We have told them that they will comply or die. Can't they hear us?

Why don't you ask the Vietnamese? Why don't you ask the Salvadorans? The Nicaraguans? The Guatemalans? The Colombians?

The Israeli peace movement and conscious people throughout the world are crying out for an end to this massacre. Here is the Gush-Shalom statement in the Israeli newspaper *Haaretz* which begins with a quote from the Israeli Defense Force.

"We warned them
And called on them To escape!"
That is disgusting Hypocrisy.
Because we have:
Bombed the roads.
Destroyed the bridges.

Cut off the supply of gasoline.
Killed whole families on the way.
There is only one way
Of preventing such disasters,
Which turn us into monsters:
TO STOP!
There is no military solution!

For information: info@gush-shalom.org
Published in *Haaretz*, August 1, 2006

Absolute Failure

September 6, 2006

Just what has the Israeli Government accomplished with its endless war crimes in Lebanon and Gaza? Here is an opinion which I share together with Noam Chomsky, Howard Zinn, Eduardo Galeano, Arundhati Roy and many others.

The U.S.-backed Israeli assault on Lebanon has left the country numb, smoldering and angry. The massacre in Qana and the loss of life is not simply "disproportionate." It is, according to existing international laws, a war crime. The deliberate and systematic destruction of Lebanon's social infrastructure by the Israeli air force was also a war crime, designed to reduce that country to the status of an Israeli-U.S. protectorate. The attempt has backfired. In Lebanon itself, 87 percent of the population now support Hezbollah's resistance, including 80 percent of Christian and Druze and 89 percent of Sunni Muslims, while only 8 percent believe the U.S. supports Lebanon.

It has now become clear that the assault on Lebanon to wipe out Hezbollah had been prepared long before. Israel's crimes had been given a green light by the U.S. and its loyal British ally, despite the opposition to Blair in his own country. In short, the peace that Lebanon enjoyed has come to an end, and a paralyzed country is forced to remember a past it had hoped to forget. The state terror inflicted on Lebanon is being repeated in the Gaza ghetto.

Meanwhile, the rest of Palestine is annexed and dismantled with the direct participation of the U.S. and the tacit approval of its allies. We offer our solidarity and support to the victims of this brutality and to those who mount a resistance against it. For our part, we will use all the means at our disposal to expose the complicity of our governments in these crimes. There will be no peace in the Middle East while the occupations of Palestine and Iraq and the temporarily "paused" bombings of Lebanon continue.

Friends, the criminal actions of the United States and Israel are eternally marked as: a moral failure, a political failure, and a military failure. The massacres of Lebanon, Gaza, Iraq and Afghanistan will be eternally remembered as the highest level of war crimes. The so-called Official Story created by the United States and Israel will be remembered as a monument to disinformation and sheer militaristic war propaganda.

The Declaration of Peace

September 20, 2006

If you are only in touch with commercial media, you probably won't know about the declaration of peace. There is a lot of money in war, so why would the commercial media want to speak of peace?

This week some 430 peace organizations throughout the United States have planned a coordinated 275 events. Here is a local example. On Monday, September 25, in Hollywood, there will be a protest gathering from 10:00 A.M. until 1:00 P.M. at the military recruiting station, 7060 Hollywood Blvd. Some of the participants will engage in civil disobedience.

The Declaration of Peace was months in the planning, it was taken from the Pledge of Resistance which we used during the U.S. wars in Central America. That pledge contributed to the United Nations conducting peace accords in Nicaragua, Guatemala and El Salvador.

Many peace organizations are faith based. The idea was to pull together both the many progressive religious peace groups together with the secular peace organizations. The unifying spiritual and political component is fasting. The month of August has been devoted to fasting, one of the most universal ecumenical practices. Hindus, Buddhists, Jews, Christian, and Islamic people all have fasting as part of their culture. Fasting is seen as a spiritual quest, and a prelude to historic or to prophetic action. The rules for the fast were completely open. Some chose to fast on water only, others on liquids only, other on lighter meals. Fasting is a time to focus attention on a mission and that is what took place.

Now the time for action has arrived. We are tired of an administration that hucksters torture while it knows that torture is simply a way of forcing people to affirm what the torturers want. Torture gave us a rationale for the Iraq war. Our tortured captives would affirm that al-Qaeda was in sync with Saddam Hussein. . . . this was a damn lie, but that is what everyone does under torture. That torture created lie led to the death of our troops and Iraqi people. We are tired of an administration that promotes kangaroo courts and denies all of our long standing legal protections. We are tired of an administration that does not have a clue about diplomacy, dialogue or truth telling.

So welcome to the Declaration of Peace. If you treated your dog the way the CIA treats its victims, you would be convicted of a felony.

Many of you were in the service. Do you remember what you were told to do if you were captured? You were to give your name, your rank and your serial number . . . nothing else. By its mentally ill focus on torture and absence of any regard for legal procedures our corrupt leaders are endangering our troops, endangering our citizens and poisoning the soul of the United States of America.

The Case Against Bush and Cheney

September 27, 2006

Why can't we just leave Bush and Cheney alone to do their job? Why all the whining about their performance? Here are a few issues. A complete list would require volumes.

1. Stealing the White House in 2000 and 2004 through outright voter fraud.
2. Lying to the people of the United States and deliberately misleading Congress in order to invade Iraq.
3. Authorizing and directing the torture of thousands of captives, leading to death, extreme pain, disfigurements and psychological trauma. Hiding prisoners from the International Committee of the Red Cross by deliberately not recording them as detainees and conducting rendition of hundreds of prisoners to "black sites known for their routine torture of prisoners." Indefinitely detaining people and suspending habeas corpus rights.
4. Ordering free fire zones and authorizing the use of anti-personnel weapons in dense urban settings in Iraq leading to the deaths of tens of thousands of civilians.
5. Usurping the right of the people of the United States to know the truth about government actions through the systematic use of propaganda and disinformation.
6. Building an imperial presidency by issuing signing statements to laws passed by Congress which negate Congressional intent. Hiding government decisions from public and Congressional view through subverting the Freedom of Information Act. Illegally spying on millions of Americans without court authorization and lying about it for years.
7. Denying global warming, and placing oil industry profits over the long term survival of the human race and the viability of the planet.

8. Violating the constitutional principle of separation of Church and State through the interlinking of theocratic ideologies and the decision making process of the United States government.
9. Promotion of U.S. dominance of the world and the building and use of illegal weapons of mass destruction.
10. Overthrowing Haiti's democratically elected president Jean Bertrand Aristide and installing an entirely repressive regime.

Friends, the CIA has made it clear that we are actually fomenting the resistance which we claim to be fighting. We call the resistance terrorists while Bush and Cheney have built a factory for creating them.

The Constitution Dies

October 4, 2006

Will our children living in the new police state understand that the Constitution of the United States died in 2006?

Yes, they will look to this as the year that our government determined we could be held indefinitely in a secret detention facility, that we could be put on trial based on unseen evidence and sentenced to death on hearsay statements or even testimony gleaned from torture.

Certainly the charges against Congressman Mark Foley are serious and should not be ignored. But to have such charges receive more coverage than the demise of the Constitution of the United States demands an explanation. The marriage between commercial media and the warfare state is obvious. Clinton was bombing Iraq and choking its people with a brutal embargo while Lewinsky held full time media attention. And now it seems that the Mark Foley matter is overshadowing the loss of the document we have sworn to defend from enemies foreign and domestic.

This is simply one more reason to participate in tomorrow's National Day of Resistance to drive out the Bush Regime. Silence in the face of legalized torture is complicity. Can you imagine that practically every picture you witnessed at the horror of Abu Ghraib Prison has now been made legal by your Congress?

Thursday, October 5 there will be a convergence at Pershing Square at Noon. This is at the corner of 5th and Olive in downtown Los Angeles. This will be followed by a rally at the downtown Federal Building at 300 North Los Angeles Street at 5:00 P.M.

Speakers at the 5:00 P.M. rally include Edward Asner, Bob Watada (the father of Lieutenant Ehren Watada, the first officer to refuse to fight in Iraq) Steve Rohde, civil rights lawyer, Jodie Evans, co-founder of Code Pink: Women for Peace and Jesse Diaz, Jr., the co-founder of the March 25th Coalition for Immigrants Rights.

This National Day of Resistance is called by THE WORLD CAN'T WAIT, DRIVE OUT THE BUSH REGIME. These demonstrations will take place in 170 cities of the United States. Full page ads in the *New York Times* and *USA Today* have announced this day of resistance. Tomorrow, Thursday, October 5, is set aside to protest the loss of habeas corpus, to protest the loss of the Constitution, to protest the on-going violations of the Geneva Conventions. And in the shadows of this destruction of our civil and legal rights is a nefarious plan to attack Iran.

It seems to me that some of the feigned shock expressed by our Congress regarding Mr. Foley is actually a cover for an even greater crime which the Congress itself has approved.

Let's Not Cut and Run!

October 11, 2006

Let's not cut and run, OK?

Tell that to someone who is going the wrong way on a one-way street. Stay the course, march over the cliff, surf the tsunami, picnic at an erupting Mount St. Helen's.

And, by the way, just order others to do this while you are at a safe distance from the action.

Please pay attention to your intelligence agencies. They are trying to tell you that al-Qaeda is in favor of our continued occupation of Iraq. Yes, al-Qaeda believes our staying the course is essential for them to have a successful future? Our intelligence people certainly must have the statement of the al-Qaeda official who said, "Prolonging the war is in our interest." Have you listened to your intelligence agencies as they tell you that most Iraqi insurgents were never previously involved in violence? On the contrary, they say it was the occupation itself which drove the Iraqis into armed resistance. The prognosis of our intelligence agencies is that the insurgency in Iraq will grow rapidly in the years to come.

Are you not aware that the isolated "Green Zone" government of Iraq is seen by most Iraqis as completely subservient to the military of the United States?

Just think of the brilliance of our leaders as they attempt to define a reality of their own making. Our Secretary of Defense predicted that the war could last six days or six weeks. Our commercial media is equally flawed. The latest *Newsweek* magazine states that there have been 45,000 civilian casualties in Iraq. But Johns Hopkins University identifies over 600,000 Iraqi dead.

And we know that imitation is the highest form of praise, so now we see the Taliban in Afghanistan adopting the tactics of the Iraqi insurgents as they grow in number and influence to the point where, after visiting Afghanistan, Senator Bill Frist recommends the Taliban be accepted into the government we have created.

The policy of George Bush and the hopes of al-Qaeda and the Taliban are quite similar. Both of them want us to stay the course. Neither wants us to cut and run.

Perhaps this is a clear demonstration of how fundamentalists think. They do not take advice, they do not change their minds when they have been proven wrong. They have only their fractured truth which is a lie.

Forgiveness

October 18, 2006

Benedictine Sister Joan Chittister has a challenge for us coming from
the Amish Community and its response to murder of its children. Here
are some of Sister Joan's words:

> In a nation steeped in violence, from its video games to its military
> history, in foreign policy and on its streets, the question remains: Why
> did this particular disaster affect us like it did? You'd think we'd be
> accustomed to mayhem by now. But it was not the violence suffered by
> the Amish Community that surprised people. Our newspapers are full of
> brutal and barbarian violence day after day after day, both national and
> personal.
>
> "Do not think evil of this man," the Amish grandfather told his chil-
> dren at the mouth of one little girl's grave.
>
> "Do not leave this area. Stay in your home here," the Amish delega-
> tion told the family of the murderer. "We forgive this man."
>
> No, it was not the murders, not the violence, that shocked us; it was
> the forgiveness that followed it for which we were not prepared. It was
> the lack of recrimination, the dearth of vindictiveness that left us amazed.
> Baffled. Confounded.

For clarification, Sister Joan might have added that the Amish were not
ignoring the need of a criminal justice system, they were speaking about
forgiveness of a deceased murderer.

Sister Joan concludes her statement saying:

> The real problem with the whole situation is that down deep we know
> that we had the chance to do the same. After the fall of the twin towers
> we had the sympathy, the concern, the support of the entire world.
>
> You can't help but wonder, when you see something like this, what the
> world would be like today, instead of using the fall of the Twin Towers as
> an excuse to invade a nation, we had simply gone to every Muslim coun-
> try on earth and said, "Don't be afraid. We won't hurt you. We know that

this is coming from only a fringe of society, and we ask your help in saving others from this same kind of violence."

"Too idealistic," you say. Maybe. But since we didn't try, we will never know, will we?

Instead, we have sparked fear of violence in the rest of the world ourselves. So much so, that they are now making nuclear bombs to save themselves. From whom? From us, of course.

The record is clear. Instead of exercising more vigilance at our borders, listening to our allies and becoming more of what we say we are, we are becoming who they say we are.

Thank you, Sister Joan Chittister.

Sectarian Violence

October 25, 2006

As Iraq is being torn to pieces, the commercial media has framed the phrase "sectarian violence" as if it were somehow unrelated to the occupation.

Actually, the occupation of Iraq by the United States is the primary cause of this so-called sectarian violence. Iraqis who have cooperated with the occupation are identified as the enemy by those who resist the intrusion of foreign troops. This phenomenon is entirely predictable. France was similarly divided in the Second World War. The French people opposing occupation fought their fellow citizens who cooperated with the Third Reich. Vietnamese people who opposed our intervention in their homeland fought against Vietnamese who cooperated with the invaders.

Division of Iraq into three parts, Sunni, Shi'a and Kurd would only make matters worse. It would be seen as the classic imperial method of divide and conquer.

It is true that the minority Sunnis who held power during the reign of Saddam Hussein now consider themselves overwhelmed by the Shi'a majority. Sectarianism is not to be ignored. But to speak of sectarian violence without identifying the cause is not acceptable.

If the cause of the violence would depart from Iraq immediately we can expect the bloodshed to decline. There would certainly be residual personal and ethnic vendettas as well as common crime but the root cause of the blood bath would be removed. The Bush administration has retreated from the slogan of, "Staying the Course." The new direction in Iraq must include the following:

- Initiate diplomacy and dialogue with Iran and all other Middle East states.
- Dismantle all permanent bases in Iraq and pledge not to build any new ones.
- Begin the withdrawal of troops immediately.

And what will we call it, "A tragic mistake?" Every intervention has been at least a tragic mistake and more accurately stated, a malicious action of cold-blooded mass murder.

Friends, there is no problem free way to leave Iraq but leave we must. Confession is good for the soul.

Let this be the last of literally hundreds of illegal interventions made by our nation.

For this to take place we must resurrect Constitutional checks and balances. For example, the 1803 decision of Marbury vs Madison made it clear that the Supreme Court had the right of judicial review over the President of the United States and could declare acts of the president to be unconstitutional. But in regard to foreign policy the Supreme Court has sat like potted plants for over two centuries. A functional Supreme Court could restrain and enjoin any war mongering administration.

Appeal for Redress

November 1, 2006

Aside from the parade of troops who are defying orders and leaving the Iraq disaster on a daily basis, there is a group of one hundred active duty military personnel who have signed an appeal urging Congress to support the prompt withdrawal of all U.S. troops and bases from Iraq. This is called the Appeal for Redress and is endorsed and sponsored by Iraq Veterans Against the War, Veterans for Peace and Military Families Speak Out.

Do you think we made any friends by breaking in to 95,000 homes in Baghdad recently?

Put yourself in the shoes of those who were following orders. Put yourself in the shoes of the families who live in those 95,000 homes as they are terrorized by heavily armed troops screaming at them in English.

Our Head Torturer and his Vice Torturer are directly responsible for every wound, every death, every mental illness that has resulted from this ill advised, morally bankrupt, and intellectually depraved and absolutely unnecessary military failure.

The time has come for our Supreme Court to engage in judicial review of such blatant crimes. The fact that the Court has remained nationally isolated in its jurisprudence does not mean that it must declare itself impotent in matters of foreign policy. Here is a quote from my father, Judge Blase Bonpane's winning oration given on January 16, 1914 when he was a Freshman at Ohio Northern University:

> Public opinion has enacted a law against murder; so should international public opinion demand a law against war, which is merely organized murder. Shall we execute a man for taking a single life, and glorify nations for slaughtering thousands? To protect justice, police powers are instituted in all realms. Why not go beyond the transitory interest of a nation and establish an international police power? Let the representatives of the world powers meet in one body! Let a world code be compiled!

My father gave that oration some ninety-two years ago. Congratulations to young troops today who understand the urgency of a speedy departure from Iraq. And today we add to their ranks two new groups, West Point Graduates Against the War and Service Academy Graduates Against the War (U.S. Air Force Academy).

These troops are the realists in our midst. Are we to carry on this war simply to save the face of the criminals who started it?

Voices for peace and outlawing war are the voices of reason. War mongers are not realists at all, on the contrary, as Bob Woodward says, they are living in a "State of Denial."

Please show your solidarity with the troops who have designed the Appeal for Redress for the prompt withdrawal of all troops and bases from Iraq.

Office of the Americas
Twenty-third Anniversary

November 8, 2006

With KPFK as a co-sponsor, the Office of the Americas (OOA) is happy to announce its 23rd Anniversary celebration to be held at the Wilshire Grand Hotel on Sunday, November 12. Our honorees this year are:

Harry Belafonte, Bianca Jagger, Gore Vidal and James Lafferty who is a well known programmer here at KPFK as host of the Lawyers Guild Show. The dinner is at 5:30 PM and the main program is scheduled for 7:30 PM. Why does KPFK co-sponsor an Office of the Americas event? Because OOA evaluates United States foreign policy and identifies any areas which appear to be illegal or immoral. This foreign policy has been dictatorial throughout our history. The Congress has frequently been a group of clappers who simply clap as the President declares another illegal intervention. And the Supreme Court remains entirely silent in the face of such aggressive behavior.

During one of the greatest scandals in United States history, known as the Contra War the Office of the Americas was founded and helped to identify this crime by being on the ground in Nicaragua for over a decade. OOA marched through seven countries calling attention to the this war fought by mercenaries and funded by illegal arms sales to the Ayatollah Khomeini. At that time our country did everything in its power to discredit and destroy the Sandinista revolution. But the goals of that revolution are still very much alive in Nicaragua today. Many U.S. operatives were convicted when this crime became known. Some of them are serving in the current Bush Administration. Office of the Americas also has worked on the ground for peace in El Salvador, Honduras, Guatemala, Panama, Colombia, Ecuador, Mexico and Iraq. When the Zapatista struggle began on January 1, 1994 OOA went to the site of the conflict in San Cristóbal de las Casas. We had the privilege of working directly with Bishop Samuel Ruiz who was the chief mediator in that conflict. Since 1991 much of our attention has been directed to the Iraq disaster which is now in its sixteenth year. OOA went to Baghdad and Babylon prior to the blitzkrieg ordered by George Herbert Walker Bush; we met with Yasser Arafat in Baghdad who was doing everything he could to avoid the coming catastrophe. We fought against the continued bombing combined with brutal and deadly sanctions imposed by the Clinton Administration and we believe that now is the time to impeach the current on going disgrace to the sovereign people of the United States, the Administration of George Bush the Lesser.

A Word to the
New Democratic Majority

November 15, 2006

When Nancy Pelosi was asked about moving forward with impeachment, she declined and said, "This is not about getting even." And this is where we must object. Nancy, of course it's not about getting even. We are neither vindictive nor revengeful. It is a matter of not being soft on crime. Serious domestic and international crimes have been committed by this administration, Nancy, and this must not be ignored. Our troops and the good people of Iraq have bled and died.

The infrastructure of the United States is rotting out and every effort has been made to destroy the public sector in the name of privatization and greed. No, Nancy, this is not about getting even, it's about removing criminals from office. And that, by the way, would leave you in direct line for the presidency. And what is Senator Carl Levin saying as he prepares to become chairman of the Senate Armed Services Committee? That we should begin a phased withdrawal of the U.S. military from Iraq within four to six months. I'm sorry Carl, we are not ready to sit back and watch the daily blood bath continue for another four to six months. There was a referendum on the ballot which emanated from 100 city councils in the United States. The question asked was: Shall the United States government immediately begin an orderly and rapid withdrawal of all its military personnel from Iraq beginning with the National Guard and reserves? Yes or No. The yes vote won overwhelmingly and was at 80 percent in Cook County, Illinois. Please pay attention, Senator Levin. We want the troops home now. No more daily blood baths.

I find it very touching to observe the feigned concern for the Iraqi people expressed by this administration and used as an excuse for continuing our occupation after years of wanton death, torture and destruction. One of the many anti-war generals said when he was asked about how we could possibly remove our troops, "we can bring them home in ships and planes." Dear new majority Democrats in the House and in the Senate, please get out of step with your favorite corporate lobbies. The people of the United States want impeachment now together with the removal of our troops from one of the greatest military disasters in

220

history. If you can't hear the voice of the people, please listen to the voices of the thousands of veterans who have in good conscience gone AWOL as a statement against this illegal and immoral slaughter.

Christian Zionism

November 22, 2006

Welcome to Christian Zionism.

This is a unique form of idol worship. It was born from the same people who made an idol of U.S. foreign policy and who identified that policy with the will of God. Call it manifest destiny if you wish. But the first commandment of God is that we should not have weird gods before us. And this one is really weird.

Using the name of the man who said, "This is my commandment, that you love one another," and who spoke of the Spirit reaching all of humankind including the Syrians and Samaritans, on October 21 of this year, Texas pastor and evangelist John Hagee had a special rally at the Church of the Cornerstone in San Antonio. You might remember the Reverend Hagee from his 1981 approval of Israel's bombing the nuclear reactor at Osirak in Iraq. Featured speakers at this year's rally were: former CIA director James Woolsey, former chief of staff for the Israeli Defense Forces, Lieutenant General Moshe Ya'alon, and Joseph Ginat, director of the Strategic Dialogue Center at the Netanya Academic College in Israel. Woolsey in his wisdom told the congregation that the United States is hated because of its freedom. Ginat told the congregation that the west has only six to ten months to take military action against Iran and he spoke of the culture of lies in the Arab world. Ya'alon expressed his belief that an ongoing war had already started between the West and radical Islam and argued that opposition to Israel has little to do with the occupation of the Palestinian territories.

Brigitte Gabriel an Arab and former TV anchor for "world News" on the Middle East Television network said, "Our enemy is in the Islamic mosques throughout the United States." Messages thanking the Rev. Hagee and the congregation came from Israeli deputy Prime Minister Shimon Peres and former Prime Minister Benjamin Netanyahu and were broadcast over two large video screens.

So here we have a nineteenth century millennial misinterpretation of the New Testament linked with the nineteenth century ideology of Zionism.

222

The only message I see revealed in such a gathering is the commonality of fundamentalist behavior. British historian Arnold Toynbee identified the problem over fifty years ago and warned us that once people are in an absolutist posture, they will kill. The goals of such behavior are void of any spiritual content. But the bastardization of religion is frequently rewarded by lucrative government funding. What is obvious here is that the name of our religion has very little to do with our performance as human beings. The name of our religion, can be used to foster a humane future or an insane future. There is no authentic spirituality which can be based on hatred, racism, and perpetual war.

Thanks to Margot Patterson from San Antonio for her article on this Christian Zionist Rally.

Out Now

November 29, 2006

Michael Moore helps us to understand why "Cut and Run" is the only brave thing to do. Here are a few of his thoughts.

We have now been in Iraq longer than we were in all of World War II. That's right. We were able to defeat all of Nazi Germany, Mussolini, and the entire Japanese empire in LESS time than it's taken the world's only superpower to secure the road from the airport to downtown Baghdad.

Let's listen to what the Iraqi people are saying, according to a recent poll conducted by the University of Maryland:

- 71% of all Iraqis now want the U.S. out of Iraq.
- 61% of all Iraqis SUPPORT insurgent attacks on U.S. troops.

So I don't want to hear another word about sending more troops (wake up, America, John McCain is bonkers), or "redeploying" them, or waiting four months to begin the "phase-out." There is only one solution and it is this: Leave. Now. Start tonight. Get out of there as fast as we can. If you invade and destroy a country, plunging it into a civil war, there isn't much you can do until the smoke settles and blood is mopped up. Then maybe you can atone for the atrocity you have committed and help the living come back to a better life.

The responsibility to end this war now falls upon the Democrats. Congress controls the purse strings. Mr. Reid and Ms. Pelosi now hold the power to put an end to this madness. Failure to do so will bring the wrath of the voters. We will fight you harder than we did the Republicans.

This is what we demand:

1. Bring the troops home now. Not six months from now. NOW. Quit looking for a way to win. We can't win. We've lost.
2. Apologize to our soldiers and make amends. Tell them we are sorry they were used to fight a war that had NOTHING to do with our national security. We must commit to taking care

of them so that they suffer as little as possible. The mentally and physically maimed must get the best care and significant financial compensation. The families of the deceased deserve the biggest apology and they must be taken care of for the rest of their lives.

3. We must atone for the atrocity we have perpetuated on the people of Iraq. There are few evils worse than waging a war based on a lie, invading another country because you want what they have buried under the ground. If you pay taxes, you have contributed to the $3 billion a week now being spent to drive Iraq into the hellhole it's become. We can receive no redemption until we have atoned.

In closing, there is one final thing I know. We Americans are better than what has been done in our name. So we will accept the consequences of our actions and do our best to be there should the Iraqi people ever dare to seek our help in the future. We ask for their forgiveness.

We demand the Democrats listen to us and get out of Iraq now.

Thanks, Michael.

Wise Men From the East

December 20, 2006

The puppet rulers within empire know where their bread is buttered and they know exactly whom they can kill with impunity. The masters in Washington say, "OK to use cluster bombs in Lebanon and the bombs fall in Lebanon and continue to tear the heads off of children long after the initial assault." And such was the case with King Herod. Imperial Rome had made it clear to him that he could kill within his jurisdiction especially if it would increase fear which is the glue holding empire together.

So Herod entertained the Wise Men from what are now called Iraq and Iran and Syria and eagerly urged them to let him know the exact location of this anti-imperialist King who was born in Bethlehem. When Herod realized that the Wise Men were on to him and had rejected his request, he ordered that every child in Bethlehem under the age of two be massacred.

The parents of the Jesus were warned by an angel that their infant son was in extreme danger so they left Bethlehem in haste and entered Egypt without papers. And there they stayed until Herod dropped dead, which may have been the most constructive act of his life.

And today the emperor residing in the United States considers the head of state in Lebanon as an ally after authorizing a blitzkrieg on that land. And the emperor in the U.S. is surprised that for some reason, most of the people in Lebanon are not pleased with their head of state. Such ingratitude!

And similarly Bush is not happy with his selected leader in Iraq so he is going to send in more U.S. troops to fight the Sadr Militia, which is simply another segment of the same Islamic sect which Bush has been supporting. Nothing could be more counterproductive.

It would also help if some Wise Men explained to Bush that the so-called sectarian attacks conducted by people dressed as Iraqi troops and Iraqi police were quite simply Iraqi troops and Iraqi police.

So what does this all demonstrate? That imperial leadership and its surrogate puppets quickly develop a serious political psychosis; we might call it sociopathic necrophilia.

This illness is indicated by a lack of concern for others be they friend or foe together with a fixation on killing. The only reality for these sickos is their own power and that power is limited by their own tenuous hold on life. Fear of losing their own life and their own power leads them to take life from as many others as possible.

Mr. Bush please step down before you destroy all life on the planet. Caesar did not have a nuclear button in his hand but unfortunately, you do.

Peace Plans

December 27, 2006

We are proud to be part of a movement for justice and peace which is ever more united and more effective. In spite of the propaganda of commercial media and the misinformation of government, our quest is being accepted by a majority while the administration babbles on with its irrational and extremely dangerous drivel.

The focus for January of 2007 will be Washington, D.C.. There are so many actions that it is difficult to list them all.

Here are a few:

- Gold Star Families for Peace and Code Pink will have a Walk for Peace campaign in the halls of Congress on January 3rd and 4th. This citizen's lobby will also be conducted at local congressional offices throughout the country.
- United for Peace and Justice in collaboration with many other organizations will conduct a major march in Washington, D.C. on January 27th.

The Occupation Project conducted by Voices for Creative Non-Violence calls upon Representatives and Senators to publicly pledge to vote against the supplemental spending bill, which will be submitted to Congress in early 2007. Civil disobedience will begin on February 5 in the offices of legislators who do not make a public pledge to vote against the supplemental war funding bill. Civil disobedience actions will continue through the month of March.

- March 17, 2007 on the 40th anniversary of the historic 1967 march on the Pentagon and the fourth anniversary of the start of the criminal invasion of Iraq, The Answer Coalition is inviting people from all over the country to once again descend on the Pentagon demanding U.S. Out of Iraq Now.

All of these national events will have local representation.

- Arlington West Memorial. Each Sunday since February 15, 2004, a memorial is erected in the sand just north of the pier at Santa Monica Beach by the local chapter of Veterans for Peace to acknowledge the human cost and consequences of war. Similar memorials are conducted in Santa Barbara and other sites.

We may have started small but currently the movement for justice and peace represents the majority of United States citizens.

What Congress is Going to Do

January 3, 2007

Yesterday's *New York Times* has a great headline. It says:

CHAOS OVERRAN THE BUSH ADMINISTRATION'S PLAN
FOR THE IRAQ WAR IN 2006.

Now we know whom to blame. Chaos is to blame that's who. If chaos had not appeared, Bush's plans would have been a great success. Right? Might we ask what caused the chaos? The press likes to call it sectarian violence. But so-called sectarian violence seems to be just a cover for the fact that people who have accepted the occupation of Iraq are fighting against fellow citizens who do not accept the occupation of Iraq.

And the same might be said of Palestine. Unfortunately some Palestinians are fighting other Palestinians whom they believe are accepting Israeli occupation.

And as the Democrats come to center stage, we must remind them that chaos just might mess up their plans as well. "We will have oversight. We will not cut off funding," says incoming speaker of the House, Nancy Pelosi. Please Nancy don't start your new job with doubletalk. If you Democrats don't cut off spending, you are fully supporting an ongoing crime against humanity. Speaking on behalf of the hopes, desires and anxieties of millions of Americans, we are asking you, we are demanding of you that you not only cut off funding for the Iraq disaster but that you immediately begin impeachment proceedings for the most criminal administration in the history of the United States. Let's stop the charade now.

We put you in power to stop the war and you are telling us that you will continue funding the slaughter of our troops by people who do not want their country occupied. You will continue the daily murder of innocent people in an illegal war? You will continue to make the United States the most hated and feared polity on earth? Congressman Dennis Kucinich put it well when he said that the war in and the occupation of Iraq will end when Congress eliminates funding for the war. This is the necessary program for the new congress. To be sure that cut off in funding takes place, The Occupation Project challenges Representatives and Senators to publicly declare that they will vote against any further funding for the war and occupation of Iraq. Failure to make this pledge will result in the occupation of legislator's offices in an ongoing project of civil disobedience during February and March both in Washington and in their home districts. Let's not have the Democrats also telling us that chaos has messed up their plans. Get out of Iraq now.

Constitutional Crisis

Yes, we are in a constitutional crisis. The President has determined that $100 billion be spent on an extremely dangerous "updating" of our nuclear arsenal. And he does this at a time when some of the nation's virulent hawks, Henry Kissinger, George Schultz, William Perry and Sam Nunn issue a statement calling for U.S. to lead the world in the abolition of nuclear weapons. See Wall Street Journal, January 4, 2007.

Our universities are being turned into houses of prostitution as the Bush Administration pumps billions into academia to design new nukes together with new horrors of biological and chemical weapons in direct violation of both the Biological Weapons and Chemical Weapons conventions and U.S. domestic criminal law.

And then there is the surge of troops in Iraq. In spite of what the poorly educated journalists or elected officials might say, there is a consensus of legal scholars that Congress has absolute power to block funding for any surge of troops in Baghdad.

Oh, yes, Bush invades Somalia with a little help from Ethiopia and then tries to assassinate a few alleged members of al-Qaeda. So he sends an AC-130 and a host of attack helicopters to southern Somalia. The AC-130 is a monstrosity designed to kill every man, woman, child and beast within its orbit. And all of this is taking place while Israel and the United States bicker over which one will be the first to strike Iran.

Friends, we currently have some options to defend the people of the United States from governmental criminality:

1. Impeachment: There are literally scores of charges that could lead to conviction.

2. The Twenty-fifth Amendment to the Constitution of the United States: This amendment is to be applied when the President is unable to discharge the powers and duties of his office. The President's behavior should make his inability self-evident.

Now in both cases the Vice President is in line to take over. Clearly similar action should be taken immediately as the Vice President becomes President because many of the high crimes and misdemeanors of the current President are directly tied to policies created by the current Vice President. This action would elevate the Speaker of the House of Representatives to the position of President. And as we petition these actions from the new Congress, the peace movement is more engaged than ever at the street level. We are joined by veterans and current members of the armed forces. And this is where history will be made.

For detailed information on action in your immediate area go to www.americasaysno.org

State of the Union

January 24, 2007

Yesterday's State of the Union left me with questions about both the President and the Congress. I would suggest that apart from being an American Citizen and having untold millions in their campaign coffers, anyone running for president or for Congress should be required to take Civics 101 and Political Science 101 and World History 101.

1. The President is not the Commander in Chief of the citizens of the United States.

    We are a sovereign people and he is our servant. When he consistently acts outside of our collective will he must be removed by impeachment or by the activation of the Twenty-fifth Amendment of the Constitution. At this point in history he has qualified for either or both of these legal remedies.

2. Comments he has made about Islamic people are similar to comments made about Jewish people by the leaders of the Third Reich.

3. He speaks of an ideological struggle. Just what is his ideology? Might makes right? The truth is anything I say it is? In any case his endless war program simply mirrors what he claims to be fighting.

4. According to the *New York Times Magazine* the death squad leadership in Iraq was imported from our death squad leaders in El Salvador.

5. The Congress has absolute authority to stop the funding and thereby to stop the war.

    There is simply no question about the legality of such Congressional action. And now some members of Congress are making non-binding resolutions? They are, however, fully authorized to make binding resolutions.

6. Corporate profits are at an all time high? What does this mean except that war profiteers are making obscene profits on the blood of our young? And this has been the case ever

234

since the Civil War. Nothing has been more harmful to our democracy than the false patriotism of war mongering greed which has always been the last refuge of scoundrels.

7. Support our troops? As they die unnecessarily, as they lose their mental and physical health, as they are denied the democratic right of redress? Are we to presume for a moment they are in Iraq because they want to be there? As most of the Bush proposals, reality is the exact opposite of what he is saying. "Support our troops," in his view is to let them die for a lie.

Paul Craig Roberts was Assistant Secretary of the Treasury during the Reagan Administration and also Associate Editor of the Wall Street Journal editorial page.

He believes that the surge in Iraq is simply an attempt to deflect attention from the Bush plan to attack Iran. Roberts concludes, "Nothing can stop the Regime except immediate impeachment of Bush and Cheney. This is America's last chance."

The Trial of
Lieutenant Ehren Watada

January 31, 2007

Lieutenant Ehren Watada will go before a military court on next Monday, February 5. On Sunday, February 4 at 10:00 A.M. here on KPFK. I will have three of the members of THE CITIZENS HEARING ON THE LE-GALITY OF THE WAR IN IRAQ. They are Professor Richard Falk, Colonel Ann Wright and David Krieger, President of the Nuclear Age Peace Foundation. The hearing was convened to present evidence that Lieutenant Ehren Watada intended to present at his February 5 Court Martial. But in a pretrial hearing the court refused to hear the evidence. As a result of the failure of this military court to hear the motives for Lieutenant Watada's refusal to serve, the Citizens' Hearing was held before a gathering of 600 people. Here are some of the points made by the legal experts who presided over the hearing:

Lieutenant Ehren Watada had not only the right to refuse to deploy to Iraq in an illegal war, but he had a duty to do so. Watada should be recognized for his courage rather than undergoing a Court Martial.

Darrell Anderson, who received a Purple Heart for his service in Iraq spoke of orders issued to, "Shoot everyone, regardless of whether they were civilians, including children."

Experts on International Law made it clear that the war in Iraq was initiated illegally. It did not comply with the United Nations Charter because it was not required for immediate self defense and it was not authorized by the United Nations Security Council. It was a war of aggression violating international law and the United States Constitution. Article 6, Section 2 of the Constitution makes treaties such as the United Nations Charter part of the Supreme Law of the Land.

The panel also received testimony regarding the systematic torture of Iraqi prisoners, and indiscriminate killing of civilians.

Dennis Halliday, former Assistant Secretary General of the United Nations described the "shock and awe" initiation of the war as terrorist act.

Law Professor Richard Falk testified that the military judge's order preventing Ehren Watada from presenting evidence on the illegality of the war was "criminally disallowing him from obeying the law."

The unanimous finding of the panel is that the United States committed crimes against peace, war crimes and crimes against humanity in Iraq. Further, Lieutenant Watada acted legally and honorably in refusing orders to deploy to Iraq, and his actions are in accord with the oath he took to uphold the constitution of the United States. The only thing going on trial on next Monday morning is the War in Iraq.

Lieutenant Watada is a victim of that war.

Light One Candle

February 7, 2007

It is better to light one candle than to curse the darkness. And it remains nearly impossible to refrain from cursing as we observe the direction our elected officials are taking.

The light we see, however, is in the streets. We see it in The Voices for Creative Non-Violence as they engage in non-violent civil disobedience at the offices of our Representatives and Senators who continue to support the rape of Iraq. The message is quite simple; if you don't stop the funding the war, you are supporting the war. And any member of Congress who does not understand the power of that body to control the purse should not be in Congress.

The peace people even occupied the office of Obama. Why should we upset such nice people? It is sad to say, but they can have smiles on their faces, love their mother, love their children and still be responsible for crimes against humanity.

These nice people must be awakened; they must do their duty to promote justice and peace. If these Democrats are not awakened our troops and the good people of Iraq will continue to bleed and die. If these nice Democrats are not activated, they will allow a pathological attack on Iran. Once the slaughter begins, the suicide bombers responsible for such an attack on Iran will stupidly wonder why their plan backfired. Is this not what we have observed in both Iraq and Palestine?

Indeed, the voice of the spirit is now heard in the streets and in the fortitude of these unwelcome visitors to Congressional offices. These are the voices of prophesy, these are the voices that give hope to a people who have lost their government, their constitution and their courage.

The current patriots in the streets whether they be Voices for Creative Non-Violence, Code Pink, or any of the thousands of peace and justice organizations now burning bright are the contemporary legacy of the Boston Tea Party. Please join me on Sunday here at KPFK at 10:00 A.M. when I will interview the founder of Voices for Creative Non-Violence, Kathy Kelly. Such leadership must not simply be observed, it must be imitated. We can do that by joining forces in the streets or by

238

supporting those who do these courageous acts. And we can also pledge that we will not vote for any candidate who currently supports the war policies of the Bush Administration or those hopelessly confused members who claim they are against the war as they continue to fund it.

Let the impeachment process begin for Bush and Cheney. We don't have to curse the darkness, we can join hands with those who walk in the light.

Why We Lose

February 14, 2007

Why is it that we have lost the Indochina War and every conflict since that disaster. In each case we fought in opposition to the will of the vast majority of the people we attacked.

We sent an army of mercenaries to overthrow the government of Nicaragua in the 1980s killing 40,000, and who is ruling that country today? The Sandinistas. We spent billions and killed 80,000 people to stop the movement for liberation in El Salvador. And what is the most powerful movement in El Salvador today? The FMLN. That's right, the very movement we tried to destroy.

And then there is Iraq. We have definitively lost that war just as we lost the Vietnam War in January of 1968 but we remained for seven more years allowing tens of thousands more of our troops to die together with millions of Vietnamese and Cambodians.

Let us compare and contrast these situations with the Cuban Revolution.

In December of 1956 Fidel Castro and his tiny invasion force landed the yacht Granma on the Cuban shore at Los Cayuelos. The Cuban Dictator Batista had 50,000 troops, an air force, a navy and a killer group of secret police. Fidel's invasion was discovered, attacked and surrounded. Few of the invaders were alive. Castro was lying flat on his back in a cane field covered with sugar cane leaves. With him was Universo Sanchez, and Dr. Faustino Perez Hernandez.

To his knowledge Castro's invasion force was now limited to the three of them. He was now Commander in Chief of exactly two rebels. Castro whispered to his two available fighters, "We are winning . . . Victory will be ours."

This message to his two troops was not blind bravado. Fidel knew that the people of Cuba were sick and tired of the Batista rule and that they would join his forces. His powerful faith and confidence were based in reality not fantasy.

240

On the contrary our mad venture into Iraq with 140,000 troops plus the surge, plus 100,000 mercenaries has failed completely. Why? The people of Iraq don't want us there.

The horrendous disaster of the mendacious Cheney and Bush is that they created a death dealing fantasy totally unrelated to reality as they march on blindly to an even more monstrous calamity in Iran. We must stop them before they kill again.

Let's Start Some New Wars

February 28, 2007

Just twenty years ago, the Reagan Administration was busy illegally and secretly selling arms to the Ayatollah Khomeini of Iran in order to fund an out of control mercenary army of thugs who were given the mission of overthrowing the government of Nicaragua. Elliot Abrams was indicted for giving false testimony about his role in this illicit money raising and was convicted of unlawfully withholding information from Congress. Yes, this is the same Elliot Abrams who covered up atrocities committed by the military forces of U.S. backed governments in El Salvador, Honduras, Guatemala and his own mercenary contra army which slaughtered 40,000 Nicaraguan civilians. This is the same Elliot Abrams who reported that the El Mozote Massacre in El Salvador was not credible.

According to the Observer, Elliot also planned the Coup in Venezuela against Hugo Chavez in 2002. Oh, yes, it was the same Elliot Abrams who flew to London under a fake name to raise more money for his beloved Contra mercenaries. He scored a heist of millions from his buddy, the Sultan of Brunei, an act specifically forbidden by the Boland Amendment. Elliot Abrams gives the following formula for covert actions:

1. Keep Congress out of it. Do not trust any friends or allies.
2. Keep the CIA out of it.
3. Do not trust the uniformed military.
4. The program must be run out of the Vice President's office.

Guess what? Elliot Abrams is now being drawn forth to help the hapless Bush Administration ignite the entire Middle East into a huge bonfire.

Abrams will use the above formula once again and once again it will be a formula for total failure. The plan is for Sunni Saudi Arabia to help the Sunnis weaken the Shiite Hezbollah in Lebanon. Aid will now go to the Sunnis who are hostile to the U.S. and sympathetic to al-Qaeda. How did this redirection happen? The unintended strategic consequence of the Iraq war has been the empowerment of Shiite Iran. So now, Bush in his wisdom, wants to empower the Sunnis to fight the Shiites, who are currently in power in Iraq. For clarification, we want to help the minority who previously ruled Iraq under Saddam Hussein and to oppose the majority who have allegedly been elected by the people of Iraq.

Friends, impeachment is the only way to stop Bush and Cheney from destroying The Middle East and creating world wide repercussions. If you find all of this confusing, please get help from the excellent journalist who is trying to help us understand it. Check out Seymour Hersh's article "The Redirection" in the *New Yorker* for March 5, 2007.

Torture Is Us

March 14, 2007

Nothing personifies our foreign policy more clearly than torture. Our policy is torture. Torture of the indigenous, torture of the slaves, torture of the poor, torture of working people, torture of our troops and torture of our purported enemies A polity of torture has no right to exist.

Torture is the work of wimps. Wimps are sadists who enjoy bringing pain to their alleged enemies. Torture is the behavior of losers who continue its performance by the endless fuel of outrageous lies. The lies are declared to be true by way of military cult leaders whose objective is to control the minds of our troops. And what form of logic do military cult leaders use? They use the logic of authority. And what role does authority have in making a legitimate argument? Zero. The science of Logic declares any argument based on authority a fallacy. Oh, yes, authority can fire you, it can torture you and it can kill you. But it is never an acceptable part of sound logic or morality.

Military leadership with all the skills of cult leader Jim Jones insists on the following:

1. By torturing these suspects, you are protecting your fellow troops.

    This is a lie. Effective commanders of guerrilla troops have understood for years that captured enemies should be treated well. George Washington identified the Hessian mercenaries as terrorists and then instructed his guerrillas to take good care of their Hessian captives who might just come over to our side.

2. Torture can save the world from nuclear war. No it can't. The only thing that can save us from nuclear war is the universal abolition of nuclear weapons.

3. Torture will make people tell us the truth. False, torture will make people say anything that might stop the torture. The truth has nothing to do with it.

In short, torture is the personification of evil. It is simply one of the many forms of rape.

So friends now is the time to impeach our Head Torturer, George Bush and our Vice Torturer Dick Cheney. And now is the time to boycott the producers of such TV Programs such as *Twenty-Four* which have brought us to the ultimate cultural perversion by picturing the torturers as the good guys and implying that some truth has been extracted by their barbaric behavior.

Join us at Hollywood and Vine this Saturday at Noon in a demonstration to denounce the torture of war.

Tanya Reinhart

March 21, 2007

This week was marked by the passing of Tanya Reinhart, a leading Israeli intellectual, an outspoken critic of Israeli government policies and one of the leading advocates for Palestinian national rights. She served as a professor of linguistics and media studies at Tel Aviv University and, recently, as global distinguished professor of linguistics at New York University and columnist for Israel's largest daily paper, *Yediot Ahronot*. Tanya had a global following for her critical perspective on the occupation of Palestine. Her books include: I*srael-Palestine, How to End the War of 1948*, and *The Road Map to Nowhere*. Tanya last appeared on my program *World Focus* on November 19, 2006.

Here are some of Tanya Reinhart's positions: Israel's policy has changed so they are now not simply defending the occupation. They are supporting the atrocities including the daily killing of Palestinians.

The recent Palestinian elections were declared to be among the best of the sixty-two which have been monitored by the Carter Center, but Israel did not like the results of the election and Israel is protected by the might makes right policy of the United States. So the Palestinian elections are not recognized and their entire population must be punished and starved.

Friends, the brilliance and clarity of Tanya Reinhart identifies something that few people in the United States understand. Tanya states that what we see now is the U.S. and Israel deliberately inciting civil wars among their enemies. They are doing this in Palestine by supporting forces like the Dahlan in Gaza. They are doing the same in Lebanon. They are doing this in Iraq. This is the U.S./Israeli policy.

Tanya was convinced that Israel is simply not willing to recognize the right of the Palestinians to exist as a state.

Just as the Bush administration has done everything possible to recklessly endanger the people of the United States, similarly, the incredibly powerful American-Israel Public Affairs Committee (AIPAC) is actually endangering the people of Israel by pushing for war in Iran, Syria, Iraq and Lebanon. Tanya Reinhart knew that the blowback from this endless war mongering could lead to the destruction of Israel. Now that she has left us it would be wise for every Israeli and every citizen of the United States to read her books and to denounce the mindless cheering sections for endless war which reside in Washington and Tel Aviv.

A Vote for Human Sacrifice

March 28, 2007

Our Democratic House of Representatives has voted to allow daily human sacrifice on the altar of the god of war until 2008.

This strange group of modern day politicians tell us that they don't support the war and therefore they will fund it. Do I hear the voice of Pontius Pilate saying, he found no guilt in the accused and then conceded to have him scourged and executed?

So our young people are marched to their death on a daily basis to embalm a lie and to serve their lobbyists, not their constituents. Would it not be better for these legislators to go on welfare, or as a Republican Senator suggested recently that they try selling shoes. Selling shoes is a legitimate livelihood, sacrificing our youth in a slow bleed policy to save the face of a criminal administration is not. So the tsunami of funds will continue to flow to international torture centers, fragmentation bombs, death and destruction of the bodies and souls of our military to say nothing about funding the out-of-control mercenaries of Blackwater and other military corporations who have made windfall profits on murder and lies.

And what about the people who live in Iraq? Some of our war promoters are acting as if they were concerned about them. If they had any concern for the Iraqi people, they never would have imposed the death sentence on them by supporting the war in the first place.

Friends what we are seeing here is a Congressional Declaration stating that the citizens of the United States are irrelevant. Just as we saw profoundly ignorant and racist members of congress change their minds on the matter of segregation and later on the Vietnam War we must now follow the lead of the Occupation Project and Code Pink in occupying the offices of current incumbents to remind them of a few things: They are to work for us, we do not work for them. We pay their salaries. It is true corporate lobbyists may contribute more than we can as individuals, but members of congress must understand that doing what lobbyists want is simply the lowest and most gross form of prostitution. Far better to sell shoes!

We demand that our troops come home now. No amount of advertising jargon is going to make the war honorable, acceptable or winnable. It began as a crime, it continues as a crime and it must end as a crime.

Conversation with God

April 18, 2007

We know that religion is often used as a cloak for malice in the political world. Here is a Liberation Theology reflection on how might remove religion from corrupt politics. It is in the form of a conversation with God.

Q: What religion do you belong to?

God: I don't have a religion.

Q: But we humans do.

God: Of course religion is a human attempt to define the indefinable and to bind a certain group of people together in that effort. Religion is a fact of Anthropology.

Q: Are religions a bad thing?

God: Not necessarily, but they are bad if they separate people from human unity.

Q: What about all those people who do not believe in you?

God: That's understandable, it may be because of all of the dumb things they have been told about me. They may not believe in me, but that does not mean I don't believe in them.

Q: Are you Jewish?

God: No.

Q: Are you Catholic?

God: No.

Q: Are you Protestant, Islamic, or Hindu or Buddhist?

God: No, those are human configurations.

Q: Some people say that you are many.

God: Perhaps they see many facets and individualize those facets as many gods. That could be called "many."

Q: How do people serve, and honor you?

God: by serving, honoring and loving each other.

Q: What about all of the religious figures that have been deified over the centuries? Jesus for example?

God: Here is where language is defective. Jesus demonstrated the unity between himself, me and all of humankind. Jesus was asking everyone to share in this divinity. He did not separate himself from the human race or deny the divinity of the human race.

Q: What religion was Jesus?

God: He was Jewish.

Q: Was he sectarian?

God: No, he was universal in his approach and made it clear that everyone who lived the truth understood his message.

Q: You mean, even if they never heard of him?

God: Of course. Anyone devoted to the truth, justice and peace gets the message regardless of their religion or lack of religion.

Q: You seem to be saying that we cannot comprehend the word God.

God: That is correct. You can only speak of me in terms of analogy, you can never comprehend me.

Q: What about all the various religious liturgies, customs?

God: These are all of value if they are celebrating the good you are doing or planning to do. Think of liturgy as a party, a celebration. The liturgy will not build the house, but it can celebrate the fact that you are going to build the house or that you have built the house. The liturgy will not feed the poor. But it can be the celebration that you are about to change the very structures that create poverty.

Q: Should we pray?

God: Yes, of course. This is a way to elevate your mind from the nitty gritty of daily life and enter into the unity of creation.

Q: Did you say creation?

God: Yes, I did. There has never been any conflict between creation and evolution.

Science is simply an effort to understand my work. People should revere science as an effort to know and then use science for justice and peace.

Q: Well, God, thanks very much for this conversation at a time when we celebrate Passover, Easter, Norwas and all the multiple celebrations of the Springtime resurrection.

God: You are welcome.

Homeland Security

April 25, 2007

When you see millions of immigrants on the streets of the United States on May 1, please understand that their issues are now your issues. Threats of terrorism and millions of immigrants are being used to justify new police-state measures in the United States. Coordinated mass arrests, big brother spy blimps, expanded detention centers, repeal of the Posse Comitatus Act, and suspension of habeas corpus have all been recently implemented and are ready to use against anyone in the U.S.

The North American Free Trade Agreement (NAFTA) flooded Mexico with cheap subsidized U.S. agricultural products that displaced millions of Mexican farmers. Between 2000 and 2005, Mexico lost 900,000 rural jobs and 700,000 industrial jobs, resulting in deep unemployment throughout the country.

Desperate poverty has forced millions of Mexican workers north in order to feed their families. In the wake of 9/11, Immigration Customs Enforcement (ICE) has conducted workplace and home invasions across the country in an attempt to roundup so-called illegal immigrants. ICE justifies these raids under the rubric of keeping our homeland safe and preventing terrorism. However the real goal of these actions is to disrupt the immigrant work force in the U.S. and replace it with a tightly regulated non-union guest-worker program. To accommodate the detention of tens of thousands of people, Homeland Security, in 2005, awarded Halliburton's subsidiary Kellogg, Brown and Root a $385 million contingency contract to build detention camps in the United States. The Military Commissions Act signed October of 2006 suspends habeas corpus rights for any person deemed by the President to be an enemy combatant. Persons so designated could be imprisoned indefinitely without rights to legal counsel or a trial. When you see those marchers next Tuesday, remember that the immigrants are marching for your rights as well as for their rights.

Thanks to Professor Peter Phillips of Sonoma State University for this information.

Immigration

May 2, 2007

Commercial media would like to give you two choices. Are you for the current immigration practices or are you for a guest worker program? The correct answer is none of the above. Do not allow them to frame you into two possibilities when there are two hundred possibilities. Current immigration practices are among the most punitive, mean spirited and counterproductive in U.S. history. Please witness the Immigration Customs Enforcement which is making militaristic raids on factories of hard working people, breaking up families and imprisoning people with the same failed tactics we have used in Iraq. This is the perfect way to make enemies and to drive substantial portions of the population underground.

What do we want? We want to amend the Immigration and Nationality Act (INA to permit parents of U.S. citizens to petition through their U.S. citizen children under twenty-one years of age to avoid deportation of their parents. Corporations which are legal persons are free to move their capital throughout the world with few constraints. But people who are real and not fictitious persons are not free to move for their security and safety. Such freedom is granted in the Universal Declaration of Human Rights but unfortunately the United States is not complying with that international accord. We also want to reinstate the jurisdiction of Federal Courts to review various agency decisions involving immigrants. The Federal Courts were striped of this jurisdiction during the Clinton and Bush Administrations.

We want to support the DREAM Act, which facilitates the education of immigrant youth and legalizes a population that would be almost certain to remain residing in the U.S. in an underground and unlawful status.

We support the Child Citizen Protection Act (HR 1176) which would allow an immigration judge to consider the well being of U.S. citizen children before deporting the immigrant parent.

We want to ensure that all workers have the right to organize and bargain collectively and to repeal international trade agreements that simply stimulate undocumented immigration. These are only a few of the changes necessary to make immigration laws humane.

You can view the entire proposal of the Unity Blueprint for Immigration Reform by going to www.mapa.org. Hundreds of civic and religious groups are supporting this Blueprint.

The Pope Goes to Brazil

May 9, 2007

Major media is covering the visit of Pope Benedict XVI to Brazil. The media consistently mentions the threat of liberation theology and the efforts made by the Vatican to stamp it out.

But as usual, the commercial media just does not get it.

Rumors of the demise of liberation theology are premature. Journalists should reflect on the fact that Jesus was born long before Marx and that Marx was probably influenced by Jesus. Pick up your New Testament and read the Acts of the Apostles:

> The faithful all lived together and owned everything in common; they sold their goods and possessions and shared out the proceeds among themselves according to what each one needed. (Acts 2.44)

History can clarify the situation. Back in the fourth century when the Emperor Constantine called the Council of Nicaea, on the Turkish coast, and paid the way for the attending bishops, imperial theology was born. The emperor had granted an Edict of Toleration to the Christians. In return we witness the emergence of imperial theology.

The sword and the cross came together in building the empire, in the crusades, the inquisition, the conquistadors and the contemporary "Christian" war mongers who can be cheer leaders for a filthy and ongoing holocaust in Iraq. Liberation theology is simply an effort to dissolve the heretical imperial theology which has tainted Christianity for centuries. Making war in the name of Jesus is heresy.

Jesus firmly embraced a preferential option for the poor. The Church must do the same.

Eighty thousand base communities of liberation theology will reverently listen to the Pope when he visits Brazil. They will show love, honor and respect for his role. However nothing and no one will ever stop them from practicing the democracy of the base community which is the democracy of the Acts of the Apostles.

The method of the base community is to first observe a situation, next to make a collective judgment about the situation and finally to enter in a praxis or reflective action. It is this kind of collective wisdom together with the fact that the empire is busy destroying the cradle of civilization in Iraq that has made it possible for the people of this hemisphere to enter into a definitive arc of liberation.

As in the case of Galileo and practically every other new concept, the Vatican, in time will begin to understand what the Spirit is doing. Both our political and church leaders must learn how to follow an enlightened people.

Luis Posada Carriles

May 16, 2007

One of Latin America's most notorious criminals, a terrorist, continues to live freely within the United States.

In 1976 Luis Posada Carriles was charged by Venezuela with masterminding the bombing in flight of an airliner and killing all 73 passengers including 24 members of Cuba's fencing team and 11 Guyanese medical students. Prior to 9/11 this was the deadliest attack on an aircraft ever to occur in the Western Hemisphere.

Posada Carriles escaped from prison in 1985 and continued his terrorism. He was linked to the bombings of several hotels in Havana. In the year 2000 he was arrested in Panama for attempting to kill Fidel Castro and many of the audience in a school auditorium.

In 2005 Posada reentered the United States illegally and took up residence in a luxurious Miami apartment. The Department of Homeland Security failed to detain him. In May of that year Venezuela formally requested his extradition from the United States so he could be tried for seventy-three counts of murder in the 1976 airline bombing.

Homeland Security claimed that Posada might be tortured if he were sent to Venezuela.

Apparently Homeland Security had confused Venezuela with our concentration camp in Guantánamo.

And now various Members of Congress have demanded to know why Attorney General Alberto Gonzalez has never declared Posada a security threat and has not jailed him under the Patriot Act.

In the meantime Cuba had decided to assist the United States in efforts to curb terrorism. Five non-violent investigators from Cuba were in the process of researching terrorism in Miami. They are, Antonio Guerrero, Fernando González, Gerardo Hernández, Rene González and Ramón Labañino.

Rather than praising the work of these Cuban citizens, U.S. authorities have detained all five of them, thrown them into solitary confinement and slammed them with sentences from fifteen years to double life in prison. This blatant hypocrisy is completely consistent with the behavior of our current Attorney General and the President who appointed him. It should be added that terrorism on the part of certain exiles from Cuba has been either supported or ignored by our government for five decades. The Bush, Gonzalez group, however has brought this issue to its apex. They not only continue to harbor terrorists but they have codified torture in their failed efforts to occupy and control Iraq and Afghanistan.

The terrorist Luis Posada Carriles must be detained and tried. The five Cuban citizens who have dedicated their lives to fighting terrorism must be freed.

How to Start a Civil War

May 23, 2007

How is a civil war started? Actually it is quite easy. Here are the directions.

First, you must be the superior military power in the region.

Next, you must occupy the territory of a weaker polity.

Third, you must establish a puppet government in the region you have occupied.

This puppet government can be structured by way of demonstration elections, that is elections which are designed for public relations reasons and propaganda regarding democracy. Once you have developed a docile, servile, dependent government in the occupied area and you begin to favor your obedient selectees with money, homes, status and armed security, a predictable result will follow.

The people who refuse to accept the new puppet government will rightfully consider the new regime to be traitors to their nation and they will revolt. Now the occupiers have the civil war they wanted in the first place. The occupying country then begins to crank out predictable propaganda saying, "See how violent those people are. They simply have no idea how to govern themselves. Think how fortunate they are that we can govern for them." And then the blood bath is underway.

There is one problem here. History tells us that the imperial state, that is the state with the power to begin the occupation, simply cannot hold on to its surrogate government.

The government they have selected will be corrupt, inept, and will self destruct. As the empire tries desperately to maintain its chosen opportunists, the opposition gains strength every day and ultimately the empire has to leave or disintegrate.

Friends, this is what we have witnessed in India as the Brits finally backed off and compacted their empire into the British Isles, this is what we witnessed in Vietnam, and Latin America and this is what we are witnessing in Iraq, Afghanistan and Palestine and Lebanon. The occupying power can foster civil wars but they cannot endure. It is so unfortunate that those who use the logic of power and authority do not yet understand that power and authority have absolutely no value and no legitimacy in making a valid argument. The occupiers have the brutality to start a civil war. But they do not have the humanity necessary to build a peaceful future. If there is to be a peaceful future, it can only be built by humanists with a functional sense of morality and ethics.

Who Are The Cuban Five?

May 30, 2007

There are five Cuban men in U.S. prisons serving life sentences after being unjustly convicted in U.S. Federal Court in Miami, on June 8, 2001. They are known as the Cuban Five.

The five were falsely accused by the U.S. government of conspiring to commit espionage on the United States. But the five never engaged nor planned to engage in espionage. They were simply monitoring the actions of Miami-based terrorist groups to stop terrorist attacks on Cuba.

For more than forty years, anti-Cuba terrorist organizations based in Miami and financed by the CIA have engaged in countless terrorist attacks against Cuba. More than 3,400 Cubans have died as a result of these terrorist attacks.

Here is a comment on the Cuban Five by journalist Mumia Abu Jamal:

> For over four decades, the U.S. empire has been waging a secret and deadly war against Cuba. They have bombed fields, poisoned grain, hijacked planes, and plotted invasion. They have trained, paid and protected terrorists who have cost the lives of thousands of Cubans and virtually crippled their economy through a seemingly everlasting embargo. The Cuban Five, young men who tried to protect their people from these instances of U.S. state terrorism, who have bombed no one, nor planned to, who poisoned no one, nor planned to, who hurt no one, nor planned to, who merely reported the plotting of crimes against their people, face the full foul fury of the empire's judiciary for trying to stop crimes.
>
> We must all protest the unjust convictions of Rene González, Fernando González, Antonio Guerrero, Gerardo Hernández and Ramón Labañino.

Here are the words of Ramón Labañino upon receiving his sentence, "If preventing the deaths of innocent human beings . . . and preventing a senseless invasion of Cuba is the reason I am being sentenced today, then let that sentence be welcomed."

The website of the Cuban Five is www.freethefive.org.

Government by Lobby

June 6, 2007

Who do members of Congress listen to most avidly before making a decision? They listen to military corporate lobbyists and that is why the rest of us 300 million people continue to wait for some representation.

Friends, the greatest structural obstacles to democracy are the corporate Washington lobbies. This conglomeration of profiteers have more political power than all of the people of the United States put together.

Now we can understand that when the majority of the people want a national health system administered in a fashion similar to Social Security, they can't have it because the insurance companies want 30 percent of those funds for profit rather than to have a system that operates as smoothly as Social Security has for eight decades while using only 2 to 3 percent of the fund for administration.

And the same lobbies function on behalf of the everlasting war system. Members of Congress sell themselves very cheaply as they become servile to the dictates of what our Republican President Eisenhower called the "Military/Industrial/Congressional complex." Take note that Ike was pressured to remove and did remove the word "Congressional," but today that word is back and we can say with clarity the Military/Industrial/ Prison/Gun and Congressional Lobby.

One of those lobbies is called AIPAC which represents the government of Israel and which has fostered the notion that people who oppose Israeli government policy are anti-Semites. Well that is a cheap shot and it has been leveled at many world class intellectuals in the Jewish community like, Noam Chomsky, Howard Zinn, Norman Finkelstein and Norman Solomon.

Government by corporate capital lobbies has no relationship to democracy and before our nation can function properly these lobbies must be outlawed. Make sure your representatives know that you know who they are listening to and that you refuse to allow them to continue to sell themselves to corporate lobbyists.

Electing a Winner

June 14, 2007

As we reach bottom at the lowest point in U.S. history, it becomes clear that people want a new springtime. Yes, in the midst of the crass corruption, violence, ignorance and obscene banality of our government, there is hope.

And how is this change going to take place? The best current example of the triumph of grass roots politics can be seen in Latin America today. In past years the representatives of corporate capital including Wall Street would select Latin American candidates useful to their interests. Some candidates would even make progressive noises for propaganda purposes. But the power of corporate capital and U.S. military interventions maintained a static status quo in Latin America. In recent years, however, Latin American candidates representing the hopes, desires and anxieties of the Latin America people have been elected. This rapid change has been helped by the fact that the United States is hopelessly engaged in losing unnecessary wars.

While the cat's away, the mice will play. And now Democrats are faced with the same problem over which Latin America has triumphed. They can work for one of three candidates who have been approved by corporate capital and Wall Street, while accepting the religion of militarism or they can go to the grass roots and make history as Latin America is making history. Latin Americans had faith enough to believe they could change corrupt systems and they are doing it.

If Democrats have the same level of faith and grass roots action, they can elect a candidate who is not acceptable to corporate capital, who will bring us a Department of Peace, a single payer health system and the return of the public sector. And to those who say, "Oh, he doesn't have a chance," are parroting just what the lobbyists for militarism want them to say as captives of false advertising.

So let's have the same faith that Latin America has demonstrated and put someone in the White House who does not bow to the corporate lobbies which are now running the United States of America.

Democracy in Action

June 20, 2007

Friends, we have just witnessed one of the world's greatest denunciations of democracy.

Eighteen months ago the Hamas Party won the parliamentary elections in Gaza.

Ismail Haniya was overwhelmingly chosen as Prime Minister. Currently the United States and Israel are recognizing Salam Fayyad appointed by Mahmoud Abbas as Prime Minister of Gaza. This Fatah group of candidates received just 2 percent of the vote.

So Fatah is recognized as the legitimate government while many of the elected members of the Hamas Parliament are illegally held in Israeli prisons.

At the time it won the elections in 2006 Hamas offered Fatah the invitation to join forces and to form a unity government.

It offered the international community a platform for peace.

It offered a ten year cease fire with the Israelis and it maintained a unilateral cease fire for eighteen months trying to normalize the situation.

Immediately after the elections of January 2006, the United States began arming militias controlled by Mohammed Declan to fight against Hamas. This policy is reputed to be that of Elliott Abrams, the deputy national security advisor, convicted in the Iran/Contra scandal. Same Elliott, same policy. But now the U.S. backed Palestinian Contras have been routed by Hamas.

As Robert Fisk says:

First we demand that the Palestinians embrace democracy and then they elect the wrong party—Hamas—and then Hamas wins a mini-civil war and presides over the Gaza Strip. And we Westerners still want to negotiate with the discredited and defeated President, Mahmoud Abbas.

Israel, with endless U.S. backing and direction, is without any doubt the most powerful element in the conflict with Palestine. Perhaps Israel could give a good example to the United States and begin a good faith negotiation with the party that won the elections in Palestine. It is true that in fits of anger both sides have denied that the other side has any right to exist. But there is no doubt that such wartime rhetoric can be dissolved by honest dialogue. It is time to make peace with Hamas, clearly the definitive choice of the Palestinian people, before Elliott Abrams and his Contras create another endless war.

To Alter or Abolish It

July 5, 2007

Two hundred and thirty-one years ago a document was written in the proper English of that time. It says:

> We hold these truths to be self-evident, that all Men are created equal, that they are endowed by their Creator with certain inalienable Rights, that among these are Life, Liberty, and the Pursuit of Happiness—That to secure these Rights, Governments are instituted among Men, deriving their just Powers from the Consent of the Governed, that whenever any Form of Government becomes destructive of these Ends, it is the Right of the People to alter or to abolish it . . .

So friends, it is time to remove the Head Torturer and the Vice Torturer from their thrones. They began their criminality as imposters on the executive branch of government. They have become the personification of malfeasance of office.

Untold numbers of human beings have been tortured, mutilated, raped and murdered in the wake of their bloody incumbency. The reason that Bush commuted Libby's sentence was to stop Libby from squealing by cooperating with the prosecution. This would have been Libby's path to avoid prison time if there had been no commutation. Yes, if Libby's sentence had not been commuted he would have sung out additional crimes of Cheney and Bush. We are dealing here with the highest level of organized crime.

So the time has come to impeach the Bush/Cheney Regime before these imposters totally destroy the United States of America and the lovely planet on which it resides.

This is the season to rid the world of this administration and to warn those who may follow that we have read a 231 year old document and we are prepared to carry out the mandate to alter and/or abolish any administration that has nothing but contempt for the citizens of the United States. And going beyond the goals and objectives of the founders, we wish to renounce the idol worship of nationalism which attempts to unite

266

God and one single empire. Our allegiance is not to the cloth of flags, our allegiance is to the human race.

Prisons as a Crime

July 12, 2007

Assembly Bill 900 is the biggest prison construction bill in history giving us 53,000 new cages for prison, jail and juvenile detention at an initial cost of $7.7 billion. It will cost $10 billion per year to simply maintain these units and we have absolutely no need of this project. This legislative monstrosity was put together in an afternoon and passed the next morning with no public hearings. It was an action of stealth.

The civilized world has discovered that non-violent offenders have no need of incarceration. House arrest, required social services, counseling and rehabilitation are far more effective than imprisonment. Actually the most effective form of rehabilitation is education. This has been proven definitively. 70 percent of those entering prison in California are non-violent offenders. Therefore 70 percent of those entering prison should not be entering prison. If we faced this reality the prisons we have now would become sparsely populated places. But the prison lobbies would not like this, the prison guards union would not like this.

So are we to accept being governed by the whims of a prison lobby?

Our sentencing laws are irrational, our parole policies are unjust. Black people are incarcerated at a rate six times greater than whites, the incarceration rate for women has doubled since the 1980s. More than 60 percent of the people in prison are racial and ethnic minorities. Families are torn apart, mothers are losing their children and young people are losing their lives in this barbaric system. I challenge anyone to find any place on earth that has more incarcerated children per capita that the state of California.

There are other states in the United States working to keep people out of prison, changing parole policy and sentencing laws. This intelligent policy has not unleashed a crime wave as funds are shifted from building cages to the necessary creation of housing, education and health care.

Friends it is important to understand that no ground has been broken for these new and unnecessary cages and no bonds have yet been sold. So it is not too late to stop this mindless and cruel theft of money from the citizens of California on unneeded and unwanted prisons. The Legislature must abolish the failed three strikes law and promote alternatives like Proposition 36.

Governor Schwarzenegger and complicit State legislators please listen, would it not be better for you personally to go on welfare and live in poverty rather than to be prostituted by the prison industrial complex?

Thanks to Mary Sutton, editor of *The L.A. Prison Times* newspaper for much of this information.

Fear

July 19, 2007

Fear of the other is used to manipulate people to sustain our permanent war economy. The Communists are coming, the Russians are coming, the Chinese are coming or is it the Cubans? The actor Ronald Reagan even claimed that Nicaraguans were about to invade the United States and he declared a National Emergency to protect us from the very people we were indiscriminately killing. So our nation came under the control of militarists and militarism by way of fear. The legislators then fall into line and vote for endless war because they fear losing elections for being, "soft on defense." And then there are the police. The reporting of crime is up 500 percent, not crime but the reporting of crime on television.

This increases the level of fear as the police continue to punish people at will. This, in spite of the fact that police may never punish anyone. That's right, police may arrest when there is probable cause of a crime being committed, they may also defend themselves as any other person may do legally. But they may never punish anyone prior to the decision of a court. But the sordid reality of police punishment continues unobstructed as part of the culture of fear.

So the national government fears the militarists, and gives in to their whims, the local government fears the police and ignores their culture of law breaking. And governors in California only get elected if they bow before the barbaric practice of state sponsored murder. Yes, we are speaking of capital punishment, that foul example of class justice which is primarily directed to people of color and the poor. And fear of crime is manipulated to sustain this ongoing atrocity. And then there is the fear of further terrorism with our borders. 9/11 remains in our minds as the unanswered questions about 9/11 create the stench of an untreated wound. And before our freedom turns to ashes through the application of the existing anti-constitutional legislation or by way of even greater repressive measures, we must use our precious time to shout out the current factory of fear now at the helm in Washington. Sadly we are at a point where we have no reason to believe anything the President might say. All credibility was killed in action with wars in Iraq and Afghanistan. Our message must be to impeach all the criminals in this administration including Bush and Cheney. Our good people can't wait, they want to construct a new and better world. After all, perfect love casts out fear.

War Is Terrorism

August 8, 2007

The current condition of our government is one of absolute chaos. Strangely, it seems that everyone outside of government knows that we have descended into a morass.

The inability of government to extricate itself from this mess is based on a failure to learn the lessons of history. Here are some of the fatal errors:

- Triumphalism: we are always right and God is on our side.
- Imperialism: the world belongs to us because we have the most bombs.
- Denial: we have always intended to do the right thing but we might have made a tragic mistake.
- Pretension: we care about the Iraqi people, if we leave there might be violence.

All of the above illusions are still in place after we have starved, bombed, tortured, imprisoned and killed the Iraqi people and their children. Violent intrusion into countless Iraqi homes has created a powerful resistance.

We have actually shown our hand by offering Iraq a plan for distribution of their oil giving the lion's share (80 percent) to private multinational corporation with U.S. and British dominance.

The President claims we are fighting a war against terror. Any sane observer can see that war is terror. Our misleaders have created a massive expansion of al-Qaeda and the Taliban.

And now, the very same lies that gave us the Iraq disaster are being used to create a war with Iran. There is even a propaganda war identifying Islam as the problem. But any balanced observer knows that there are fanatics in every religious culture without exception. Our nation has no authority to attack other countries based on their possession of nuclear weapons. We have signed the Nuclear Non-Proliferation Treaty which was designed to abolish nuclear weapons. And now our administration, together with some silly Republican and Democratic candidates with all the banality of evil, say, "Sure we can nuke Iran if we feel like it."

Hiroshima and Nagasaki are the markers of our descent into perpetual war. Our brutal international interventions since August 6 and 9 of 1945 have been consistently backed by nuclear threats. Militarism remains as the final phase of each previous culture. It will be the end of our culture if the people do not create a total regime change in the United States. A malicious polity representing 4 percent of the world's people will only create resistance on the part of the remaining 96 percent.

The Peace Movement

August 22, 2007

People who are confined to commercial media are simply not in touch
with the actual history of 2007. Among these unfortunates are those who
say, "Where is the peace movement?" or "The peace movement is dead."
   Much of the media and especially TV is delivered in a timeless bubble
with no past and no future. The current movement of resistance in the
United States is simply censored out of the equation.

* In the Southern California area there are more than fifty peace
  vigils each week.
* The Occupation Project has sat in the offices of thirty-nine
  Representative and Senators demanding an end to the Iraq
  disaster. 320 of their members have been arrested.
  <www.vcnv.org>
* From September 14–21 the Declaration of Peace will coor-
  dinate a week of nonviolent actions in every Congressional
  District in the United States to defund the war.
  <www.declarationofpeace.org>
* September 15 There will be a National March on Washington to END THE WAR NOW and to impeach George Bush.
  <www.answercoalition.org>
* September 21 and every third Friday of every month, the
  Iraq Moratorium Campaign will conduct an escalating series of actions demanding an end to the war.
* October 21–23 NO WAR NO WARMING will have a massive intervention in Washington, D.C.
  <www.nowarnowarming.org>
* October 27 there is a coordinated plan for ten huge demonstrations across the United States.
  <www.unitedforpeace.org>
* Currently citizens are walking and biking across the country
  to end this war now.

- Then there is the giant annual manifestation by School of the Americas Watch at Ft. Benning, Georgia scheduled for November 16–18.

All of the aforementioned plans are accompanied by the actions of our troops who have shown the courage to resist an illegal war. Thousands have left their units and many have gone public. Sadly, scores of troops have committed suicide. Veterans have established memorials all over the country, including Arlington West at Santa Monica Beach, to call attention to the ongoing bloodbath that is sustained by an unconscious and spineless Congress.

And all of this is just a sampling of what the movement for justice and peace is doing throughout the United States.

Seasons of Discontent:
A Presidential Occupation Project

August 29, 2007

There are many people out there who understand that we do not live in a monarchy. We are citizens, not subjects of the king.

So here is the message of The Voices for Creative Non-Violence. The project is called SODaPOP which stands for Seasons of Discontent: A Presidential Occupation Project.

The project begins this fall and will continue through January.

The offices of all Presidential Candidates who do not comply with the following demands of these citizens will be occupied in protest:

- A complete halt to all ground, air and naval military actions against Iraq and Iran.
- Full funding for the reconstruction of Iraq to repair the devastation caused by seventeen years of warfare by the U.S. and its allies.
- Full funding for the Common Good in the United States to: rebuild our public education system; to promote a living wage, to provide a universal single payer health care system; to rebuild our country's deteriorating infrastructure and to re-organize the entire public sector of our society which has been devastated by an ideology of privatization.

Friends, we are not interested in seeing and hearing multi-billion dollar advertising campaigns with meaningless political babble, especially from so-called liberals like Hillary and Obama. Just think, they are going to give us better wars, more effective wars; more funds for the military/industrial/prison/congressional and pharmaceutical lobbies. And, oh yes, they want nuclear weapons to remain on the table as a threat to the human race.

Voices for Creative Non-Violence in their Seasons of Discontent does not accept the double talk platforms of political power seekers. Voices is quite simply saying, here is a platform that expresses the hopes and desires of our people. We are tired of having our intelligence insulted on a daily basis by a corrupt and failed administration. We deserve better than that. And if you can't offer something beneficial to the common good of our people, we will occupy your campaign offices to make our point.

Any candidate who wants to be elected in 2008 must affirm a dedication to the Constitution of the United States, all existing International Law, and to the Universal Declaration of Human Rights.

Supreme International Crime

September 5, 2007

Chris Hedges is a Pulitzer Prize winning reporter and served as Middle East Bureau chief for the *New York Times*. He frequently reported on Iran. Here are his thoughts on the upcoming war of aggression which the Cheney/Bush Administration has planned against Iran. It was exactly this kind of premeditated murder that was clearly identified as the "Supreme International Crime" at Nuremberg.

The Pentagon has reportedly drawn up plans for a series of airstrikes against 1,200 targets in Iran. The air attacks are designed to cripple the Iranians' military capability in three days. (Why not say thirty years?)

This outrage will be accomplished by U.S. and Israeli warplanes.

But then what? We don't have the troops to invade. And we don't have anyone minding the helm who knows the slightest thing about Persian culture or the Middle East. There is no one in power in Washington with the empathy to get it. We will lurch blindly into a catastrophe of our own creation.

It is not hard to imagine what will happen. Missiles which cannot reach the United States, will be launched at Israel, as well as American military bases and the Green Zone in Baghdad. We can expect massive American casualties, especially in Iraq, where Iranian agents and their Iraqi allies will be able to call in precise coordinates. The Strait of Hormuz, which is the corridor for 20 percent of the world's oil supply, will be shut down. Chinese-supplied anti-shipping missiles, mines and coastal artillery will target U.S. shipping, along with Saudi oil production and oil export centers. Oil prices will skyrocket. The dollar will tumble against the euro.

Hezbollah forces in southern Lebanon, interpreting the war as an attack on all Shiites, will fire rockets into northern Israel. Israel, already struck by missiles from Tehran, will begin retaliatory raids on Lebanon and Iran. Pakistan, with a huge Shiite minority, will reach greater levels of instability. The unrest could result in the overthrow of the weakened American ally President Pervez Musharraf and usher into power Islamic radicals. Pakistan could become the first radical Islamic state to possess a nuclear weapon. The neat little war with Iran, which few Democrats oppose, has the potential to ignite a regional inferno.

Hundreds of demonstrations are taking place now and throughout the months ahead. The international organized crime syndicate in Washington can either listen to the voices for sanity in the streets of our nation or we can all perish together.

What Happened On September 11, 2001

SEPTEMBER 12, 2007

A growing number of experts are calling for a serious investigation of what happened on September 11, 2001. This week Dr. Lynn Margulis, a Member of the National Academy of Sciences and world renowned scientist called the official story of 9/11 a fraud. She is joined by a host of structural engineers. Dr. James Quintiere, former chief of the National Institute of Standards and Technology has joined his voice with this host of scientific professionals. A new investigation of 9/11 is also called for by Congressman Dennis Kucinich. Citizens have a right to know.

The FBI states that Osama Bin Laden is not on the most wanted list because they have no evidence he had anything to do with 9/11.

The art of revolution is the art of uniting forces so it is our task to integrate the events of 9/11 into the wider movement for justice and peace. As we do this we must remain in sync with the experts who have rejected the official story. But we become our own enemy if we confuse fact with opinion. Many people in the movement for justice and peace are turned off by those who do not make this distinction.

The 9/11 issue reminds me of the hundreds of books and articles written about who killed John Kennedy, who killed Robert Kennedy and who killed Martin Luther King. Many of us said, "Of course these were inside jobs but we have a war to stop in Vietnam." And we will not be at all surprised if 9/11 is proven to be an inside job.

We must see 9/11 in the context of 1200 targets identified by the Pentagon to be obliterated in Iran. This simply means more and more massacred children together with their innocent parents.

We must see 9/11 in the context of oil companies which have already divided up Iraq for the privatization of petroleum. We must see 9/11 in the context of corporations which have no loyalty to the people of the United States or anywhere else. They are not opposed to the obliteration of the cradle of civilization in Mesopotamia nor to murder at home. The criminals who attacked our country on 9/11 will be identified. The criminals who have destroyed Iraq and Afghanistan have already been identified. So stay together, the art of revolution is the art of uniting forces.

Resistance

September 19, 2007

The fruition of the movement for peace and resistance is well underway. Last Saturday 100,000 marched against the Iraq War in Washington, D.C.. This massive gathering was organized by ANSWER and led by Iraq veterans, and military families marching from the White House to the Capitol and demanding an immediate end to the occupation of Iraq. The march concluded with a solemn ceremony to memorialize the U.S. soldiers and Iraqis killed and wounded in the destruction of Iraq. This ceremony was followed by 5,000 marchers surrounding the Capitol and prostrating themselves in a symbolic "die in." When the marchers then attempted to deliver their message of peace to the Congress some 200 people were arrested including former U.S. Army Colonel Ann Wright. Did you ever stop to think about the historic accuracy of the peace movement? On every major issue from Vietnam to Central America to Afghanistan and Iraq, the people in the streets have spoken the truth and the government has lied.

Back in 1990 here in Los Angeles there was a demonstration in front of the UNICAL Building demanding NO BLOOD FOR OIL. And now after sixteen years of devastation, Alan Greenspan finally says, "Oh, yes that is what the war is about." Well the peace movement knew that even before 88,000 tons of bombs were dropped on Iraq in January of 1991. Criminals in office speak of freedom and democracy while they simply want absolute control of the world's resources.

The September 15 demonstration in Washington was timed to coincide with the long awaited report for General Petraeus which was actually a report by Cheney and Bush parroted by General Petraeus.

George Bush went to Anbar Province to meet with Abdul-Sattar Abu Risha leader of the Anbar Province. David Petraeus told the U.S. Congress how Anbar Province was a model for Iraq. Abu Risha was subsequently assassinated. People who ally themselves with the U.S. in Iraq are in danger of being assassinated. Is this a sign of success? War Monger Cheney is fanatically beating his drum for war in Iran. Such a war will lead to the devastation of Israel as well as our green zone island in

Iraq. Such a war with Iran includes the very real possibility of a nuclear attack from Israel or the United States. Apparently there is no limit to what a failed, discredited, and pathologically lying administration will do. Resistance is essential.

The Monks Did It!

September 26, 2007

The Monks of Myanmar have given a course on resistance to the rest of the world. This course must be a required one for every Bishop, Mullah, Rabbi and any other type of religious leader in the United States. Even George Bush can hear the message for the people of Myanmar. It would be nice if he could make the transition to people in his own country.

Just as China blocks the international community regarding Myanmar so Bush blocks the international community in Iraq and Palestine. Both of these great powers must recognize their stupidity. The militarists of Myanmar also declare themselves as Buddhists and the Bushites in the United States also declare themselves as Christians.

Both attempts are oxymoronic. Bushite Christians are a contradiction in terms just as Myanmar Buddhist Militarists are a contradiction in terms. The Buddhist Monks have a simple message, "We do not worship strange gods and the state is the strangest god of all!"

And we must not forget the message of these Buddhists for the international justice and peace movement. They project the power of presence power of spiritual conviction. They refuse to let their lives be ruled by fear.

And as we proceed as U.S. citizens to understand that a general strike may be required to stop the Republican and Democratic Party militarists, let us reflect on the power of not working which is called a "strike," and the power of not buying which is called a "boycott."

Oh yes, we know the barbaric military of Myanmar killed it own people when they marched in 1988. And perhaps that is why Mrs. Aung San Suu Kyi was weeping when the Monks walked by her home in Yangon. We also know that the ongoing lie which is militarism will lead the Myanmar Generals to dress up agent provocateurs as Monks and have these phonies initiate an armed attack leading to a brutal response. Well Dr. Martin Luther King solemnly reminded us that there are casualties in the peace movement but these casualties would never equal the slaughter of imperial war.

We must follow the endurance and courage of the Myanmar Buddhists. Imitation is the highest form of praise.

Who Do We Call?

October 10, 2007

Would anyone have the 911 number to call? Criminality is rampant in the current administration of the United States.

The Chief Executive is lying through his teeth about no torture as we routinely practice horrendous forms of torture. It's true the Congress can and should impeach. But the Congress has passed away and is effectively not in session. The Supreme Court is on an early "long winter's nap"

Well then, do we contact the Attorney General to report such crimes? Should we call the FBI? The local police? The CIA? Certainly many public officials have been arrested while in office; Governors, Mayors, Members of Congress and State Assemblies. There is no problem with such arrests.

But here we have the Chief Executive and his cronies clearly out of control. Are they to be exempt as they wantonly break national and international laws?

Millions of people are saying no, they are not exempt, as we observe thousands of daily vigils throughout the United States as well as dozens of major mass mobilizations.

But the criminality goes on as if there were some divine right of kings in our land. And now the justice and peace movement in the United States has taken a creative approach; leading Americans are asking our military to refuse orders to attack Iran.

This is an effort to create a kind of coalition that makes history.

Soldiers know the horrors of war, death, severed limbs, blindness and mental illness. They have seen the genocide in Iraq and they are not apt to romanticize about its repetition in Iran. A Pentagon consultant told Seymour Hersh, "There is a war about the war going on inside the building."

So while mindless thugs are doing everything possible to create an illegal war with Iran, elements within our military establishment are in opposition to another armed disaster.

We are not asking the Pentagon for a military coup in the United States. On the contrary, we are asking them to support and defend the Constitution of the United States. They do not need to show any loyalty to international crime.

God Made Me Do It

October 17, 2007

Have you ever wondered how people can adjust to genocide? Our citizens have made such adjustments on numerous occasions. There was a spirit of Manifest Destiny as we conducted genocide against the indigenous people of this hemisphere in the eighteenth and nineteenth centuries. We declared ourselves called by God to rule from sea to sea.

Then there was the terrible swift sword of the civil war which gloried in the death of 600,000 Americans among the small population of our country in the 1860s. We never have lost so many citizens as in the Civil War.

In the Spanish American War, President McKinley informed us that we were going to Christianize the enemy. He seemed to have forgotten that the enemy was already Christian.

Oh yes, World War One was the war to end all wars. As that mindless slaughter concluded some intelligent people formed a League of Nations. But our warfare state Senate destroyed the League by 1920 and opened the way for a Second World War, the most calamitous event in the history of the world. Had there been a functional League of Nations there would have been no World War II. The intelligent people came back again once again after World War II and established a United Nations to end the scourge of war forever. But with our power as victors in World War II we decided to use the U.N. as a weapon for conquest and we manipulated a war with Korea as a United Nations Action. Our citizens were carefully propagandized to translate the word communist as, "OK to Kill."

The OK to kill definition was so successful that we used it to conduct genocide in Indo China and Latin America. As the Soviet Union collapsed, a new word was coined, "terrorist." Starting with Ronald Reagan this word became the battle cry for new wars in Central America. And when we were actually struck by terrorists in 2001 we immediately attacked a nation that had never attacked us, Afghanistan. This error was compounded by an attack on Iraq which our head of state has attempted to blame for the 9/11 tragedy. In one of his recent speeches we heard the word al-Qaeda mentioned ninety-five times. Bush clearly had purposely tried to confuse our people by calling the Iraqi resistance, al-Qaeda.

And as our long standing addiction to war continues, the women and men in the armed services are discovering the criminality of this administration. Washington Post reporter Dana Priest recently said in an interview that she believed the U.S. military would revolt and refuse to fly missions against Iran if the White House issued such orders. A score of Generals have spoken against this endless war. General William Odom former director of the NSA said, "The invasion of Iraq, I believe, will turn out to be the greatest strategic disaster in U.S. history.

With plans for war with Iran on the table, we must organize mightily that the ancient myth of Manifest Destiny will die on the sands of Iraq.

Put Out the Fire

October 24, 2007

One dinky DC-10 is available to attempt to put out fires on the West Coast of the United States. Hundreds of manned and unmanned aircraft are ready for a mass murder of Iranian citizens.

It seems we have a problem of values here. We are completely unprepared for disasters here at home while we create endless and unnecessary disasters overseas.

Apparently we have a toxic group of individuals who are happy with the flames in Iraq and anxious to see Iran on fire. The profundity of racism we see in this group seems to prefer the destruction of the cradle of civilization over the saving of thousands of homes in the Southland. We could easily have a fleet of fire dousing DC-10s that could have saved thousands of homes in a few hours if we simply put aside our global warring.

The stench of neo-Nazi racism arrives this week at the University of Southern California. It is called Islamo-fascism Awareness Week. The program is dedicated to hate and fear as it perfectly mirrors the tone of Germany in the '30s. One of the distinguished guests at the university for Islamo-fascism awareness Week is Ann Coulter who says we should invade Muslim countries, kill their leaders and convert them to Christianity.

Indeed we are fortunate that Islamo-fascism Awareness Week came at a time when Southern California is burning. Let this remind the racist perpetrators of Islamo-fascist Week that their position as represented by our corporate designed foreign policy has made Iraq into a hell on earth as they now are drooling to do the same in Iran. The corporate mind, not being human, has no concern for any human values.

On the side of the humanity, however, we congratulate Ted Glick who organized a convergence on the U.S. Capitol Building this week to protest the wars in Afghanistan and Iraq. The theme was, "No War, No Warming." Ted and sixty other patriots were arrested in acts of non-violent civil disobedience.

And now it is our turn to come out on this Saturday, October 27. We will meet at noon at Olympic and Broadway and March to the Federal Building. Our troops must come home from Iraq and Afghanistan now and there must be no war in Iran and then we can begin a program of disaster preparedness in the United States.

A Call to the Supreme Court

October 31, 2007

We had hoped that the new Democratic Congress would help us to end the war in Iraq. They have not. They have even seemed unmoved and frequently supportive of a planned suicide mission on Iran. In view of this impasse we are turning to what we consider the most powerful branch of government, the Supreme Court. Here is a letter coming from the Office of the Americas to that court:

> We are writing with a sense of urgency on behalf of the people of the United States and the sovereign state of Iran.
>
> Our President and Vice President appear to be in the process of conspiring to commit an illegal war against the people of Iran. Such aggression would mean the likelihood that innocent millions will die and possibly result in attacks on the United States. An overwhelming majority of our citizens do not support the current occupation of Iraq and most certainly would not support an attack on Iran.
>
> The plan seems to include the following:
>
> The United States and Israel will strike at Iran. Iran will respond immediately with strikes on Israel, and Iraq. In the wake of such a disaster there is a real possibility of Israel and the United States resorting to nuclear weapons. China and Russia will come to the aid of Iran. The President has recently made reference to World War III. His plans for Iran could actually give us World War III.
>
> The President stated our need, "to defend Europe against the emerging Iranian threat."
>
> But Europe does not share his concern.
>
> Mr. Fareed Zakaria, former editor of *Foreign Affairs* concluded, "the American discussion about Iran has lost all connection to reality."
>
> As we review Article III, section 2 of the Constitution we can see the broad powers of the Jurisdiction of the Supreme Court regarding, "Controversies to which the United States shall be a Party;—to Controversies between two or more States; . . . or between a State, or the Citizens thereof, and foreign States."

This imminent crisis requires a full exercise of the power of Judicial Review regarding the conduct of the President and Vice President at this critical moment in history. Indeed the legacy of this Supreme Court will be determined by its action on this matter of utmost importance. The lives of our citizens and citizens of the international community are in the balance. We are urgently asking your cooperation.

Friends, we are also asking that willing individuals file at the Supreme Court for an injunction against military action. This is the legal remedy to stop an action before something terrible and irrevocable happens.

Civics 101 Requirement

November 7, 2007

Much of the work of the Office of the Americas over the past twenty-four years has been trying to stop our government from killing people. The focus of our work is on the foreign policy of the United States. We have found that policy to be dictatorial and counterproductive. The daily outrages of the current administration have reached a state of intolerability.

We firmly believe that our nation must go through an exercise of international repentance. Over a space of time we have been responsible for far more unnecessary deaths than the Third Reich. But Germany has gone through a long and effective period of national repentance. The horrors of the Fuehrer's rule are now forbidden by law.

We must follow the example of Germany's repentance. The list of terror tactics developed by the presidential imposter George Bush must be codified as federal offenses. Yes, this includes so-called preventative war, rendition, torture and most certainly one of its ugliest forms called "water boarding." Any aspiring public servant who cannot identify water boarding as torture is unqualified for office and most especially for the office of Attorney General . . . thank you for your interest Judge Michael Mukasey. You are incompetent and morally challenged.

And in a new era of repentance, a list of required Federal Crimes will be forthcoming. Any plot of citizens or office holders to bomb another nation should be taken as seriously as a plot to attack our own country.

All people intending to go into public service should be required to take a course in Civics 101. This would help them to understand that they are seeking to become a servant of the people, not a Godfather of organized crime.

The current brood of nut case neo-cons conspiring to attack Iran should all be arrested for their intent to foster terror against civilians.

We at the Office of the Americas, together with a massive and like-minded international movement for justice and peace, are dedicated to confronting the daily outrages in which we live. You are the people who make this critical work possible.

We look ahead to a new era of planetary justice and peace.

The War on America

November 14, 2007

In a new era of planetary consciousness, nut case fanatics in and out of government must receive the same indictment for plotting the bombing of Tehran as they would receive for plotting the bombing of Chicago. We in the United States don't have any more of a right to live than anyone else on the planet.

And at this moment of crisis who are the people closest to the trigger of a nuclear holocaust?

According to Michael Weinstein, the founder and president of the Military Religious Freedom Foundation, the highest levels of the Air Force, Air Force Academy as well as other branches of the military's highest brass are riddled with cult like members of a warped, exclusionist and ersatz Christianity which Chris Hedges identifies in his book *American Fascists, The Christian Right And The War On America*.

Cadets are clearly and officially pressured into a mind set based on sheer fiction. When you think of it, how else can they be prepared to abolish millions of innocent lives unless such repulsive action can be sanctified as a Godly act?

In this very wide spread and illegally authorized cult the United Nations is deemed to be the Anti-Christ.

Sadly, the President and many of his cronies are in this same loop of nationalistic and fundamentalist religiosity. The very same style of demonization that hypnotized the Germans to accept the holocaust is now being directed to the world of Islam. It remains our task to accept and understand the Anthropology which has given us a plethora of religions on this earth and to realize that the name of ones religion tells us little or nothing about their integrity.

How then can there be any planetary unity with such a wide variety of religions?

Actually it is entirely possible. We know people by the fruits of their lives, not by the name of their religion.

Rather than trying to convert others to rigid sectarian views, we must accept their non-theism, their atheism, agnosticism, Christianity, Judaism, Islam, Hinduism, Buddhism or Animism And within their enlightened consciousness they can begin to understand a universal and non-sectarian approach which is based on a conversion to peace, justice, joy, courage, endurance, love, compassion and repentance.

The conversion to these universally accepted virtues can unite the planet into one family of admirable diversity. And this was the basis for the establishment of the Universal Declaration of Human Rights in 1945.

Friends, it is clear that we are the realists and that our current political leadership is lost in a hopeless miasma of delusion.

Final Commentary

November 28, 2007

It has been a privilege to speak to you during the Evening News for many years. However, KPFK has a new policy stating that programmers with an existing program will not also have a scheduled commentary.

While I do not want to interfere with your Church attendance on Sundays, I do want you to know that my program, *World Focus* will continue to air every Sunday Morning from 10:00 to 11:00 A.M. This Sunday I am fortunate to have Father John Dear, a Jesuit Priest who has authored and edited twenty-five books on justice and peace and who has been arrested some seventy-five times in acts of civil disobedience. I will also interview Arlene Inouye, founder and coordinator of the Coalition Against Militarism in Our Schools and Gregory Sotir, multimedia director and web designer for the Coalition Against Militarism in Our Schools.

My commentaries for Pacifica Radio are now published in two books. The first book is called *Guerrillas of Peace on the Air*. These are Pacifica Radio Commentaries and my personal reports from the field on international direct action for justice and peace.

The second book of my Pacifica Commentaries is called, *Common Sense for the Twenty-First Century*. This book includes my Pacifica interviews with Chalmers Johnson, Reverend James Lawson, and Jonathan Schell.

These books are available at the Office of the Americas which has produced my Pacifica Commentaries by way of KPFK. You can reach us at (323) 852-9808.

The books are also available at Amazon.com.

So my friends, I want to thank you for listening to these commentaries during the KPFK news for these many years and ask you to tune in on Sundays at 10:00 A.M. to listen to my program, *World Focus*.

This program is also podcast and available 24/7 at: www.kpfk.org, click on *World Focus*.

This is Blase Bonpane.

World Focus

Interviews

Selected from

November 15, 2005 to June 4, 2007

Robert Fisk

I

November 15, 2005

BONPANE: Hello and welcome to *World Focus* coming to you from KPFK Los Angeles where we are now podcast and available 24/7 and internationally at www.kpfk.org, click on *World Focus*. I'm Blase Bonpane, your host. Today I am very honored to have as a guest Robert Fisk, who is a Middle East correspondent for the *Independent* of Britain and has been working out of Lebanon for three decades. He holds more British and international journalism awards than any other correspondent; I believe he is one of the world's great journalists. Thank you so much, Robert, for being with us.

FISK: Thank you. You're going to become my PR man.

BONPANE: Sure, I'll be happy to do that. So happy to see this great book, over a thousand pages, *The Great War for Civilisation*, your father had that written on his medal.

FISK: Yeah, my father was much older than my mother; died in 1992 at the age of ninety-three, born in 1899, century before last. He was a soldier in the last months of the First World War, in 1918, third battle of the Somme. And, when he died, as I said, in 1992, I inherited his campaign medal. And he believed, during the First World War, he was fighting the war for civilization, and on the back of that medal was inscribed "the Great War for civilisation." When I saw it I thought that has got to be the ironic title of my book.

BONPANE: Oh yes, because we are still fighting the Great War for civilisation.

FISK: Aren't we just?

BONPANE: Are we not? Now who are the civilized, please?

FISK: Well, we always talk about civilization, when we talk about western civilization, we're always talking about the present. I've noticed when commentators, or journalists, or politicians talk about Arab civilization, they're always referring to the fourteenth century. The same with Persian civilization. And they don't acknowledge, and the whole system of semantics is such that we don't acknowledge, that civilization still exists and does however slowly progress in other parts of the world.

BONPANE: We hear our politicians speak about the civilized world. They're referring to the part of the world that drops fragmentation bombs and the part of the world that uses white phosphorus on people.

FISK: Don't mince your words Blase. Look, I think they are also talking about those people in other parts of the world who do what we want them to do. We'll include various dictators in our civilized world, like Mr. Mobarek, King Abdullah of Jordan, and even King Abdullah of Saudi Arabia, providing they keep their people under control. They're meant to represent them, but that's not the same thing as controlling them. And providing they basically do what we want, particularly in resource areas of the globe, like, for example, the gulf, the Arab-Muslim world.

BONPANE: It's so amazing how we go from friend to enemy so fast with Manuel Noriega, Osama Bin Laden, Saddam Hussein, and on and on.

FISK: Oh, you can go back further than that. Nasser originally was favored by Anthony Eden, the British Prime Minister, until he nationalized the Suez Canal, then we had to bomb him. The foreign office in London and the United States thought that Khadafi was much better than King Idris in Libya until, of course, he started setting off bombs in American discos in Berlin, then they had to be bombed. Saddam, we supported him right through the 1980 to '88 war. Donald Rumsfeld was there in '83 shaking hands with Saddam. The Americans are so frightened of that bit of history that the trial of Saddam has been so framed by the Americans that he is not allowed to mention that period and that hand shake with Rumsfeld.

BONPANE: It's amazing. 1972, Iraq nationalized its oil production. And that is what we wanted Saddam to turn around, but he refused.

FISK: He really got involved. I mean Saddam took over the Baath party effectively in '78–'79, and just before that the United States had given the Baath Party the names and addresses of all the leading communists in Baghdad who were then liquidated, of course.

BONPANE: Yes.

FISK: So from that date Saddam could look upon the west, in general, particularly the French under Chirac, who welcomed him to Paris and gave him an honored state dinner, or at least he was the mayor then, and then took him to a bull fight in Southern France. So this is Saddam, you know. And now we bestialize him, of course, and he was a wicked, cruel man, but he was a wicked, cruel man then too. Once he invaded Iran we supported him, but when he invaded Kuwait, wrong country to invade, we hated him, we turned him into Hitler, the beast of Baghdad, and so we do this all the time.

300

BONPANE: Well, '80 to '88, one of the great wars of the twentieth Century, we sided with Saddam, and then apparently, Mrs. Glaspie, our ambassador in Iraq, said that she, or that we, as the United States, were not concerned about his problem with Kuwait.

FISK: I think we said we were not involved with inter-Arab disputes. Yes, and that remains an astonishing remark given the fact that we knew by then that large forces of the Iraqi military, both special forces, special guards, and indeed the ordinary infantry were right on the Kuwaiti border. I don't think there was a big plot, I don't think this was. I think it's part of the inability of western governments to comprehend and seriously study what goes on in the Arab world, and our ability constantly to see, particularly the Muslim world, in ideological terms. I mean, you can say Bin Laden does that, he does see things in ideological terms, but once you look at a part of the globe through the spectacles of ideology, you miss out on all the information that conflicts with your view.

For example, five weeks before the British and Americans, or shall I say the Americans and the British, invaded Iraq in April of 2003, five weeks before, Bin Laden issued an audio tape in which he said that Muslims, who would favor him in Iraq, should guard their weapons and have an alliance with the socialists. He meant the Baathists and the ex-soldiers of the Iran-Iraq war. Socialists remain infidels, but in history it has been in our interests sometimes to make such allowances. Now there was the detonator pin for the insurgency that would have on the one hand the Wal-Mart suicide bombers of al-Qaeda and the army of the shadows which had trained for eight years fighting the Iranians. And we missed it; the Pentagon, the State Department, American journalists, British journalists, me. We asked all the usual questions, "Is that Bin Laden's voice?" "How long ago was the tape made?" "Is he ill?" "Is he still alive?" "Where is he?" We didn't listen to what he said, because it didn't fit in with our ideological view of the war, because we were going after weapons of mass destruction, which didn't exist, links between Saddam and 9/11, which didn't exist, and then in the background, maybe democracy, which still doesn't really exist because the whole of Iraq is in chaos and anarchy.

BONPANE: This is one of the problems with power. Power tends to define the truth. Now we've had so much success in Afghanistan that we have the number one opium producer/operative today, we have the Taliban apparently quite visible, we have al-Qaeda, we have Osama Bin Laden. What have we accomplished in Afghanistan?

FISK: We've managed to create new warlords whom we've paid and put into the government, lots of little Saddams for the future. I was asking myself the other day how soon a new little Afghan Saddam will invade Uzbekistan or Kazakhstan and we'll have to go in and rescue those former southern Soviet Muslim countries. The beast of Kabul has invaded, but what can we do? We've got to fight to get him out, and we're going to have another series of long wars always in the same resource area, and the saddest thing, or the most tragic thing, or the most ridiculous thing is that we always go there saying we're coming to liberate the people. Napoleon said he was coming to liberate the people of Cairo from the Pashas in the eighteenth century, when the French expeditionary force landed in Egypt. General Angus Moore, British commander of the British invasion force in 1917, put up a big proclamation on the walls of Baghdad. I've got a copy next to my desk when I was writing this book, saying, "We, the British, come here not as conquers, but as liberators to free you from generations of tyranny."

BONPANE: Yes.

FISK: I bought that poster for $2000 from the daughter of the British soldier who took it off the wall thinking, "Maybe that will be valuable one day."

BONPANE: Oh and I think it will be. We liberated the Philippines; we liberated Cuba. The first president of Cuba was General Leonard Wood. A U.S. general was the first liberator . . .

FISK: And one of the few journalists who was doing his job at the time was Mark Twain.

BONPANE: Yes, indeed.

FISK: He was the guy that went after the whole . . . .

BONPANE: He helped create the anti-imperialist league. The press says he died a bitter old man. He wasn't a bitter old man . . .

FISK: He got the Middle East completely wrong and the Philippines completely right.

BONPANE: He was very, very angry that our troops would get all these medals for killing people in the mouth of the volcano, most of whom were civilians in the Philippines.

FISK: Shot down as soon as they got up. I remember that.

BONPANE: Exactly, and he was bitter about that. Now torture and war have gone together for centuries, and we see torture in our behavior over many, many years, certainly in Vietnam, certainly having lived so long in Central America, we saw it constantly. Now we have the effort to codify torture. And we have a Vice President who is campaigning for torture.

FISK: CIA only. We'll not let the military dirty their hands in such shameful affairs, but the CIA, they're the right guys for the job.

BONPANE: It is really. I think you mentioned in your book here about torture, that it's counterproductive for one thing. First of all, it's immoral, but that it creates resistance, and this is what's happening. It is so obvious. You know, we have had people who are outside agitators in Iraq.

FISK: Of course.

BONPANE: But it seems media is claiming that the whole thing is outside agitators, and I think we are dealing with resistance here, don't you?

FISK: Look, we say the word "outside". Those Arabs who come from say Saudi Arabia or Syria or even Lebanon, in quite a few cases I know of. They don't consider themselves as coming from outside. They live in the homeland of the Arabs, right? They would say that there are 148,000 foreign fighters in Iraq, and they are all in American uniform. They are the real foreign fighters from the outside, and that is their argument. Now, I think the point is this, the actual Iraqi insurgency when you have a hundred men in company strength wiping out whole police units. In one case, in the spring of last year at Ramadi, a twelve man marine outpost guarding the mayor's office was simply overrun and eliminated by hundreds of armed men. These guys are not from outside Iraq. These men are terrorists, insurgents, call them what you like. These are the soldiers of the Iran/Iraq war who learned to live and die and fight suicidally against an infinitely superior force, the Iranians, for eight years. Many of them were captured, held ten years in POW camps in Iran, twice as long as any World War II POW. Then came home to see their families starving under U.N.-U.S. backed sanctions; men who could take no initiatives in that war, because the only man who could take initiatives was a guy with a mustache who lived in a palace in Baghdad. Now suddenly they can take on and use those skills they had learned, deadly skills, against another superior army, but with taking the initiative themselves.

BONPANE: Well, you brought out how the resistance includes many of the Sunnis who were officers under Saddam Hussein, who have now become the resistance.

FISK: Well, it's not in the book, because it's too recent to do so, but not so long ago I met three leaders of the insurgency, Iraqis. I met them in a neighboring country, not Syria, actually it was in Jordan. The first one walked into the room, he was called a "general," and he said, "Ah, Mr. Robert, we meet again." I said, "We've never met before? Come again." He said, "No we have." He said, "You were under fire in the Iraqi front line in 1980 when we were invading Iran, and I took the first tanks as a tank major across the Al Karon River bridge, and you climbed on my tank, and interviewed me: I said, "I don't remember." Gone back to Beirut, looked up my files, and there he was. Now this is a guy who was a major, and presumably when the Americans invaded in 2003, he reached the stage of general. Then the army was all disbanded courtesy of Paul Bremer, the second U.S. pro council in Iraq, but he still holds the rank of general. He was the man who was commanding Fallujah when the U.S. went in in November and destroyed much of the city. The other two men were also officers in the Iran/Iraq war. So what you've got in this insurgency is the Iraqi army in plain clothes, the army of the shadows. The whole al-Qaeda issue is separate from that.

BONPANE: Yes.

FISK: Of course it's a danger. I mean these are the suicide bombers who don't mind how many Shiites they kill, how many Iraqis they kill, and somebody in Iraq wants a civil war. I don't think there will be, but that is a different issue. But it's the Iraqi army which is fighting the American army, these are the Guerrillas.

BONPANE: Now something is happening, Jordan is attacked. It seems that countries that are allegedly supporting the United States are now going to be under attack.

FISK: Well, they have been for some time. Australians in Bali; July 7 tube bombings in London; we had the Spanish bombings of the trains which had its effects, the Spanish withdrew from Iraq, and now we've had Jordan. Jordan was training Iraqi policemen. U.S. Special Forces officers were involved in that training inside Jordan. U.S. Special Forces officers live in Amman and some are involved in training other elements of the U.S. military in Jordan. Of course Jordan was bound to be a target at some point. It was inevitably going to be a target. What we are seeing now is that the attacks are not going against just Saudi Arabia, which they have been for some time, but they're going against other Arab countries which are clearly allies of the United States.

BONPANE: Seems very obvious with the Jordan action. Now, after being so many years in all of this, it seems that you have felt a certain sense of depression with this ongoing, endless, stupid bloodshed.

FISK: I guess it is partially personal. For the three or four years I was a Middle East correspondent, then for the *London Times* before Murdock took it over. It was a great adventure to me, watching the second invasion of Afghanistan, the descendants of the battle of Stalingrad in the snows fighting Mushahada tribesmen, the Iranian revolution, which was on a par with the French revolution in terms of its shockwaves around the world, the holding of the American embassy hostages, the beginning of the Iran/Iraq war. But about page 200, 199, there is a story where a colleague of mine, John Snow, British television, rescues the crew of a British ship, in which I had a small, extra part. And it's a happy story because it ends with the crew being successfully rescued, and me chucking all of their duty-free television sets back in to the river because we couldn't take them with us across this island which was under fire. I said to a very dear friend of mine that that is the last happy story in this book, because the rest of the book is torture, death, injustice, genocide, ethnic cleansing, and secret policemen. An unrelieved story of pain and destruction, and I became quite depressed writing it. I remember my French researcher came down to my library one afternoon. She was going through 328,000 files, pages, records, diaries of mine, and she said, "Robert, we are going for a walk on the beach. I am taking you for a pint of Guinness in the bar and we're going to get you out of here."

BONPANE: Yes.

FISK: And it was. I was finding myself very depressed, because as a journalist you find you go to the front line in Iran, you spend three weeks in the trenches, or you go to the Iraqi side, and then you go home for Christmas, you have holidays, you go out to dinner, and then you go back and cover the war again. But, if you chop out the bit of you and push it together, you realize the extraordinary suffering that that region has gone through. And I actually finished the book, and this may seem odd to hear, I actually finished the book, astounded at the restraint of Muslims, at the blankets of injustice which we partially were responsible for laying over them . . . amazed.

BONPANE: Yes their restraint. You know the beginnings of this came through some ideologues who, we won't give their names, like Wolfowitz, Perle, their communication with Benjamin Netanyahu, the Likud party, then somehow, the United States accepting this as policy. How in the world did this take place?

FISK: Well, I've been trying to look at it from a different angle. We attacked Afghanistan, we were going to hunt to the death Bin Laden, and we didn't get him. And at some point, although journalists in Washington knew or didn't point this out, Bin Laden was faded out and Saddam Hussein was faded in, and suddenly Saddam was responsible for 9/11, which he wasn't. And we knew he wasn't. And all of these bogus intelligence reports, and then we have aluminum tubes, etcetera, etcetera. And I asked at a lecture I gave in New York a year and a half ago. When did Bin Laden go away and be replaced by Saddam? Because the press didn't tell us. And a history professor in

New York wrote me a letter said, "I think I found it Robert." He said, "I was at the lecture, and I listened to that, and I put into my computer all the articles that mentioned Saddam and Bin Laden in the *New York Times, The Washington Post, Los Angeles Times,* etc. for that period." And he said the changeover came exactly at the moment of the Enron scandal. So there's another thing to think about.

BONPANE: Of course.

FISK: Another way in which history is manipulated.

BONPANE: Yes.

FISK: And, part of my book, part of what I've been trying to say, and I realize it now that I have finished it, not when I wrote it, is that we must refuse to accept the narrative of history laid down by our betters, by our prime ministers, and our presidents, and our generals, and our journalists.

BONPANE: In Africa they say if history was written by the lions, it would be entirely different, you know.

FISK: I shall use that in the future without crediting you.

BONPANE: So we have an occupation in Palestine, we have the leaving of some of the people who were residing in Gaza, and we have an increase in those who are going into the West Bank. So if we compare and contrast the occupation of Palestine with the occupation of Iraq, what do we come up with?

FISK: Well, one thing you haven't actually mentioned which is tangential to this is that we claim we've got democracy in Afghanistan, and democracy in Iraq, and democracy in the West Bank. All those, because there were elections, all those elections were held under foreign occupation, either American, British, or Israeli.

BONPANE: Even Bush says you can't do that.

FISK: I mean, I more and more come to the feeling that the issues of peace between Palestinians and Israelis goes back to U.N. Security Council Resolution 242 of 1968, which said effectively there must be a withdrawal of Israeli troops from territories occupied in the '67 war in return for the security of all states in the area, which, of course, includes Israel. The same resolution insisted on the nonacquisition of territories through war. That does not, therefore, give Israelis the excuse for saying, "Well, we'll keep that bit, and we'll keep the settlement and let you have that bit." But the Oslo agreement of '93 effectively allowed the Israelis to do just that, to renegotiate 242, and now we have a situation where George W. Bush, who calls Ariel Sharon "the man of peace" says publicly that there are some facts on the ground, i.e. Jewish settlements on Arab territory for Jews and Jews only, which are not going to change.

In other words that is tearing up 242. If that is really the foundation of the Oslo agreement, and all the other attempts for peace in the Middle East are gone only by returning to it, I think, Israelis will have the peace that they deserve, and Palestinians will have the state that they deserve, since Israel already has a state. But as long as you keep this wall separating east Jerusalem, which surely can be the only capital for Palestinians, as long as you have these massive secular roads which Palestinians can not even cross or drive on across the West Bank, and as long as these settlements continue to expand either within their existing areas or outside of it, there isn't going to be a peace between Israelis and Palestinians, and that, I'm afraid, is the raw truth. Many Israelis will tell you that, many Palestinians will tell you that, but again we have leaders, I'm talking about our own dear Prime Minister as well as your President, who have embarked upon an ideological world project, and this does not take into account the realities that you see if you go there, and I see when I live there and very often I find it difficult to write.

I have a weekly column as well as writing my own reports in the paper. I think I've reached a point where there are two different levels of reality, and they don't connect anymore. What can I say? You know, you hear this thing, "things are getting better in Iraq, democracy is coming, the people are happier, Saddam is gone," but when you live in Iraq, I mean, I go to the mortuary and pull out the computer, which it is illegal, because the Ministry of Health has been told by the Americans not to let journalists see the dead, and find that in July alone 1100 Iraqis, just in Baghdad, just in July alone, 1100 died by violence. I went on a Monday morning to the mortuary, by nine o'clock there nine dead, by midday there were twenty-six bodies brought in, covered in flies. One was a young woman with her hands tied behind her back shot three times in the head, there was a baby shot in the face, there are death squads at work, not just insurgents fighting. This is the Iraq which is apparently getting better, and when you question British or U.S. officials, they'll tell you, "It's only getting worse 'cause it's getting better."

BONPANE: We've got our death squad leaders from El Salvador, especially Mr. Steel, now in Baghdad training Iraqis in death squad behavior similar to those of El Salvador.

FISK: I have not reported on that . . . that's nonsense . . .

BONPANE: It was in the *New York Times Magazine*.

FISK: Then it must be true. Hold on a second.

BONPANE: Your Dad wrote about the Great War for civilization at the same time my father was part of World War I, and he wrote about the need in 1914 of international law and order, now are we making any headway? We had the League, and then we had the United Nations. We have a craving for international law and order, we can't deal with the oceans without international law, we can't deal with the air, how are we going to make more progress?

FISK: I don't think we are making progress. You see, 9/11 opened a door and the breeze that blew through that door effectively destroyed all those lectures we used to give to what we used to call the third world, the Soviet Union, the eastern block countries, and to the Arabs about human rights, no more torture, no more secret policemen, no more dungeons, no more torture chambers. When we have, as you rightly say, Vice President Cheney effectively saying, "Ok the military doesn't do the torture, but let's let the CIA," you know what happened, strangely enough, in Iraq.

Abu Ghraib was a symbol of Saddam's shame, the torture of women, the mass rape of women in front of their husbands, the hangings of all the political prisoners, this is what Abu Ghraib was: a torture, a death, it was a hell disaster, a hell sentence for Iraqis. But what we did when we went into Iraq is said, "Well, we're not as bad as Saddam." We just used Abu Ghraib to sexually abuse them, beat them up, threaten them with dogs. Maybe we killed one or two at Bagram in Afghanistan. Once you use Saddam as the moral compass of what you can do, you will start saying, "Give the CIA but not the military permission to torture because we are not as bad as Saddam, we're not as bad as him. He used to hang women. We don't hang women, we just kill men occasionally during torture by accident." Once you do that you're on path to perdition because you are no longer the United States and Britain is no longer Britain.

BONPANE: Well Cheney is right in league with the Torquemada and the others of the great inquisition.

FISK: That's what you say.

BONPANE: Well, sure, because they would say, "Look, we don't do the killing, the secular authorities do the killing," so it's like saying, "Let the CIA do it: You know they are the secular authorities, but we of the religiosity of the United States . . .

FISK: Yes, yes but what you are also not taking into account is the contamination that this causes in so many other countries. For example, you now have the British warlords ruling, with certain of them dissenting, that although we mustn't torture anyone, it's ok to take the evidence given by people under torture in other countries. You have in the little country of Ireland, beautiful, little, friendly Ireland, where rendition planes from the CIA are taking shackled prisoners from the

United States, refueling in Shannon Airport. The plane isn't touched by local police, of course, and it is then taken on to Uzbekistan, or other countries, where prisoners are fried alive, in fact, to make them talk. So this is what we're now contaminated with. We can say, "Oh, it's only the CIA, it won't happen in the United States, we'll do it somewhere in, I don't know, South America," or actually the two places which we're not supposed to mention, which are Poland and Romania, which is another country where the torture goes on in a secret basis. Astonishing, who would ever believe on the 10th of September, 2001, that we would ever see this going on in our lifetime.

BONPANE: Rendition is a crime. If I'm in a U.S. court and I said, "Look I am innocent because I had my victim taken to Uzbekistan to be killed," does that mean that I am innocent?

FISK: It might do so, if you remember the U.S. administration at the moment or if you remember the Blair government. But the real problem as I say is that we are now involved in deeply immoral acts. And just imagine how it looks to the Iraqi, who says, "But what are you blaming us for?" But this is different, 9/11 has happened. 9/11 has become the excuse to tear all our laws to pieces.

BONPANE: Oh yeah, just to do anything.

FISK: And because Bush said, "9/11 has changed the world forever," I'm not going to let nineteen Arab murderers change my world. Why does he allow you to believe that it's going to change yours?

BONPANE: Well, so he's made a criminal state out of our country, and we are very upset about it. We look forward to him going before a court of law, we look forward to . . .

FISK: Blase, you are more radical than I am. Hold on a second . . .

BONPANE: Well, that is what we would look forward to because we are very, very upset with the behavior of our government.

FISK: Well, we do feel the same way in Britain, as I'm sure you realize, but the problem in Britain, and it's a little bit the same with you, is I get this in correspondence from readers, is that more and more British people feel that the democratic process is breaking apart. That they go and elect people to go into the British Parliament to represent them, but the moment the MPs get into the British parliament they don't represent them any more, and they take the country off to war. And to some extent that kind of hoax democracy fear exists here in America, but for different reasons.

BONPANE: Very definitely. I don't know what happened to the time. This has been such a great experience, and I so appreciate what you are doing, and have done, and what I hope to see is a happy ending to this disaster which you have witnessed for so long.

309

FISK: So do I, but it'll be a shorter book, I promise.

BONPANE: Thank you so much.

FISK: Thank you very much.

BONPANE: Really is a joy having you. Well, just hope that you have a great return, and we're so glad you came to LA.

FISK: Thank you very much.

BONPANE: And you were at UCLA last night, you're going to be at USC today?

FISK: Yes, I am.

BONPANE: Wow, and on and on.

FISK: I'm afraid it is on and on. Right the way through next October.

BONPANE: Well, we much appreciate your book and we hope that everyone will read this magnificent book, *The Great War for Civilisation: A Conquest of the Middle East* by Robert Fisk.

Greg Palast

June 4, 2006

BONPANE: Hello this is Blase Bonpane with *World Focus*. I am privileged today to have Greg Palast as a guest. Greg's latest book *Armed Madhouse* will be released on Tuesday of this week. A cross between Sam Spade and Sherlock Holmes, Greg Palast has become a persona non grata in the United States and his reports have been exiled to BBC's top current affairs program, *News Night*, and England's *Guardian* newspapers. Welcome Greg.

PALAST: Blase, glad to be with you.

BONPANE: What a title you've got here. I mean, it take a half hour to read it. *Armed Madhouse: Who's Afraid of Osama Wolf, China Floats, Bush Sinks, the Scheme to Steal 2008, No Child's Behind Left and Other Dispatches From the Front Lines of the Class War.* That's just the title. That's not the whole book, right?

PALAST: Well you don't have to read all of that that after the title.

BONPANE: OK.

PALAST: But, I mean, yeah, because the class war, there are so many fronts. We're talking about you know, who's afraid of Osama wolf, and that's of course your war on terror. China floats, Bush sinks, that's the international flow of currency that goes from everything from the Chinese's yuan to Hugo Chavez's oil. The scheme to steal 2008 for the conspiracy nuts out there who think that Bush didn't win 2004, well here's the evidence that he didn't. No child's behind left is part of the educational state. And of course, that doesn't even include the secret history of the war over oil in Iraq. That's all it is, about the movers and shakers versus the moved and shaken and it's all about them and us it's class war.

BONPANE: Well I think it's important to use the word class war because so often those in power imply that the poor start the class war. The class war is a fact by virtue of the distribution of goods and services. The fact that in a town, like the one you're coming to, Los Angeles, we have people working two and three jobs a week who cannot get a first and a last and a security deposit and they are homeless, working poor, mixed in with billionaires in the same town and apparently no one sees the problem.

PALAST: Well, you know Blase, I grew up in the kind of ass-end of the valley before I moved to England and there's a Chevy plant there my father used to sell refrigerators made by the General Motors there. Where is it man? I'll tell you where it is. It's fallen victim to the class war. And by the way, there is a lot about George Bush here. But you know the democrats had their hand in that one, too. In fact, I know people have recently fallen in love with Mr. Gore but please read the section about NAFTA. And if you wonder where the GM parts went, ask Mr. Gore. Again, it's not just where the auto parts are but the body parts and body bags. The war in Iraq is another front in the class war.

BONPANE: There's no question about that, we have two parties of corporate capital, the Corporate Capital Republicans and the Corporate Capital Democrats.

PALAST: You have a problem with that Blase?

BONPANE: (laughing) I do, I do have a problem with it. I'm very sickened by the comments coming forth from the Democratic party and I find it very hard to identify with anything they do, they are hawks, they are trying to out-do the hawks of the Republican party and they are supporting this massacre in Iraq and here we are.

PALAST: One of the reasons why I wrote this book, and you'll notice it has like fifty illustrations in it . . .

BONPANE: I caught that.

PALAST: And I did it for good reason, you know, because in a way I feel like I am Joe McCarthy, you know he was always saying, "I've got documents here!" But you know the difference between me and McCarthy is that I actually have the documents. I thought I'd better show them so these people don't say, "Oh there's another black helicopter guy." And for those who don't know me, I do investigative reporting for BBC TV, which is of course I guess is illegal under the Patriot Act Three, and one of the things we got out of our investigation in Iraq, was you know, for the nuts who think that George Bush had a secret plan to grab the oil fields in Iraq, that wasn't true, he had two plans. We got them both and they're in here. And I think people should actually see what the hidden policies are. I mean, we talk about the rulers of the planet getting together and planning our future based on the oil. Well here it is, and you should know its contents and who put it together and why. And I gotta tell you that the fate of Iraq's oil involved no Iraqis. That's to begin with.

BONPANE: Right.

312

PALAST: Most important is that the guys in Washington were shunted aside. The real plan, the kind of winning plan, because there was competition you'll see between the two sides, there's a 323 page plan, which, and I show you one key page of it in the book. This was written, and even though it says it was written by the U.S. State department, it also says not for public release, public review, completely confidential, blah blah, how I got it another story of course, but, it was written in Houston, by the oil boys.

BONPANE: You know, we have a problem coming up and that is the limitation on whistle blowers came out this week from the Supreme Court. Very interesting that there is a limitation on First Amendment rights here. In the U.S. I know there have been many problems here, and in Britain as well.

PALAST: Oh yeah.

BONPANE: With freedom of speech, but this seems to be increasing as of yesterday.

PALAST: Well, yeah. The idea is to put a chill also on sources. But if you are out there, you got a document that says confidential, do not see, burn this, go to <www.gregpalast.com>. I love brown envelopes with stuff in them. I can't say I'll be to act on all of them very quickly, but we really do raw journalism. And that's what you'll see in the book. I mean, you'll see. And you of course do have to authenticate everything but that's the fun part. And people will remember, some people saw my BBC reports on the Bush Family Fortunes, remember when I had the documents showing the scrub of the black voters before the 2000 election. And when I confront Katherine Harris' henchmen with the list he literally does a runner. I have to chase him with the cameras into his office. Then he called in the state police and had me marched out of the state building in Florida. You know, one way to authenticate these things, is to confront them.

BONPANE: I see on your chapter 5, "The Class War, I Hope I Die Before My Next Refill." Is that oil, or gas, or diesel?

PALAST: I wrote the book out in the woods on a small path at the end of Long Island. And I go to the pharmacy and an older guy is getting his prescription drugs, under George Bush's wonderful, new drug program. And the woman behind the counter hands him a credit card slip and says, "I'm sorry." It was like, $1,200 for his medicine, right, and he hesitates and he signs, of course, right, I mean what is he going to do? He signs for the medicine, and then he says, "I hope I die before my next refill."

BONPANE: Because he's in the donut hole, you know, and everybody's gonna be in the donut hole. That's where you pay the max and this program was simply designed for the pharmaceutical companies with the ultimate goal of destroying MediCare.

PALAST: You have lots of complaints, don't you Blase?

BONPANE: Oh, it's just terrible. I hate to be so negative.

PALAST: Look on the sunny side. When Bill Clinton came in, oil was eighteen to twenty bucks a barrel. Now it's seventy! And that means your stock in Exxon's just gone straight through the roof, man.

BONPANE: Yeah.

PALAST: It's mission accomplished, and that's one of the things that I was trying to show in that Iraq chapter. That was the plan, it was not blood for oil. It was blood to make sure we didn't get the oil. That was the big shocker for me is finding out that we weren't there to get the oil. They don't want us to get the oil. They love three dollar per gallon gas at seventy bucks a barrel. We're paying it, they're collecting it. And that is what the plan was for. It was, as they said, to enhance Iraq's relationship with *OPEC*. They were afraid that Iraq would bust the *OPEC* quotas. That Saddam was out of control. You bust the OPEC quotas, you bring Saudi Arabia and OPEC to their knees.

BONPANE: And you bring the euro into the market as well and that's another reason to have a war, isn't it?

PALAST: Well, you know, I have to say, with the euro, after all, Bush is trying to wipe out the dollar. That's one thing that's happening. The dollar is dying and that's one of the reasons, by the way, that they wanted to privatize social security. They got to get that money the hell out of this dying nation. Our nation is choking to death. It's choking on high interest and high oil prices care of the Bush clan, the Bush cabal. And that means that capital has to get its money out, and its doing it quite quickly. When you look at the death of the auto industry, General Motors heading into bankruptcy, every single U.S. airline in bankruptcy court. And think about it, Bush and Gang, they just love it. And this is one of the things that I explain in the class war, this is part of the program.

Now, why do they want high oil price? I mean, why do they want to choke off the prices? I mean the venal and obvious thing is that $10 billion every three months for Exxon in pure profit and I mean no one has seen profits like that since the Pharaohs man. But even more, that $3.00 per gallon charge at the pump is an effective gas tax, which goes through the oil companies. They take a big slice. And then King Abdullah, over there in Saudi Arabia, Abdullah gets his little slice for another Rolls Royce. The remainder does come back to the United States in the form of treasury bills and treasury bond purchases. George Bush has run up a $2 trillion addition to the national debt. $2 trillion, which he says he spent stone sober.

BONPANE: Yes.

PALAST: Where is he gonna get it? And the answer is that he's gotten it from the *petrodollars*. Basically, instead of taxing the rich, they are dropping the tax on the rich and they are charging us through the oil pump.

BONPANE: Well, isn't the idea here to be able to ultimately say we don't have money for social security, we don't have money for MediCare, we can't afford any programs for health. In other words, let us destroy the public sector of the United States of America. Let's do that. Isn't that, isn't that the goal?

PALAST: Well that's only part, remember they've got to destroy the manufacturing sector too, and they are doing that very, very nicely. Because don't forget, because when King Abdullah lends us his *petrodollars*, we lend him in return the Eighty-second Airborne Division which is pretty expensive. But that's not all let's not forget, the entire increase in national debt, the entire increase, has now been bought up by foreigners. With money that we sent out to China, to Saudi Arabia, to the Arab Emirates. They hold our debt. But, the Koran says you can't charge interest, that's usury.

BONPANE: Yes, it does.

PALAST: But that doesn't bother King Abdullah to charge an extra pound of flesh. General Motors is dying, but their entire loss is accounted for by an increase in their cost of their interest payments. You know, they keep saying, "It's the greedy auto workers!" You know the Japanese auto workers get paid a lot more and their industry is doing very well. What we are getting killed with is the price of oil and the price of interest rates, but remember who is the winner in this. The banks are collecting the interest rate. Abdullah is collecting the oil money and the interest, and the Bush family is getting their slice. And that is why, talk about bringing something from left field, I have a chapter called "The Assassination of Hugo Chavez" because, there is only one guy out there who can upset the petro-cycle game.

BONPANE: He's got a beautiful plan here. He's been looking at a nation with 80 percent of his people in misery, and he said this is kind of silly, we are one of the richest nations in the world, it might be nice to have a little bit of balance here, to have a little bit of distributive justice. But why in the world do we go to your appendix here, not your appendix as an organ, but the appendix in your book, and see, "Return to Hubert's Peak, Why Palast Is Wrong?" Why are you wrong?

PALAST: Well OK, that's a joke and a punch-line you'll have to get by reading *Armed Madhouse*. It starts with Chavez and the Hubert's Peak. Let's put it this way. What happens is that this guy Hubert, who people say talked about a peak. He never used that term, he said that in about 2006 we're going to shift from white oil to heavy oil. He never said anything about running out of oil. In fact, he said we will not run out of oil. We will run out of light crude, and we are moving to the era of heavy oil.

BONPANE: And oil peaked in the 1970s.

PALAST: Yes, it did. What he's saying, and it was very prescient and was very very important because tomorrow, Hugo Chavez, and I just met with him last month in Caracas, President Chavez is going to demand that *OPEC* recognizes Venezuela, not Saudi Arabia, has the world's largest reserves of oil. And that's just not boasting. That just has a lot to do with who has control over *OPEC*, who sets the quotas, you know, who's in charge. That is an earthquake because the Bush family is completely tied up with Saudis.

BONPANE: Here comes Citgo, you know?

PALAST: And so this is really important stuff because you know, here's what's happening, and you'll see this in the book. I just spoke to you about petrodollars. Remember that film *Network*?

BONPANE: Sure.

PALAST: "The oil, Mr. Biel, the Arabs have taken billions of dollars from us and now we must take it back." That's that whole cycle of getting the *petrodollar*s back. Now I talked to Chavez , and you'll see this in the book, I talked to Chavez and he said I'll give you the oil cheaper than the Saudis, fifty bucks a barrel. That's his opening bid. That's a buck a gallon off the price, is what he's offering us. Now you would think, given the death of American manufacturing, given the rip off of the average consumer, that George Bush would be down in Caracas kissing Hugo Chavez's bottom, and say thank you for cheap oil, cheaper oil. But no, the response of the Bush administration is basically given through Reverend Pat Robertson, who said, you know, "Hugo Chavez thinks we tried to assassinate him and I think we should just go ahead and do it."

BONPANE: Cold blooded murder piously recommended by a "holy man."

PALAST: Well, but the important thing here is what you'll see a chart in the book that I got from the inside of the U.S. Department of Energy, and they asked BBC where did you get that and I wouldn't tell them. Now that we released it they've made it public. But when Chavez says we have more oil than Saudi Arabia, he's actually being modest. He says he actually has 50 billion more barrels than Saudi Arabia.

They say he has five times as much as Saudi Arabia. It's heavy stuff, OK, but as the price of oil rises, and as we move away from the light, we go to the heavy. But they hate Chavez because he says "I'll drop the price of oil. I've got a lot of it. And if you want to open up my oil field, then fine, I'll drop the price. But you ain't getting the money back George. I'm not funding you're oil wars. I'm not funding your tax cuts for the rich at the expense of my poor. I'm keeping the money in Venezuela and in Latin America." And to underscore the point, he withdrew $20 billion from the U.S. Federal Reserve and gave it, and lent it, to Argentina and Ecuador, and those nations in turn, told the IMF to go kiss their Latin behind. Now that's an earthquake, because the IMF and the World Bank were instruments of financial colonization. And they just smashed those financial colonial links. They're now, in fact, instead, linked in an alliance with Chavez and that's what's happening all over Latin America. That's why they need to get rid of this guy because there ain't no more *petrodollars* coming out of Latin America. But Chavez says I'll give you cheap oil, and in fact, for your poor neighborhoods, I'll give you a discount. People to people, he says I'll give you people to people discounts, I'll give you the entire nation cheap oil but you are not gonna get the oil money and you are not gonna have troops in Latin America.

BONPANE: Well that's the whole issue and that's why there's been this tremendous shift in Latin America. The very interesting thing about this shift is that people are coming from different ideologies but they are in solidarity on their focus on the needs of the people of Bolivia, Ecuador, even Argentina, Uruguay, and Brazil.

PALAST: If you look in the book, in fact if you look on John Perkin's website, a segment about my book on Ecuador, I met with the President of Ecuador, who's a conservative guy. He used to live in the United States, he was a cardiologist in California . . .

BONPANE: Yes.

PALAST: Then he became the President of Ecuador. And he said he would have been a Republican here. He says, you know, "All I want is to keep the little wealth of my nation. They have oil there. I just want to keep 20 percent of our oil. Not 100 percent, 20 percent." The IMF said no way and they choked that nation. They bled that nation. Ecuador didn't have $5 million for vaccines for kids and then Hugo Chavez wrote a check for a quarter billion dollars and said get the IMF off your back, get the U.S. oil companies off your back, and you know, this guy normally, like I was saying, would be a Republican in America. He is now signed up with Chavez.

BONPANE: Combined with this is the awakening of indigenous people who can get rid of a president in a matter of weeks, by storming the capital in Ecuador. It's amazing how they can do this and how they have done it time and again, he also has to keep that in mind.

PALAST: That's a very important point about Chavez. And you'll find it in the book. Let's not forget that Chavez is, as he says, Indio y Negro. He's black and Indian.

BONPANE: Definitely.

PALAST: And that is the first time you'll find someone who isn't a white Spaniard running Venezuela. And that makes a big difference. But even more important is that, that puts him on the other side of class divide from the Bush oil gang. And that's really what the book is about. I mean we're all, we're all indigenous. When they bust the levies in New Orleans the people tried to keep their head above water, economically and physically. And I mean you do have the real story of New Orleans in there too, the class wars. It actually goes to everything from social security to Iraq and of course to . . . you can't, you can't steal Venezuela's oil, you can't control Iraq's oil on behalf of Saudi Arabia. And they can't grab your social security until they take your elections away.

BONPANE: I'm speaking today to Greg Palast, the author of *Armed Madhouse*, which will be released Tuesday of this week and the full title is *Who's Afraid of Osama Wolf, China Floats, Bush Sinks, The Scheme to Steal 2008, No Child's Behind Left and Other Dispatches From the Front Lines of the Class War*. Here's a little comment on Ecuador, it says the people will be whacked with a light bill based on the price of oil set by *OPEC*. And that's not all, the World Bank has also required Ecuador to raise prices on basic foods. No wonder Joe Stiglitz mentioned that this program has destroyed every country that it has dealt with, and he happened to have been the vice president of the World Bank.

PALAST: Yes, the Chief Economist, yes. In fact, I have spoken to Stiglitz about this stuff. And what was interesting for Stiglitz is that I showed him, and he was able to confirm. He didn't give it to me, people were wrong to think he was the leaker, but I have the secret plans for basically the financial coup d'etat drafted by the World Bank and IMF for seizing control of all of Ecuador's assets together with those of Argentina and Brazil. Let's see, who else, Tanzania? And I actually show these plans in the book. And there's also a recipe for shrimp curry.

BONPANE: I have a question about the international monetary system. It seems to all be fiduciary. What I'm saying basically is we're talking about ink blips here, it seems as long as people put their faith in the blips it will work but there's, in effect, nothing there.

PALAST: This is one of the things we have to face, which is that the blips work if you think of them as chips that represent an economy, but if the economy goes, the blips don't mean anything and that's one of the problems we are running into with Social Security. As our economy is dying we have on account books a huge number of treasury bills which back our security payments. We can't make it because the social security funds rely on treasury bills which can only pay as much as the United States is worth. And as soon as the United States' productivity begins to die, that's the end.

BONPANE: I observe that everyday and I often wonder how the international monetary system can continue. Only eight countries are involved when we discuss the economy of almost two hundred nations. Eight counties have real money, the rest apparently have Monopoly money. I don't think you can conduct an international monetary system in that fashion.

PALAST: Well it's very interesting. I have President Bush announcing with great pride that he's forced the Chinese to revalue the yuan. As I explained in the book, that means he's basically said he successfully got the Chinese to devalue the dollar. Imagine waking up thinking, "I successfully devalued the dollar, today your pensions are worth less, you have less purchasing power, your future is looking dimmer and the jobs are going to China, but congratulations to me." And the American newspapers are like, "Oh, he revalued the yuan!" They didn't even know what the heck that means, they just got this "is that brilliant or what!"

BONPANE: What you do is change the Secretary of the Treasury and bring in a new one right out of Wall Street. That solves the problem!

PALAST: I mean, why am I laughing?! Because you have to laugh. Because that's why I have so many jokes in the book, because it's so grim. Especially the chapters on the theft of the 2004 election. And of course, like I said, the story of New Orleans.

BONPANE: We really appreciate your being with us, and it is important, I think, to try to bring in a certain amount of levity to an impossibly horrible situation. We just had a great massacre in Iraq and now they are trying to say it was a few bad apples and what we have here is a massacre that's gone on for sixteen years.

PALAST: It's not a bad apple, it's a whole forest that has gone rotten. And that's why we need the kind of informational bullets that you provide to protect ourselves. Without your show, without this information, they've got us because the only way they can pull this off is by lying.

Just remember, the positive thing is that they had to steal these elections, that they had to lie, lie Americans into a war, that they have to make up silly stories about the evil man Hugo Chavez who, unlike our president, was elected. They have to tell you fairytales about how free trade is going to set us free. And hence the continuing system of lies and disinformation. And you'll see all these documents that they don't want you to see in my book.

BONPANE: Oh, I think so. And I'm just sorry that we're out of time. Greg, we want to thank you for being with us and we're going to continue with *World Focus* after a brief break.

Peter Laufer

June 4, 2006

BONPANE: Hello, this is Blase Bonpane with the continuation of *World Focus*. I'm privileged today to have Peter Laufer as a guest, a Vietnam War resister and author of many books, a former NBC news correspondent who has won numerous awards, including the George Polk Award for overseas reporting and the Edward R. Murrow Award for study of the Vietnam War and post-traumatic stress disorder. Welcome Peter.

LAUFER: Blase, thank you very much.

BONPANE: It's a pleasure and I have your book *Mission Rejected: U.S. Soldiers Who Say No to Iraq* and you wrote it and Norman Solomon wrote the forward. Can you tell us how you happened to do this book?

LAUFER: Well, I was pleased to connect with the publishing house, Chelsea Green at a point when they were making a pointed decision to expand their list from books about sustainable living to sustainable politics, a couple of years ago. And, so, we worked together to come up with this title. It's something that is dear to my heart because it is so frustrating, upsetting, ghastly, to watch the replication of so many of the mistakes that this country made during the Vietnam era now with the Iraq war.

BONPANE: We see hundreds of thousands of dead. My goodness we go from '91 to the present, we're talking about fifteen years here of massacre, and of course there's been some discussion about a recent massacre that will be, will put various troops on trial. But . . .

LAUFER: By the way, what you just said Blase is that we talk about it across that timeline. This is something that goes back in terms of the overshooting war to '91. You're absolutely right, and so often as long as it's been since this most recent invasion we talk about it as something separate but of course that war went on in its own way from '91 on.

BONPANE: Well, the bombing went on, the sanctions went on, thousands and thousands of children died, and we're aware over Memorial Day of the cost to our young people, the thousands of them who have died and the many thousands wounded. And I noticed also we're now doing a comparative study of the cost of the war. The war up to this date, the recent Iraq war under young Bush, would pay for 37 million children to attend a year of Head-Start, or would give 170 million children health insurance, or would 4 million, practically 5 million children would actually increase the number of school teachers in public schools by 5 million. These costs are leading to the destruction of the public sector of the United States, as well as losing our soul before the rest of the world I believe.

LAUFER: Well what a sad commentary when that comparison is studied and then when you add to it the horrific losses of life and property to a lesser concern on both sides. And that's the kind of thing that motivated me to write the book. The stories that these soldiers tell, the ones who come back from Iraq and choose not to go again and to work against the war as well as those who refuse to go in the first place. I hope these stories are tools to help us figure out a way to stop the war, to help us figure out new ways to engage in dialogue with those who are still proponents of the war because the credibility of these people really can't be impugned, these are heroes, these are people who volunteered for the service and they're coming back and saying it's wrong. That's very different than when you and I say it.

BONPANE: That's true. Take the case of Aidan Delgado Here he is, an MP in Iraq. He becomes aware of what's going on in Abu Ghraib, and he says, "Not on my watch." He said, "I am out of here, I am now a conscientious objector." He gets his status of CO in Iraq, which is really amazing, and then of course he is isolated and they even took away his body armor, said well you won't need this anymore, and comes home. And he's been all over this country explaining what he saw.

LAUFER: Indeed, and he has an intriguing history beyond what you just recounted. He had a working knowledge of street Arabic because he grew up in part in Cairo, his father was in the foreign service. So this was a fellow who understood what was going on from a lot of facets and realized that not only that he could not do it himself but that he wanted to come back and tell these stories to anybody who would listen.

BONPANE: Well he is a very compelling speaker. And you have the case of Joshua Keys and he saw what was happening to the Iraqi people and he relives this saying he's been fighting a war for months and months. All I'm seeing is death, destruction, and chaos.

LAUFER: Joshua Keys is an example of what we've come to call, many of us, the poverty draft. He never had any kind of ambition to be a soldier. He was looking for a job, he had a wife and kids, and he found the army and he was seduced into the army in expectation that this was going to be a job. Now of course that brings up something interesting to analyze, and something I talked about alot with these guys, and that is you can't go into the army as a volunteer even during peacetime without realizing that it's a machine designed for killing, that's what its purpose is, and why should they be surprised when they find the army doing something that they don't like, and that is killing. And I think of the soldiers whose now opposed to the war up in Canada really says it best. This is Jeremy Hinzman and he is trying to achieve refugee status up in Canada and he says "I was told in basic training that if I'm given an illegal or immortal order then it is my duty to disobey it. I feel that invading and occupying Iraq is an illegal and immoral thing to do." And it's lines like that that I think can help empower people to realize that the war is wrong and to figure out new ways to talk about it and deal with it.

BONPANE: I'm speaking today to Peter Laufer, who's just written a book, *Mission Rejected: U.S. Soldiers Who Say No to Iraq*, published by Chelsea Green. Now we look at Indo-China and we want to compare and contrast. That war was ending in a mutiny when General Westmoreland said, "All I need is 750,000 troops." He had no idea he had not a clue what was going on and apparently a mutiny was taking place.

LAUFER: Well there certainly is no mutiny now. And the numbers who are speaking out are relatively small. It's hard to quantify and of course who knows how many are opposed to what's going on and are just accepting the fact that they have signed up and they are going to fulfill their obligations and their commitments. But there are the parallels, there are the gross differences and of course one of the most important differences, is that there is no draft now and these people all did volunteer. Unless we talk about the poverty draft or the backdoor draft of the Stop Loss program that doesn't allow the soldiers to leave after their tour of duty if the army decides it wants to keep them.

BONPANE: It seems to me that we can not continue internationally with a war system because at its base the wars are fought historically by slaves. It becomes a matter of involuntary servitude and as people become conscious of this it would seem to me that we would have to develop a functional peace system, which we thought we did with the establishment of the United Nations after World War II. But apparently we have developed an enormous hostility toward the United Nations.

LAUFER: Yeah, and one of the soldiers profiled in the book says just what you said and I think the language is such that we can say it on the radio. This is Clifton Hicks and he was talking to me in Germany as he was waiting to figure out how to get out of the military hoping for "conscientious objector status" which he ultimately did receive. And I said, "what's going to happen if you don't get it, will you go back?" He said, "it's not that I won't go back, it's that I can't go back." And now these next lines, you get a feeling for just how gross the problem is that has been created there. He says "I can't go back, I just hate that place so much. The sad thing is that I hate those people. I hate the reason we're there. The whole place is just so foul, it's a cesspool of pure evil, the insurgents are evil, but we're evil too. The insurgent who is killing me, he is being used just like I am. They say these guys are mindless, look as us. We joined up too. We're both violent peers fighting each other. Once we volunteer we can't leave. We become con-scripts. We're just pawns, we're being used. It's a war," Clifton Hicks said, "fought for filthy rich bastards too cowardly to do it themselves, who want more money, fought by us, the masses of uneducated fools killing each other."

BONPANE: I think well put, and very mildly put. He could have stressed that even more because to me it looks like a cult situation on both sides. We have pathetic individuals like General Boykin who told the troops that they were fighting the devil, isn't that lovely? I mean, what is that but a cult leader speaking to people with a mind control situation, telling them we're fighting the devil. You know?

LAUFER: Absolutely, and of course many of these soldiers went over there with so little prior knowledge of the region, of the culture, of the language, and so under those circumstances it had to have been easier for the military to demonize the opposition.

BONPANE: And it's absolutely necessary because how can you open fire on people, especially civilians, unless you feel you're killing the devil. And this has been a long standing problem with young people who go out of the twelfth grade who've been poorly educated, have no sense of history and they go off to die as the enemy in a place where they are not wanted. That to me is an enormous tragedy and I think it's important that your book realizes that consciousness is developing. *Mission Rejected: U.S. Soldiers Who Say No to Iraq* by Peter Laufer who worked with NBC News as a correspondent and has won the George Polk award and won the Edward R. Murrow award and did a great study on post-traumatic stress disorder in the Vietnam veterans and we find those veterans on our streets here in Los Angeles, approximately one-third of our homeless are veterans. And in regard to the cost of this war, we have great shortage of housing, someone who did the math said the cost of this war, just the young Bush war, and not his daddy's war, but the young Bush war, the cost in housing is 2,563,944 new homes.

LAUFER: The numbers are just so staggering and it's all but impossible to comprehend the amount of treasure, past the human treasure that is wasted on both sides over there, particularly at a time when we all know that this money is needed at home. Not to mention the soldiers at the time of Katrina, there were soldiers from the Louisiana National Guard watching television in Baghdad in frustration because they could not do what they signed up for in the National Guard and that is to help their neighborhoods.

BONPANE: That, and New Orleans still sits there unfixed and the new levies are entirely under question in terms of their efficacy. We don't believe, and many engineers don't believe, they've done a right job even on the few levies that have been fixed. So we have a tremendous domestic problem and we see our young people so pained and so injured and so killed in this process. I have another figure here which says the cost of the war, just under George the lesser, is the fully funding of anti-hunger for the whole globe for eleven years. We could have taken care of the whole international hunger problem for eleven years with the cost of the Iraq war, just the recent war.

LAUFER: Amazing numbers. But you know, one of the things I came away from talking to these soldiers Blase, is that is some cause for optimism, there really are some heroes that these that men and women can stand up to the monolithic U.S. government and U.S. military and say no, this is wrong. That should give us, I think, some sense of some optimism, the beginning of a feeling of some turnaround in this country toward the war. If those right in the heart of it who volunteered for the military, are saying no. And also I think, it kind of gave me as I was working on the book, a sense of really being amongst heroes. It is difficult to imagine the problems with individual faces going up against the peer pressure, not to mention the authority of the military and saying no, you're ordering me to do that you're saying it's a lawful order and I'm saying I won't do it because I don't think it's a lawful order and I'm answering to a higher authority.

BONPANE: It's entirely legitimate. And one thing that's happening, and I don't know if you notice this, is we're seeing a similar response among the officers. I had the good will, the good fortune, last week of talking to Colonel Ann Wright who left in disgust. And I asked her why she joined the military in the first and she said I wanted to get out of

Arkansas. And many have said, even Colin Powell, when he was asked why he joined the military, he said "$260 a month, that's why."

LAUFER: Yeah, Joshua Keys said we had two boys at the time, this is when he joined the military, and my third one was on the way, there was no work in Guthrie, Oklahoma where they were living. He says, "You know what I mean? There wasn't going to be a future. Of course you can get a job working at McDonalds but that wasn't going to pay the bills."

BONPANE: Yes.

LAUFER: "And the local army recruiting beckoned and he says I started thinking, hey, you always see it on TV. I'll go up and talking to them and see what they have to offer."

BONPANE: We have a wonderful coalition against militarism in the schools here in the Los Angeles area which the young people spend their time explaining the lies that take place in the matter of recruiting, how many young people have been lied to. Some were told, well if you join the reserve you never have to go overseas. All kinds of things, that you are definitely going to get help with education and they've been trying to instruct the young people the realities of joining because the recruiters are very, very strong in the poverty areas.

LAUFER: Absolutely and the lies that you talk about are blatant because it is in the contract that eventually they recruit signs where the line exists that says any of the promises made are moot if it is determined that there has to be some sort of change because of the status of circumstances on the ground. It is an incredible contract to read and in fact I quote from that line in the book just because it's so amazing to think that these recruiters are, as you say, promising and then the contract itself says all promises null and void. There was at the University High School in Los Angeles a very strong op-ed piece by a student in the *Wild Cat Newspaper* there that draws attention to just what you were saying. The way they seduce with lies but also they had put a Hummer all jazzed up to look like a hipster car into the campus and they were appealing to the Spanish speaking students by giving out t-shirts and writing that had the legend and the same legend was written on the Hummer, "Yo soy el army."

BONPANE: This is going on on a daily basis, especially in our high schools. Some like Garfield have 97 percent Latino student body. And the pressure is on, they're called at home and they are in every way told that this is the only thing for them. I think this is really a tragic moment. Then we read of the massacres that are taking place. The massacre uncovered by *Time Magazine*. We reflect on it and seem to feel that the whole things been a massacre. It's not just the indi-

326

vidual Haditha massacre. It's a day by day issue that's going on. We compare it to My Lai and then we think that Vietnam also was a massacre of some 3 million not just My Lai.

LAUFER: Absolutely, and I think you're correct that the peace movement is going to be, already is, stimulated by these soldiers who are rejecting the mission. They are creating their own organizations. They are joining organizations that already existed. They're working with outfits like Vietnam Veterans against the War. They've created Iraq Veterans against the War. They're joining up with Veterans for Peace. Again, the numbers still seem small by our memories of what occurred in Vietnam but unfortunately we're still relatively early in this mess. I must say though that many of the veterans that I've spoken with say that they were surprised by how quiet the peace movement was on the home front and how quiet their generation is and how little disruption the war is causing to regular life in the U.S.

BONPANE: I think there's a lot of truth in that. In terms of many of the activities of the peace movement, we have the problem that people won't know about it if they're watching commercial media. They'll rarely hear of the day to day work. For example, in a place like L.A., we have forty and fifty vigils a week going on here. But the commercial media doesn't know about it or doesn't want to know about it let's put it that way. So there is a lot of activity occasionally the really large demonstrations are reported but the smaller activities are non-existent unless you're listening to Pacifica or some alternative media and that's a problem. We've seen the Iraq Veterans against the War develop and Tim Goodrich's work in that development, and how important these veterans have been in establishing, for example, Arlington West on our beach here in Santa Monica and many other beaches.

LAUFER: That's a great visualization that communicates so thoroughly so quickly.

BONPANE: It's truly awesome because they have a marker there for everyone, for all the going on 2,500 of ours and then a sign which says, if we counted every Iraqi there wouldn't be room enough on this beach. And they also try to make a note of the number, the total number, of wounded. Another figure in terms of cost of this war. is that, this is unbelievable, the children of the world could have basic immunizations for ninety-four years with what we have spent in the second Iraq war. So the disaster goes on. Media, apparently, wants to continue to support the war, in spite of all of this. We have a war culture and we have to work very hard to build a peace culture, I think.

LAUFER: Absolutely, but again as we try to search for some optimism the very low popularity figures that the President is suffering currently, the growing number of those who believe the war is wrong. This has to give those of who are opposed to the war and working against the war optimism, hope, and fuel to continue the struggle.

BONPANE: I would think so because it's a situation where many people are not speaking. They don't realize that silence is approval and by their silence they are approving. And many people are in a situation of fear and the manipulation of fear is one of the lowest forms of corrupt politics and we've become experts at it. The people of the United States have been recklessly endangered by this war. And they should realize that the administration who brought it about is responsible for endangering not only people overseas but those of us here at home as they threaten a nuclear war on Iran. I mean this is beyond belief.

LAUFER: It's beyond comprehension and you're so right about not being silent. And you're so correct Blase about the importance of media such as Pacifica and stations like yours. But I think, in addition to that, it's incumbent on us to act one on one. If we're in a supermarket line and the guy behind us has an American flag pin on the lapel and it's not upside down, it's an opening to engage somebody one on one and just build this dialogue person by person. And that's why, again, I hope that the stories in the book are of value because it's so difficult, if not impossible, to impugn the credibility of somebody who's been over there, done what they were told to do, and come back and say this was wrong.

BONPANE: It's absolutely a necessary and I do think that one to one is important. I've seen the president of our board, Alice Powell, a woman in her late seventies began giving out bumper stickers and began a vigil at Veteran and Wilshire. And that vigil has continued now for years. She has personally given out more than 50,000 bumper stickers which say, "War is not the answer." So it is important to do that one to one work and realize that it can be, can have a multiplier effect very, very quickly. Would you care to say a final word about *Mission Rejected: U.S. Soldiers Who Say No to Iraq*. This is a book by you with a forward by Norman Solomon and it's published by Chelsea Green. Any final thoughts on that?

LAUFER: Well I'm just so pleased for the opportunity to talk about the message that I am lucky enough to transmit from the soldiers that talked with me about their experiences. I think that it is so important for us to look for new devices to talk about the war to those who still are proponents of it. And I think the voices of these soldiers do it in

328

a compelling and poignant manner, and as I said, with the kind of credibility that as much passion as you and I have Blase, we just don't have the type of credibility that they have and that's why their stories, I believe, are so important.

BONPANE: I do too. I think they're the vanguard of peace in our country. I've been speaking today to Peter Laufer, a former NBC news correspondent whose won numerous awards including the George Polk award and the Edward R. Murrow award and who has just written this wonderful book *Mission Rejected*. Thanks so much for being with us Peter.

Robert Fisk

II

February 4, 2007

BONPANE: Hello this is Blase Bonpane with a continuation of *World Focus*. I am privileged today to have the best-selling author and journalist Robert Fisk as a guest. He's speaking to us from Beirut where he is based as a Middle East correspondent for The Independent. Robert is one of the world's most awarded journalists. He has won seven British International Journalist of the Year awards, his book *Pity the Nation* is a history of the Lebanon war and has received wide critical acclaim, as does his most recent book, *The Great War for Civilisation: The Conquest of the Middle East*. Welcome Robert Fisk.

FISK: Thank you.

BONPANE: I read your recent article in *The Independent*, "The World Ignores the Signs of Civil War in Lebanon." Would you care to comment on that article?

FISK: Well I wrote this actually in Paris when I went to Paris for one day for what is called here "The Paris Three Conference." It was a meeting of world leaders, including your own Secretary of State Condoleezza Rice, to try and raise money to offset Lebanon's appalling public debt, which stands at the moment at around $41 billion. Don't ask me how the Lebanese managed to spend that much money. And I was very struck by the fact that in the west, in Europe, which is, I am European, I come from Britain, we simply don't seem to be in touch with reality. I don't say this just because President Bush thought the Israelis won the last war in Lebanon, but the fact that everyone thought that they were backing the Fouad Siniora democratically elected government of Lebanon. This money, all of which of course had various pins attached to it like "you must win over the Hezbollah," which handed over, almost part of a package deal, to get the Lebanese to fight the Lebanese.

When Fouad Siniora, the very pleasant, gentle Prime Minister of Lebanon, was being asked questions of Lebanese residents in Paris and journalists, and they were asking about the agricultural industry in this country and about the tourist industry in the next twelve months without realizing that Sunnis and Shiites had been fighting in the streets with guns in Beirut, and Christians versus Christians were hurling thousands of stones and rocks at each other. It was as if the unreality, the mythical world in which your President now appears to live had spread to Europe. No one understood the gravity of the situation here, which is very serious to the point where, for example, a few hours ago I had lunch in Lebanon with a very well to do, educated family. A woman crossed the restaurant they were eating in and said to my host, who's a Shiite, "Don't you think your son Hussein should change his name in order to be safe?" In fact there are two realities, there's real reality here, and there's a mythical reality in Europe and America. That's what I was writing about.

BONPANE: Well, is there not something behind so called "sectarian violence" in Iraq and in Lebanon that is a matter of, "are you with the occupiers or are you with the opposition?" Is that not behind sectarian violence?

FISK: Well I'm not sure who the occupiers of Lebanon are, they usually seem to be the Lebanese. I don't believe whenever you have a conversation in this country, in Lebanon, I always say there must be a special chair reserved at the conversation for "the plot." The Lebanese more than any other Arabs believe in "the plot," that there is some massive international conspiracy producing civil unrest, civil conflict, civil war in Iraq, in Afghanistan, here, wherever. And I always say, to the displeasure of my lunch or dinner guests, that the Americans have screwed up everything in the Middle East for years, don't tell me they can work "the plot" well, don't tell me they're behind civil conflict, they're not. I do think that it is in our culture, in our habit to constantly point out the differences between sectarian, confessional, religious groups, call it what you like, in a way we won't do with our own society.

I am so tired and sick of maps of Lebanon that show Shiites at the bottom, of course, the Sunnis in South Beirut, and the Shiites in South Beirut, and then the Christians in North or East Beirut, and then the Shiites in Beckar and the Sunnis in Tripoli, which is a Lebanese city to the north. Just as I am sick of maps of Iraq which show Shiites at the bottom and the Sunnis have this famous triangle, actually it's an octagon, maybe a pentagon, in the middle, and the Kurds in the north. You know there are always maps.

BONPANE: And sometimes they don't really tell the story.

FISK: Well it's not so much that. The problem is we don't draw maps of our own cities. I remember when I was in Northern Ireland as a correspondent, the British Army would have colored maps of Belfast. The Catholics, of course, were colored green, the Protestants were colored orange and the middle classes who intermarried have themselves a brown color. But we don't draw confessional maps of Birmingham, England showing the Indian areas or the Pakistani areas or the Muslim areas, and you don't show maps in the Washington Post, for example, of the ethnic origins of Washington, though I could draw you a map. You don't show maps of American cities, New Orleans for example, which show color of citizens. You don't do that because you are all good Americans, but in the Middle East it is perfectly permissible for us to draw these maps and we do this with Lebanon.

We do it all the time. We constantly emphasize and reemphasize and remind the people who live here, in Beirut for example, of which group they are. It was very interesting today, at the same lunch I was at, there was a girl who said to me, "You know when I went to school," she said, "we simply did not know why the other girl was called Elizabeth," which is of course a Christian name. But now everybody talks about whether they're Christians or Muslims or Shiites or Sunnis, and partly I think this is because of us. Westerners are constantly reemphasizing to people in this region how different they are from each other.

BONPANE: Well if we compare and contrast the Protestant/Catholic situation in Northern Ireland with this situation that we see in Lebanon . . .

FISK: You can do that in New York by the way.

BONPANE: Yes, of course.

FISK: If you don't mind me saying so, you could do it in New York. I could draw a map of New York for you if you want.

BONPANE: But isn't behind that religious difference a political reality that is dominant over the ethnic side of it?

FISK: Well, we want it to be. I mean I don't think it's a lie to say divide and conquer.

BONPANE: Yes.

FISK: The Romans did it, the British did it, we still do it. We "the west" whether it be the Americans, our own dear Mr. Blair, or anyone else. We're always stressing every military ministry of defense in London, Pentagon briefing talks about Shiites, Sunnis, Kurds, which the Muslims are, which the Christians are, it's incredible the way we do this. We don't think there's anything racist about it, we think it's quite normal, and of course these differences exist, of course they do. But who's emphasizing them is the question, why are we doing that?

BONPANE: I was going to shift to some comments by one of your colleagues, John Pilger, who said the war begins in Iran, and that's quite a frightening statement.

FISK: I know John Pilger quite well and we are good mates, but I don't necessarily prescribe to what he writes and says.

BONPANE: Sure.

FISK: There is a civil war in Iraq. We are told by the *New York Times*, so it must be true. Right? I don't think Iraqis want a civil war. I don't think Iraqis get up in the morning and have some humus for breakfast and say let's go kill a Sunni or a Shiite or whatever. Somebody wants a civil war in Iraq, that's certainly true. Let's wind the movie back to Saddam Hussein's period. He maintained, without an active support, an eight year war against Iran, and the majority of the Iraqi army, like the majority of the Lebanese army actually, were Shiites fighting Shiites in Iran.

BONPANE: Yes.

FISK: And they didn't break apart and start killing each other. So there is some incendiary element that wants a civil war, a civil conflict in Iraq. And if you can sufficiently kill, bloody, make suffer, or torture another community to your own, you'll bring it about eventually. You had a civil war in your country, but mercifully quite a few decades ago. It's not difficult to have a civil war.

BONPANE: You know in regard to the surge on page . . .

FISK: Oh the surge, the wonderful word surge. Where's that come from? Who first used surge? Was it Bush?

BONPANE: Yeah, I believe so, on page . . .

FISK: Be sure the *New York Times* has used it as well.

BONPANE: Oh, definitely. Page 1022 of your book, *The Great War for Civilisation*, you point out something that has already been a surge. If we have 124,000 troops and then we have 100,000 mercenaries, that's 224,000 troops. Isn't it so? It seems . . .

FISK: What I call foreign fighters, but yeah . . .

BONPANE: Yes.

FISK: But that's a phrase that has just been appropriated by your country about people who are from the Arab world but are not of Iraqi nationality.

BONPANE: You mention 8,000 came from Britain, more than British troops . . .

FISK: Indeed they did, didn't they? That's right.

BONPANE: And 300 security firms in Britain.

FISK: No, I mean the point is this. Who are these mercenaries? What are their rules? Who do they work for? I don't know. Who burned the libraries of Baghdad in 2003? Who destroyed the museum? Who looted the heritage of Iraq? I don't know, and we don't know, and we don't ask. Don't tell me the west wasn't in some way involved in this mass looting. Of course we were because many of the elements, many of the icons that were looted turned up in western countries, not least your own and mine by the way. But the fact of the matter is that we don't ask the right questions. We don't challenge authority. We are still taking the narrative of history from the State Department or the Pentagon or the British Foreign Office or the British Commander in Chief or the American Commander in Chief of whatever it may be. And I still don't understand why the Iraqis would want a civil war.

Now if you look at, for example, the history of the French in Algeria and the war for independence, which did win Algeria independence, which lasted from 1954 to 1962. The French went around deliberately trying to get what was then the FLN, who eventually won power and are still in power in Algeria, and the ALN, which was the other opposition force, to fight each other, and they were successful. And one Algerian historian has told me they think Algerians killed half a million of their own people in a civil war designed by the French to relieve the pressure on the French army to maintain control of Algeria and to get the Algerians to fight each other. Now I don't know if that is correct. I suspect, given some of his evidence, it might be, and I'm not saying the Americans are trying to engineer a civil war in Iraq, but I am saying that one of the principles of counter-insurgency is to get the insurgents to fight each other.

BONPANE: Well in the meantime, we hear the same arguments for a war in Iran as we heard for a war in Iraq being repeated in a different way, and today we have Uri Avnery terribly concerned that this would be suicidal for Israel. He's asking his own people in Israel "What's going on here? We're not going to come out of this unscathed." He says Iranian missiles will rain down.

FISK: The fact of the matter is I don't know if I believe in a future war with Iran, but then again I'm the fall guy that didn't believe there was going to be an invasion of Iraq, and got it completely, totally, bloody wrong. There may be a bombing of Iran, I don't know. But it seems to me what we've got here is another part of the official narrative which is accepted by our colleagues in journalism. You know the nuclear instillations in Iran did not begin under the Mullahs of the Islamic republic. It began under the Shah of Iran. And the Shah actually wanted nuclear power and Siemens built the Bushehr plant, the German company. Western companies were standing on each other's shoulders bidding for nuclear rights to build Iran's nuclear industry because at that stage, at that time, the Shah was our policeman in the Gulf.

The Shah actually said on American television he wanted an atom bomb because the Soviet Union, which existed then, and the United States have atom bombs. Nobody told him he couldn't visit the White House. When Khomeini took over Iran, the first thing he did was close down, and I was present at the speech when he said this, the nuclear installations, which he said were the work of he devil, Satan. Only when Saddam Hussein, who was working for us at the time, used gas against the Iranians, did the Iranians say, under Khomeini's Islamic revolution, well hold on a second, if he's got gas, he'll use nuclear weapons next, we better reopen the nuclear installations. That is the background for the nuclear crisis in Iran, which you are not being told and *New York Times* is not remembering, because it has a faulty memory on things like this.

BONPANE: Well I think what happens is that historically wars are started by contrivances, we see almost a contrivance for each war and now we hear that the Iranians . . .

FISK: You could go further than this. There is one country in the Middle East region, generally, which has a large number of al-Qaeda supporters in it, whose security services have worked with al-Qaeda, who have a large number of their populations supporting the Taliban, which have a nuclear weapon. It's called "Pakistan."

BONPANE: That's the Wal-Mart . . .

FISK: We're told that the President of Pakistan, General Perez Musharraf, is a friend of ours, so that's ok.

BONPANE: It's unbelievable, I mean they've become the Wal-Mart of nuclear weapons for the world and there is no problem . . .

FISK: Pakistan's dear Mr. Khan, who is a friend of Perez Musharraf . . .

BONPANE: Yes.

FISK: Gave the blueprints to both Iran and Libya for nuclear weapons and we still forget it.

BONPANE: This is a horrendous violation of the nuclear nonproliferation treaty which was designed to lead to the abolition of nuclear weapons entirely, and now we're extending that use, saying ok to India, ok to Pakistan. You have them, you can use them, but Iran, who doesn't have them, can't use them. I'm worried about a contrivance when we hear that our troops are threatened in Iraq by Iranians. No one has proven that, but they're starting to say if our troops are going to be attacked by Iranians in Iraq, we are going to have to fight back, another contrivance: Tonkin Gulf, remember the Maine . . .

FISK: Well it's a double contrivance because the Iraqi government, made up of SCIRI and the various other parties, were all parties that were created in Iran during the Iran/Iraq War when we were supporting Saddam, who later we were happy to see hanged. You know the problem here is not just the perversion of reality now, from which your president does suffer, frankly, it's also the perversion of history. And what amazes me, I mean I come to the United States a lot, I love coming to America. You have all these universities, all these departments of Middle East studies, and Islamic studies, and Arabic studies. You have this massive intelligence operation, with all of its supercomputers, and you keep getting it wrong. Can you account to me how this happened?

BONPANE: Yes I can . . .

FISK: No, I'm not saying the British Foreign Office is top of the league in this. We lie like everybody else does, but how do you get it so wrong?

BONPANE: I've been in academia for years and I would like to say that over half of the governmental aid to academia, in the United States, is for military purposes. They're now doing more research for some wonderful new models of nuclear weapons at the University of California. This is a prostitution of academia, and I'm really quite upset about it.

FISK: Well don't mince your words, as they say in England. I'm not interested in the prostitution of academia, I'm interested in how they get it wrong. I was on a program for *Al Jazeera* International the other day, which the new English language *Al Jazeera*, and two very odd things happened. In the Beirut studio live I can't see the person speaking in Washington or wherever, and there was this guy in Washington who was basically running the Bush line, and I wasn't sure from the program whether he was a spokesman for the Israeli government or the American government. I mean I genuinely didn't know. He could have been a member of the Israeli embassy staff in Washington or the Israeli consulate in New York. And I realized after about ten minutes it didn't matter because he spoke with the same voice anyway. You couldn't tell the difference.

But what struck me particularly was that the person who was speaking, who I later understood was actually a U.S. administration spokesman, was saying constantly things which he must have known his audience would not believe. That we all wanted democracy in the Middle East, that we always hated Saddam. Things that were total perversion of the historical record. And at one point he said to me, I mean we are on a live circuit, "Why do you think this war continues?" And I said, "Because you say the things you say and nobody, absolutely nobody, believes you. And you constantly think there is something wrong with the presentation of U.S. policy in the Middle East. It's not the presentation that's wrong, it's the bloody policy that's wrong."

BONPANE: The first victim is . . .

FISK: And it didn't get across . . .

BONPANE: Is the truth . . .

FISK: I didn't expect he would, but I was amazed at the fact that this was the person who was talking, mainly, I suppose, to an English speaking Arabic audience, by and large probably a Muslim audience, but he actually thought it would work.

BONPANE: Well it's really a tragedy and there's so much covered up and I'm looking at an article of yours, "The Mystery of Israel's Secret Uranium Bomb," could you speak to that?

FISK: I'm going to tell you about this article, and I'm going to tell you about what happened. In the war last summer Israel used, and so did the Hezbollah by the way, a number of previously unused weapons.

BONPANE: Yes.

FISK: I think that very much the war last summer was a war for Iranian and Israeli and, of course, American armaments manufacturers trying out new weapons. After all, the Hezbollah used a new Iranian missile to hit an Israeli warship which had never been used before. It didn't exist during the Iran/Iraq war between 1980 to 1988. And there's no doubt the Israelis used new weapons, bunker busters, whatever you want to call them, against Hezbollah targets which largely failed, but, then again, that's part of the story. On two locations, one particularly the town of Al Khiam, there appeared to have been uranium residues, enriched not depleted, in the craters. I have gone down and taken pictures of the craters, I've talked to all of the scientists who were involved, I've studied all of the U.N. reports on the craters. I ask in my story, was there a new secret weapon? Certainly, there was a bomb dropped on the village of Al Khiam, or town of Al Khiam in southern Lebanon, and in the area around it dogs have fallen sick, people have fallen sick, and a small British team has claimed there were enriched uranium traces in the crater.

BONPANE: Yes.

FISK: I have since spoken to a Lebanese scientist who assisted that British team, who says he does not believe there was more than the natural amount of uranium. Uranium, of course, exists in rocks, stones, water, whatever, and I am not convinced that the Israelis used a uranium weapon of any kind mainly because it was used so close to the border of Israel. If it was used, it would endanger Israelis as well, so I don't

337

necessarily think that's correct, but I still would like an explanation of the nature of the weapon that was used. For example, at one point the Israelis said they did not use phosphorus in southern Lebanon, and later on they admitted they did. So just saying denial, denial doesn't work. But in the case of this alleged uranium missile, I am not yet totally convinced that it was a uranium based or a uranium enriched weapon. In fact I actually remember I was in America at the time talking to my office about these claims and said we will begin the story with a question mark; we will not begin it with a statement.

BONPANE: We do have the problem of depleted uranium throughout the area, however, I mean throughout Iraq especially, and it seems, according to many scientists, that it is not terribly depleted; it is actually quite radioactive and may have a great . . .

FISK: This occurred in the Gulf War of 1991. We used depleted uranium in Kosovo and parts of Serbia in the war over Kosovo when NATO was bombing Yugoslavia. We used it again in this war. And in fact American generals are boasting of it about 2003 in Iraq. And there is clear evidence in southern Iraq from the first Gulf War, if you call it that, I mean 1991.

BONPANE: Yes.

FISK: And there is growing evidence in Kosovo of cancers caused by the use of these weapons. It is too soon to know, and we used them, by the way, in Afghanistan as well, whether they have caused diseases or sicknesses in Afghanistan and Iraq this time round.

BONPANE: You also wrote an article in *The Independent* on the Roman Empire is falling. It was after the Baker report. I think that was quite significant as well. Would you care to comment on that article?

FISK: Well, all I can comment is that not that many months ago I was in Kufa, in central Iraq, big Shiite religious city, and I was talking to NATO soldiers, not Americans. While I was chatting to them an American armed civilian walked up to me in their military barracks. I assume he was a CIA, I don't know, I don't care, and he wanted to ask me about the Roman Empire. You just mentioned it. And I, for my PhD, did modern Irish history, but for my first degree I did Latin and linguistics. Most of the books on linguistics are by a man called Noam Chomsky, whom I've come to know quite well. I can read Latin books, and what was very interesting, I said to him you've made a big mistake when you came to Iraq.

When the Romans captured a foreign country, when they entered a new land, they crucified all the insurrectionists and offered Roman passports to everyone. Not a real passport of course, they offered Roman citizenship. I said if you had come to Iraq in 2003, made every Iraqi an American citizen, you would never have a bloody insurrection. He didn't understand what I was trying to say, which was that if you treat these people like they are exactly the same as you, they will love you, not hate you. But we didn't offer them American passports, we didn't offer them British passports, we told them they could have new Iraqi passports, and we would like their oil, please. That's the problem with the new Roman Empire.

BONPANE: Yeah, well it seems to be quite obvious that is the problem all right. Now we're getting a little short on time, and I wonder if you have some final thoughts for us in regard to how we can achieve peace in the Middle East.

FISK: Oh, we are going in the wrong direction. We're going towards more and more war. You know I was asked this twice in the last three days . . .

BONPANE: Yes.

FISK: . . . and without wanting to stick my neck out or say something I might later be abused for, I think people who are interested in the Middle East should go to the Middle East and have a look at it.

BONPANE: Yes.

FISK: I think that Americans who are deeply concerned about what's happening and they shouldn't go to Iraq or anywhere that is warlike and dangerous, of course not. But they should go to Israel, they should go and talk to Palestinians, they should come in to Lebanon when it is safe. But people should come from the United States and talk to the people here. Don't worry about the ministry of fear. We have one of those places in England as well, which constantly says danger, danger, danger, terror, terror, terror, terror, terror. Come and talk to the Arabs and the Israelis.

BONPANE: I think it would be enormously helpful. I know how much it has meant to me to go to Iraq, and it has meant so much to others to go to the Middle East as well. I couldn't recommend anything more highly if they have the chance to see it themselves. I just want to thank you so much for being with us today.

FISK: But don't forget to tell them to read the papers before they turn up. Don't get involved in a war, but come and talk to the people who live there. They know what's happening, and you don't have to read the *New York Times*.

BONPANE: You know what is happening. You are one of the most awarded journalists in the world, and we are so honored to have had you on today. We hope that your listeners will read your amazing work, *The Great War for Civilisation: The Conquest of the Middle East*, taken from a medal your father had in World War I, the great war for civilization. I want to thank you.

339

Chalmers Johnson

March 4, 2007

BONPANE: Hello. This is Blase Bonpane with *World Focus*. I am privileged today to have Chalmers Johnson as a guest. Dr. Johnson is President of the Japan Policy Research Institute and is author of the best-selling *Blowback* and *The Sorrows of Empire*. His latest book was released this month and is entitled *Nemesis: The Last Days of the American Republic*. That completes the trilogy. And he has also been a contributor to the *Los Angeles Times*, *The London Review of Books*, *Harper's Magazine*, *The Nation*, and he appears in the prize-winning documentary film *Why We Fight*. Welcome Dr. Johnson.

JOHNSON: Thank you very much. It is always a pleasure to talk with you.

BONPANE: Well I certainly enjoyed reading your book and I can't help but think that every Greek drama seems to focus on hubris and here we have the remedy of hubris coming from *Nemesis*.

JOHNSON: That's the way the Greeks in their system of gods imagined it. That she was the goddess of retribution, of vengeance; the punisher of arrogance and excess, and above all hubris. She was a very important figure in the Greek pantheon, and my contention is that she noticed the things that we've been doing as a country, and she's probably here by now, biding her time, awaiting her opportunity to reform her divine mission.

BONPANE: Well all of the indications are there. We have a dramatic drop in the stock market today. It appears that Iran has turned to the euro, and many other countries are doing so as well, and then we have the Chinese relationship there. So do you feel that this is part of this nemesis at this time?

JOHNSON: Absolutely. It seems to me, though, we have numerous problems of militarism, out of control imperialism, the weakening—serious damaging of our constitutional system, imbalance within our government. In many ways one of our most serious problems is we're facing bankruptcy. We have a record setting trade deficit, among the largest ever recorded. We are continuing to spend more on armaments than all other nations on the Earth combined, we're engaged

340

in continuous wars of choice, almost invariably, and the possibility of bankruptcy is very much there. People have asked me, what are the triggers that would set it off? It could be if China decided to quit absorbing so much of our borrowed dollars because they obviously found they were becoming less and less valuable. One other obvious indication would be that the oil producers began to shift and demand payment in euros rather than a weak currency like the dollar. All of these are signs that it could be approaching. Bankruptcy would not be funny. It would not be the end of the United States, any more than it was for Germany in 1923, or China in 1948, or Argentina just a few years ago, but it would mean a drastic lowering of our living, the collapse of our stock exchange, the end of our influence in the world, and would produce social disorder in the United States that might be rather difficult to control.

BONPANE: Well, we have this very optimistic comment coming from Dean Baker, who is the co-Director of the Center for Economic and Policy Research. He said, "A lower stock market is good for a lot of people. If corn prices fell 30 percent that would be bad for you if you were a corn farmer, but good for you if you weren't and ate a lot of corn. Stock ownership is highly concentrated, 75 percent of the population holds little or no stock, including retirement accounts, and so if stocks go down, and you don't own any, you are better off."

JOHNSON: These are just clichés and circular reasoning. It's what we get from our so-called economic sciences all the time. Meanwhile we've lost well over 3 million manufacturing jobs since the year 2000. We have record-setting trade and current account deficits that are adding up to 6 percent of gross domestic product. Your listeners who did economics back in college years ago will remember it always used to be thought that when that figure approached 3 percent of GDP, you were in extremely serious trouble, as was the economy. Well, we are already at twice that yet we continue to spend money on worthless weapons.

We know there are worthless weapons for warfare in outer space and airplanes that are basically designed to fight the Soviet Union despite the fact that it disappeared fifteen years ago, these kinds of things. And we've been putting it all on the tab. We are financed by China and Japan, who continue to accept dollars basically for the sake of their own domestic employment and their own strategies of building up their power as major nations, and they're willing to pay a certain amount for that, but time is running out on that gimmick.

BONPANE: I see you use the words "military Keynesianism" accurately when you are building so many useless items every dollar is looking for something of value and that means too many dollars are looking for a house, and a $10,000 house is a half million dollars. So this is already something people should be able to read, but apparently they may wait until it is too late.

JOHNSON: I think they might. The speculation in the press this morning about the huge sell off yesterday around the world, what's fascinating to me is the analyst said, "We don't know why it happened. It's psychology and the public is moody and worried. Too much speculation in China." This, that, and the other thing. I don't think it's rocket science to say obviously the public is worried about the way the world is going, worried terribly about the leadership in this Country. The President's poll numbers are now below Harry Truman's and he's being held directly responsible for the utter disaster of Iraq. Our congress isn't working well; it's hardly working at all. There's ample reason to be worried and to sit down and have a family talk about should we continue to be in the stock market or wouldn't it be better to move our money into something more secure.

BONPANE: I'm really shocked at the decline of both the courts and the congress. The congress doesn't seem to realize that it has the power of the purse. They were talking about a symbolic resolution. I don't know where they studied Political Science 101.

JOHNSON: It is absurd. It really is, that is to say, it is easier, if unpleasant, to explain Bush and Cheney's desire to enhance the Presidency, to provide even more power than is already there, to resort to even more secrecy than is already there, and to behave as if they were monarchs. But still that is not too hard to explain. Many presidents have been behaving in this manner for a long time now. What's hard to explain, almost impossible, is just the total failure of the key institutions of our separation of powers. Where are they? What do they think they're doing? Why no oversight?

I live in the 50th district of California where we just saw our Congressman, Randy Duke Cunningham, going to prison for eight and a half years for taking the worst bribes in the history of the Congress, and it is significant that the bribes all came from defense contractors to corruptly receive Pentagon funds for things nobody wanted. That is to say we have constitutional procedures for getting rid of political leaders that are unsatisfactory or for some reason or another need to be changed; it's called "impeachment." Last November the public elected the opposition party to begin to address this issue. The first thing they say is that impeachment is off the table.

BONPANE: That was a shock really.

JOHNSON: If impeachment is off the table then maybe democracy is off the table.

BONPANE: Apparently so. I feel the same thing applies to the courts back in 1803. We had the declaration of judicial review after Mayberry versus Madison, and now we are seeing the court doesn't seem to realize, or doesn't care, that it has the power to declare acts of the Congress or the President as unconstitutional.

JOHNSON: The willingness to tolerate executive branch torture. The willingness to tolerate executive branch secret kidnappings in cities in Europe and flying them to countries where they know they will be tortured. The willingness to tolerate the suspension of habeas corpus for people we hold in what's obviously an American prison at Guantánamo Bay, Cuba. If the constitution doesn't apply there, then it doesn't apply on any of our 737 American military bases around the world. People who join the armed forces have just given up their constitutional rights, which is also absurd. Indeed it's the lack of courage that is so appalling. Canadian citizen, Maher Arar, who was seized at Kennedy Airport, basically because he is Islamic, he is a Canadian citizen, seized by our agents, flown to Syria, tortured for ten months, and then released on grounds that we made a mistake. He's sued the Attorney General over this, and the case was thrown out by one of the district courts on grounds that we can't take cognizance over this because it's foreign affairs, that that is the President's responsibility. It's hard to imagine a more incompetent decision or incompetent reasoning.

BONPANE: You mention on page 37 there is widespread agreement of officials in the field, including FBI agents stationed at Guantánamo, that information extracted under torture is usually worthless. That torture largely compels its victims to say what the torturer wants to hear, and the use of torture precludes the building of a legal case against a particular captive. The Spanish Inquisition found the same thing to be true.

JOHNSON: I think that's true. And even recently we have new legislation recently passed by the congress and demanded by the President that allows these military tribunals they're setting up to use evidence obtained under coercion. There isn't a system of jurisprudence on Earth that believes that is even slightly fair. By definition, when that enters the case, then the trial is a farce.

BONPANE: You quote the Dean of Yale University Law School and former Assistant Secretary of State saying, "The notion that the President has the constitutional power to permit torture is like saying he has the constitutional power to commit genocide. It's just erroneous legal analysis."

343

JOHNSON: There is no question about it. Yes the President goes around repeatedly saying in public "I am the decider." It is hard for me to think of a statement that is more antagonistic to our constitution where he is anything but the decider. He is one of a collegial process in which we set leaders and people with different sorts of power to balance each other. This is the single greatest defense we have against the rise of a dictator or tyranny, and the President seems to be simply opting out of that. That may be George Bush's personality or something of that sort, but where are the American citizens? Where is the press? Where are the people who should be doing elementary oversight on our government? Don't they know what they are about to lose?

BONPANE: The press doesn't do fact checking on government officials, it takes their word. It may, in fact, check you, and it may, in fact, check me, but they're not fact checking what the President says or they would have had a much more critical situation.

JOHNSON: They don't understand our constitutional system. The First Amendment, giving freedom of speech, freedom of press, was not enacted in order to protect salacious magazines or gossip. It was, as Benjamin Franklin made absolutely clear; it was done to empower the press to be a watchdog over the bureaucracy, over the secrecy of the executive branch; to penetrate it, to expose it to public scrutiny so that the public itself could exercise elementary oversight on its government. It doesn't do that, and the public doesn't do it either.

BONPANE: It is an enormous loss to see the lack of critical thinking that is going on and the inability to identify the shallowness of the approach we've taken. And I know you deal with our situation, trying to understand the banality of evil and the level of shallowness that can be there in people that are incapable of thinking. I think someone could go through a school system and do a lot of memory work and be quite incapable of critical thought. That is a serious problem that pertains to our education system as well, I imagine.

JOHNSON: Interesting enough Arendt, in the book she wrote on the trial of Adolf Eichmann in Jerusalem, called *Eichmann in Jerusalem*. In the last line of the book she used a famous phrase that he represented the banality of evil, that is, by which she strongly implied he was a bureaucrat. He was doing the job that was assigned to him by his government. It was to efficiently transport prisoners across Europe to death camps in Eastern Europe. But she said we have ample evidence that he was educated, that his mind functioned properly, things of this sort. So in later years she contemplated this phrase when she said she did not have theoretical intent in mind. As she contemplated it, she said what we are talking about here is a man who has failed to think, a man without critical judgment, a man without a conscience. I use this in *Nemesis* to try and illustrate the mindset of both the officers, the political leaders, the Secretary of Defense, as well as the ordinary torturers in Abu Ghraib prison that led to this unimaginable scandal for our armed forces. This was all revealed to the world well before the 2004 presidential election.

We may, in this country, be able to argue that George Bush's policies in the first four years of his administration were his and not the American people because we did not elect him. He was put in office by a 5 to 4 decision of the Supreme Court. He did not win the electoral vote. However in 2004 he clearly won the electoral vote by 3.5 million ballots, making his war, his torture, his prisons, his budgets ours in the eyes of the world, and this was very costly. But I did use the Arendt idea. She was attempting to explain otherwise very highly educated Germans and their behavior during World War II, to show that this is also very much our case in Iraq. I was then interested in the case of Sergeant Darby, the man at Abu Ghraib prison, who got a disk of the pictures of torture being inflicted on helpless prisoners, and it turns out he hadn't stopped thinking. He sent it to the army criminal investigators and said that this portrays behavior that I simply know is illegal. I'm a citizen of the United States. Darby is not particularly praised for this action.

BONPANE: I see these people as "yes" people. They learned to say yes in Kindergarten and all through school. And they really didn't know how to say "wait a minute." You mentioned long after Arendt's death Jerome Kohn, a colleague, compiled a volume of her essays entitled, *Responsibility and Judgment.* Arendt concluded, in one of those essays, was man's inability to think for himself. And this seems to be the key here. We have a lot of nice "yes" people who will say yes to torture. Whatever teacher tells me must be correct, and, therefore, I will proceed. Very, very dangerous and very much part of the militarism that has taken over our culture.

JOHNSON: I believe so to. One of the things I am trying to issue, without question, is a strident warning, but a warning to the American public, of the threat to our constitutional system and to also recognize the root cause of our problem now is not who we elected to office or which political party, it is the collapse of our system of oversight, of checks and balances, of ensuring that we do not have something like an imperial presidency in which they can get away with anything they want to do.

BONPANE: I'd like our listeners to know I am privileged today to have Chalmers Johnson as a guest. Dr. Johnson is president of the Japan Policy Research Institute and is author of the best-selling, *Blowback*, and *The Sorrows of Empire*, and also his latest book just released this month is entitled, *Nemesis: The Last Days of the American Republic*. Now thinking of saying those words, I can't help but concentrate on your final observations here saying the combination of huge standing armies, almost continuous wars, military Keynesianism, and military expenses have destroyed our republican structure in favor of an imperial presidency. So we can either keep our democracy or keep our empire, but we can't have both.

JOHNSON: That is one of the main themes of my book, that there is no more unstable configuration, history tells us, than the one we see in the United States today. That is a domestic democracy and a foreign empire. You can do one or you can do the other, but you can't do both. The empire itself has a, you can't avoid it, militarism. Standing armies, huge expenditures, these armies are needed to acquire the empire in the first place, then needed to expand it, to police it. Empire, one must understand, is a pure form of tyranny. It never seeks the consent of the governed. It is an absurdity to talk about spreading democracy at the point of an assault rifle. The choice, historically, is probably best seen first in the Roman Republic. That was a genuine democracy and on which many of its institutions we copy for our constitutional system. It decided that when pressed by the military interests that grew up because of the Empire, it decided to retain its Empire after the assassination of Julius Caesar. As a result of that it lost its democracy and became a military dictatorship. It lasted a fair length of time, but no one would ever call the succeeding emperors a good government.

I try to offer an alternative to this. It seems it's not quite as clear cut as in the case of the Roman Republic, but it is, I think, clear enough. The British after World War II, in light of the war that had just been conducted against Nazism, they realized that in order to retain the jewel in their imperial crown, namely India, this could only be done through administrative massacres. They had used them often enough in the past. They realized that that is what would be called for—to keep such a huge population forever under the thumb of a foreign country indefinitely. The result, I believe they realized, would be Britain would have to turn itself into a tyranny. It would lose its democracy. I believe the British, to their credit, chose democracy over empire and liquidated the empire.

BONPANE: I see where you mention here the only way you could regard Britain's willingness to join the United States in its invasion of Iraq is as an atavistic response.

JOHNSON: There are still people in England, as we know the propaganda goes on endlessly about how wonderful the empire was without going into the settlement of Australia or the kinds of wars carried out against defenseless Africans, and things of this sort, but certainly the English did not have to be part of this crazy neoconservative idea that the United States was the new Rome, that we were the lone superpower, that we were beyond good and evil, we could do as we pleased, and we were going to demonstrate that to the world in a war of our choice, namely the invasion of Iraq which has come back to haunt us.

BONPANE: The 737 military bases currently maintained by us seem to me to be the reason for our inability to offer medical care to tens of millions of our people, and also the decline in education, and also the enormous decline in the public sector, and the infrastructure of the United States.

JOHNSON: It's absurdly expensive and, in my opinion, we don't need any of them, but we certainly could simply dispose of 700 of them tomorrow, and be rid of them. Instead we are talking about creating a new command like CENTCOM and PACCOM; a new command for all of Africa. It would probably be located in the horn of Africa, in Djibouti, or in Gulf of Guinea, where we have interests in oil. But of all the things we don't need is an American military presence in the huge continent of Africa. They're not going to do any good. It's just plain ambition, even hubris, on the part of our now professional military.

BONPANE: Can't we see we are creating the very thing that we are allegedly fighting: the growth of the Taliban in Afghanistan, the growth of resistance in Iraq. Shouldn't it be obvious, and now actually we allegedly are going to support the Sunnis in Lebanon to fight Hezbollah Shi'as in Lebanon. This is incredible.

JOHNSON: We have people who simply know nothing about that part of the world. They apparently didn't know until two years after they invaded Iraq the true difference between Sunni and Shi'a divisions within Islam, and that Iraq, under Saddam Hussein, was a Sunni minority government. If you overthrew it and kicked it out, the Shi'a will come to power. They did and they, of course, will ally themselves with their neighboring Shi'a superpower, Iran, which they are in the process of doing. All of this seems to defeat even the stated purposes of the neoconservatives. The 9/11 Report tells us that the Army had four Arabic translators.

BONPANE: Yes. They simply didn't know what people were saying. In the midst of this we're complaining about the possibility of Iran developing a nuclear weapon when we have 9960 of them. I mean, this exceptionalism is simply not acceptable in a world where there is to be international law.

JOHNSON: This kind of thing, this sort of imperialism, will ultimately, as it did with the former Soviet Union, lead to imperial overstretch, to ideological rigidity economically, as we see in our country today, the inability to reform, and finally the union of anti-imperialists around the world against us. I'm sorry to say if the United States went the way of the USSR right now, I don't believe there would be any more world wide grieving over it than there was at the departure of the Soviet Union.

BONPANE: Exactly. We have created a great deal of hatred throughout the world and after an attack on our country that led the world to show enormous sympathy for us after 9/11. They came forward to want to help and then we started striking in all directions instead of saying, look, a crime has been committed against us, would you help us to apprehend those who were responsible.

JOHNSON: This is the bungling of the sort for which the impeachment clause was written.

BONPANE: Absolutely. Just so grateful to you for being with us today, Dr. Johnson. I want to recommend your book, *Nemesis: The Last Days of the American Republic*, and to let our people know that this is an extremely serious moment and that we do have a duty to impeach Bush and Cheney at this time because they are just threatening the entire world, and they can turn the Middle East into one giant bonfire if they continue the way they are going and that will have repercussions internationally. Thank you so much for being with us.

JOHNSON: Thank you for inviting me. I appreciate it.

348

Noam Chomsky

June 24, 2007

BONPANE: Hello this is Blase Bonpane with *World Focus*. I'm privileged today to have Dr. Noam Chomsky as a guest. Noam Chomsky is institute professor at the department of linguistics and philosophy at the Massachusetts Institute of Technology but more than that he's one of the most influential thinkers of our time, or of any time. He has revolutionized the study of linguistics and fosters the moral consistency that should be the international rule of law. With linguistics and ethics Noam observes the corruption of language and logic that has become part of our daily lives. He shows us how consent is manufactured through the misuse of language and by identifying crass jingo as fact. Noam has written over seventy books and his name brings instant terror to the halls of CBS, NBC, CNN, ABC, and the *New York Times*. They seem to be literally afraid of him. What amazes me about you Noam is your profound humanity and your identification with the human race. Welcome to *World Focus*.

CHOMSKY: Glad to be with you again.

BONPANE: Thanks so much. There were elections in Palestine. What happened?

CHOMSKY: Well, there were elections in January 2006, free elections carefully monitored but the people in Palestine committed a crime. They voted the wrong way. They didn't vote the way their masters told them to vote. And the result was that instantly the United States and Israel were reflecting the deep hatred of democracy that is really a profound feature of the Western intellectual culture, liberal culture too. They instantly turned to severe punishment of the Palestinians for this crime.

Whatever Israel does it's doing with U.S. authorization. They imposed a harsh siege, and withheld funds that they are legally obligated to provide. They even went so far as to cut off a small flow of water that they control into the arid Gaza strip. The United States imposed a harsh embargo, and the European Union sort of went along, tepidly, but nevertheless did. The U.S. and Israel immediately, along with Egypt, who is very much opposed to Hamas, which is kind of an off-shoot of the Muslim brotherhood which probably would win a free election in Egypt if anything like that were allowed. They began a process of the standard operating procedure for overthrowing a civilian government that you don't like which is to arm the military, to prepare for a military coup. This has been very common in Latin America and throughout the world.

So they began arming their own favorite, Fatah which was defeated in the election. Fatah also refused to allow Hamas, which was the plurality which took over the parliament, to function. That led last couple of weeks to a vicious internal struggle in Gaza.

Gaza, is what Israeli human rights groups call the largest prison in the world. It's a pressure cooker, with no food, no jobs, a lot of guns coming in, and probably with Israeli approval. This turned into a violent civil strife, in which Hamas emerged victorious, but in a pretty ugly way which really lost them support.

For the United States and Israel this is a short-term failure. They had hoped for the military coup to overthrow the government. It didn't, it strengthened the government in Gaza. Those who have overwhelming power have many ways to snatch victory from defeat and they're doing it.

Now, the current stand is to tighten the noose on Gaza so that the "animals" will suffer even more and turn on each other and Western humanists will be able to cluck their tongues about the savagery of the barbarians who they are crushing. Meanwhile Israel and the United States will continue to pursue their extensive policies of takeover of the West Bank which is much more valuable. Gaza is a hell hole after years of occupation. But the West Bank has resources, it has a substantial water resources which Israel is annexing with U.S. support. Israel is proceeding to annex effectively the Jordan Valley, which is about a third of the West Bank which imprisons whatever is left. And what's left is being, you know, maybe roughly half of the West Bank much of it arid and unlivable is being broken up into unviable cantons separated from one another and from East Jerusalem, what's left of East Jerusalem, the center of Palestinian commercial, educational, political life, now all separated.

Huge infrastructure projects, major highways now allow Israeli settlers, meaning Jewish settlers, and tourists to travel throughout the West Bank and maybe see an Arab with a donkey up in a hill somewhere. That's effectively taking over whatever they want.

BONPANE: Well, it seems that there's a great awareness now among many Israeli intellectuals and the people themselves there even pushing now toward the consideration of a one state solution. I was looking at Brian Klug's reviews of four books on the state of Zionism. Brian Klug is senior research fellow of philosophy at Saint Bennett's Hall, Oxford and a member of the faculty, the philosophy faculty at Oxford and he's cofounder of the independent Jewish Voices in the United Kingdom. He identifies these four books that are quite striking on saying what Zionism was about in the first place and how it has changed. For example, he quotes the Declaration of the Establishment of the State of Israel and proclaims complete equality of social and political rights to all of its inhabitants. It's almost like a First Amendment. And many people are saying, what happened?

CHOMSKY: Well, you might ask what happened to the First Amendment?

BONPANE: (Laughing)

CHOMSKY: I mean look, James Madison once pointed out that a parchment barrier, as he called it, is no defense against tyranny.

BONPANE: Yes.

CHOMSKY: Stalin's constitution was beautiful too. The First Amendment really became enacted in a serious way in the 1960s. I mean that's the first time that the Supreme Court set a really high standard for the protection of freedom of speech, actually the highest in the world. But that was in the context of the civil rights movement.

BONPANE: Yes.

CHOMSKY: I mean free speech cases didn't even get to the Supreme Court until the twentieth century and then they were very weakly defended. But in the context of popular struggle, major popular movement, the court did establish a high standard. Well, yes, it's two centuries after the Bill of Rights. The same is true of the Israeli declaration. It sounded nice, but the Palestinians were intended to be second class citizens at best.

The basic law of the states established by the Supreme Court, kind of like the Constitution, declares that Israel is what it calls, "the sovereign state of the Jewish people." In Israel, in the Diaspora, that means, it's my state but not the state of its Palestinian citizens. They have some rights but are deprived of many others. For example, over 90 percent of the land was reserved to, people of the Jewish race, religion, and origin. Now technically that's been modified but not effectively, we know what technical revisions mean by virtue of our own history of suppression of blacks and so on.

BONPANE: Please continue.

CHOMSKY: It's true that the country changed but you can't look at the words and draw such conclusions. In fact if you really look at the history of Zionism, really, commitment, formal commitment to a Jewish state wasn't made by the Zionist organization until 1942, and that was at a meeting in the United States. And, as late as the time of partition, there was still a substantial part of the population, especially the cooperative movements, the kibbutz movements, who were committed at least formally to bi-nationalism. It was not incidentally a one state settlement, that doesn't make any sense.

BONPANE: Yes.

CHOMSKY: But a bi-national federation would make sense and that was a substantial, you know not a majority by any means, but a substantial part of the Jewish settlement in Israel. The issue of pre-Israel settlement was informally in favor of bi-nationalism, some kind of federal arrangement of Jews and Arabs, Palestinians. Now from 1967 through, about the mid-seventies, that could have been, there could have been moves toward that and it would have been, I think, a very healthy development that would have meant Israel and Palestine, whatever you want to call it, next to it, the two of them joined in some Federal arrangement, maybe with closer integration as circumstances permitted.

Actually I was writing about that a lot between '67 and '75, when it was really feasible. And at that time it either was suppressed or it just elicited total hysteria. In the late nineties and recently a one state proposal has been revived and it's greeted with considerable sympathy. You can read articles about it in the *New York Times Magazine* and the *New York Times* book reviews, the books you mentioned. So at the time when it was feasible it was anathema, now it's relatively popular and I think is it's completely unfeasible.

BONPANE: Well Brian Klug in his review of Yakov Rabkin's book, *A Threat from Within*, which is a century of Jewish opposition to Zionism states that, "Rabbis generally spurn the new movement. Some strands, especially among the ultra-orthodox, still do," as Rabkin meticulously documents then, "a useful reminder at a time when it almost seemed as if Judaism has been converted to Zionism." Are you aware of a transition there?

CHOMSKY: Well, I know Rabkin's work and it's interesting. But you have to remember that this is a very marginal thread. It's true that there is, the original settler Jewish community in Palestine before the immigrations, before the European immigrations came in, the big ones, mostly in the early nineteenth century and since. There was a Jewish community there; it was mostly very orthodox and very anti-Zionist.

BONPANE: Yes.

CHOMSKY: And it remains so. But these Jews, for what they regard as religious reasons regard Zionism as heresy. In fact the remaining

Jewish community of this group in Jerusalem, has actually called on Jordan to take over Jerusalem again so that they can have religious freedom. But in the current scene that's an extremely marginal group. If you go back to the early part, a century ago, Zionism altogether was a very small strain in the world Jewish community. Especially, the main Jewish community was in Eastern Europe.

Well, that was all wiped out by the Nazis, but you know, or else many just emigrated to the United States, mostly like my parents, but Zionism was a very small part of that. It was secular, secular and leftist a lot of it, secular and socialist, the religious Jews didn't want to have anything to do with it. They did settle in Palestine with the aim of establishing a national home, as it was called formally. In the back of their minds it was a Jewish state but it wasn't formally proposed. And then over the years things changed I mean the comment that you quoted about contemporary Judaism being essentially Zionism, that's pretty much since 1967. It wasn't true in the 1950s for example, so we see a journal like Commentary which today is a rabid ultra-nationalist Zionist journal but if you go back to the 1950s it was non-Zionist.

BONPANE: What I'm wondering about is the future. I was speaking to the Israeli consul and I said, "What do you think about a First Amendment in Israel?" And he said, "Well tell that to the Saudi Arabians." He felt there wasn't going to be a First Amendment in the Middle East. How do you see this thing resolved?

CHOMSKY: Remember, I think it's worth remembering that there wasn't a First Amendment in the United States either.

BONPANE: Yes.

CHOMSKY: In an effective sense until pretty recently.

BONPANE: That's right.

CHOMSKY: And it's not just the First Amendment it's general civil rights. Of course he's correct, I mean Saudi Arabia is a brutal tyranny. It's a major U.S. ally, the oldest and most valued U.S. ally in the region and traditionally the U.S. has tended to support extreme Islamic fundamentalism. Saudi Arabia is a case in point. By comparison with Saudi Arabia, Iran looks like a free society. But the United States has never had anything against brutal tyrannies that suppress freedom that are religious extremist as long as they play their proper role. And the role of Saudi Arabia is to permit the U.S. to effectively control much of the world's energy system with the Saudi elite breaking off plenty of profit from it. That's the arrangement and so its been tolerable. But his point about Saudi Arabian civil liberties are, of course, correct. And the U.S. and Israel too have supported Saudi Arabia, in part because it is playing the role of suppressing independent Arab nationalism. However that has nothing to do with what goes on domestically inside Israel or domestically inside the United States.

BONPANE: Right.

CHOMSKY: Israel cannot become the state of its citizens as long as it is committed to being a Jewish state. I mean that's just a contradiction in terms and always has been. Similarly, if the United States were, if the Supreme Court and the United States were to declare that the United States is the sovereign state of the white Christian people

BONPANE: Ay!

CHOMSKY: OK, well but it's a democracy. What would that mean?

BONPANE: It wouldn't mean much. You know, in March, the Arab League reiterated its commitment to peace and normal relations with Israel if Israel withdraws from the land it has occupied since 1967 and agrees to both the creation of a Palestinian state and a "just solution" for displaced Palestinians. Ay, what has happened there? Has that been dismissed?

CHOMSKY: That's a reiteration, as you say, of the Arab League position of 2002.

BONPANE: Yes.

CHOMSKY: And that itself was a proposal that goes back to the mid-1970s and it's kind of all suppressed here because it's unpopular to look at the facts, but you can discover them. In January 1976 the major Arab states, Egypt, Jordan, Syria and others, introduced at the Security Council of the United Nations a resolution, a formal resolution, calling for pretty much for what the Arab League is now asking for, calling for a two state settlement on the international border, internationally recognized border. And then the resolution incorporated the wording of U.N. Resolution 242 which everyone accepts as the major document which said, the solution would include guarantees for the right of every state in the region, including Israel and a new Palestinian state – every state in the region, to live in peace and security within secure and recognized borders.

Well that was the Arab position in 1976. The PLO Palestinian organization supported it. Most of the world pretty much agreed. The United States vetoed it so it's a U.S. veto, a double veto. First of all, it isn't enacted and secondly it's vetoed from history. The Carter administration vetoed a similar resolution four years later meanwhile there were almost annual resolutions in the general assembly passed by overwhelming majorities, 150 to 2 or something like that, U.S. and Israel objecting, calling for recognition of Palestinian national rights. Well the U.S. has just been blocking it.

354

BONPANE: Well, the highest ranking U.N. official in Israel warned that American pressure has pummeled into submission the U.N.'s role as an impartial middle east negotiator, I'm speaking of Alvaro Desoto who is the U.N.'s middle east envoy, that's a fifty-three page statement which he made which I think not only applies in the case of Israel but it applies to the hostility that the United States has had toward the U.N., don't you think?

CHOMSKY: Well it does, that's a very good and important statement. Among other things he quotes U.S. envoys as looking forward to violence in the occupied territories, that's pretty much what happened just a couple of weeks ago. Remember it's part of a much broader pattern.

BONPANE: Yes.

CHOMSKY: If you look at U.S. relations with the United Nations since its formation back in the '40s, the U.S. was instrumental in creating the United Nations. We have to distinguish here between U.S. public opinion and U.S. elite opinion. They're very different. The public tends to be very supportive of the United Nations, still, calling for higher funding, letting the U.N. take the leading role in international crises and so on. That's the public. The public has very little influence on policy. If you look at policy and the elite opinion it has undergone a transition.

In the late '40s and the early '50s it was very favorable to the U.N. And that was a period when the U.N. was virtually at the service of the United States just because of the nature of the post-war system. Through the 1950s decolonization began, the general assembly became more representative of the world at large. The other industrial centers began to recover from wartime damage and destruction. By the mid-1960s the United Nations was no longer under effective U.S. control and attitudes shifted strikingly. Up until the mid-60s the United States never vetoed any resolutions. Since about 1965 the U.S. is far in the lead in vetoing Security Council resolutions on a wide range of topics. Britain is second and nobody else is even close.

BONPANE: Well I think that it would be interesting for people to realize that much public policy is made privately by lobbies and that we have government by lobby and as you say the U.N. among the citizenry is popular but among those making policy they still are in a nineteenth century nationalistic mode when the whole world is looking for planetary thought so we have a problem here.

CHOMSKY: And it's a problem that goes well beyond this on a wide range of issues. Both political parties in the United States are well to the right of the general population. The U.N. is only one case of it. But I wouldn't call it lobbies; it's basically the corporate sector, the elite intellectuals, what's sometimes called the "political class," the small, maybe 20 percent of the population, that's actively engaged in a public discussion and policy formation and decision making, either in government or in the business world or in the ideological institutions.

BONPANE: But how could anyone in their right mind want to support the idea of a war with Iran. I mean we hear this from, what AIPAC seems to be saying, our candidates like Mrs. Clinton saying well that's not off the table. This to me seems like a form of crass insanity. What's going on here?

CHOMSKY: That's what most of the world believes. They believe it to be insanity.

BONPANE: Yes.

CHOMSKY: But it's both political parties here and it's the elite political class with a few exceptions. Actually this is another case where public opinion, in my view, is very sane. Now there have been careful studies of public opinion in the United States and in Iran by the most prestigious U.S. public opinion agencies and it's striking. If Iran and the United States were functioning democracies there probably wouldn't be a crisis. There's just overwhelming agreement among the populations as to how to resolve it by very large majorities, like three quarters, 80 percent.

In both countries, Iran and the United States, it's agreed that Iran should have the right to nuclear power like any signer of the non-proliferation treaty but that it should not have nuclear weapons. There's again overwhelming agreement that the whole region from Iran through Israel, and that would include U.S. forces deployed in the region, that the entire region be nuclear weapons free. Furthermore there's even stronger agreement in the United States, it's 82 percent of the population, that the nuclear powers, primarily the U.S. should live up to their legal obligation to move toward elimination of nuclear weapons.

BONPANE: I think if we look toward these issues we see a new springtime in the making because people want healthcare for all, people want peace, people are not interested in attacking a place like Iran, people want to eliminate nuclear weapons. It seems that the will of the people has been so restrained, so ignored that we have to just proceed regardless of what government wants to make sure that these things happen.

CHOMSKY: Well what we have to do, and this is a very large scale problem, the examples that we've been talking about are illustrations, is to turn the United States into a functioning democracy.

BONPANE: That would be fantastic.

CHOMSKY: In which public opinion makes a difference.

BONPANE: That would be really a beautiful thing. I want our listeners to know that today I've had the privilege of speaking to Noam Chomsky, Institute professor at the department of linguistics and philosophy at Massachusetts Institute of Technology. We're so grateful that you've been with us today.

CHOMSKY: I'm very delighted to have a chance.

BONPANE: Thanks Noam and I do hope that people will read your new book *Interventions*.

I want to thank my engineer Mark Maxwell, my producer Melinda Moran, and Blase Martin Bonpane for the music. You can access *World Focus* by going to www.kpfk.org any day, any time during the week, and internationally or go to www.officeoftheamericas.org. Thank you very much for listening.

This is Blase Bonpane.